MathFlare

Name: ______________________

Class: ___________

Teacher: ______________________

Introduction

As parents and educators, we recognize the pivotal role mathematics plays in shaping a child's academic journey and future success. Yet, the path to mathematical proficiency can often seem daunting, fraught with challenges and complexities. That's where the transformative power of MathFlare Workbooks shine through, illuminating the way forward with clarity, precision, and purpose.

Introducing MathFlare Workbooks – a beacon of guidance, a testament to excellence, and a catalyst for achievement. Crafted with meticulous care and expertise, MathFlare Workbooks stand as paragons of educational excellence, designed to nurture young minds, ignite a passion for learning, and develop a deep-rooted understanding of mathematical concepts.

Picture this: your child eagerly delves into the pages of Mathflare Workbook, greeted by a step-by-step guide illuminated with vivid examples that demystify complex mathematical concepts. With each turn of the page, they embark on a journey of discovery, encountering thoughtfully curated practice questions that reinforce learning and hone problem-solving skills. And when they unveil the answers to those very questions, a sense of accomplishment blossoms within them – a tangible reward for their hard work and dedication.

But MathFlare Workbooks are more than just tools for learning; they are pathways to comprehension, fostering a deep-seated understanding of mathematical concepts through a sequential, logical flow. From fundamental principles to advanced problem-solving strategies, every chapter builds upon the last, ensuring a robust foundation upon which future knowledge can be constructed.

As parents, we yearn for nothing more than to see our children thrive, to witness the spark of inspiration ignited within them as they conquer academic challenges with confidence and poise. MathFlare Workbooks serve as partners in this noble endeavor, offering not just practice questions, but the keys to unlocking a world of opportunity.

And for teachers, MathFlare Workbooks stand as invaluable allies in the quest to cultivate mathematical proficiency in the classroom. With answers readily available, instructors can focus on guiding and nurturing their students, confident in the knowledge that MathFlare Workbooks provide a solid framework upon which to build.

In the pages of MathFlare Workbooks, we find not just the promise of academic excellence, but the seeds of a brighter tomorrow. So let us embrace the power of mathematics, let us champion the journey of learning, and let us pave the way for a generation of young minds poised to shape the world. With MathFlare Workbooks as our guide, the possibilities are infinite, and the future, bright.

Table of Contents

MathFlare
MATH WORKBOOK
Grade 2
Step by Step Guide and Essential Practice with Answers
Addition Subtraction
Multiplication
Place Value and Expanded Notations
Geometry
MathFlare Publishing

MathFlare
MATH WORKBOOK
Grade 2-3
Step by Step Guide and Essential Practice with Answers
Addition Subtraction
Multiplication and Division
Place Value and Expanded Notations
Geometry
MathFlare Publishing

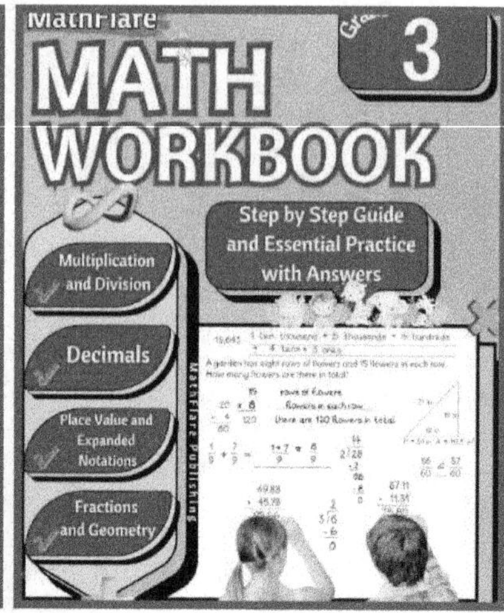
MathFlare
MATH WORKBOOK
Grade 3
Step by Step Guide and Essential Practice with Answers
Multiplication and Division
Decimals
Place Value and Expanded Notations
Fractions and Geometry
MathFlare Publishing

MathFlare
MATH WORKBOOK
Grade 1
Step by Step Guide and Essential Practice with Answers
Counting and Numbers
Addition and Subtraction
Place Value and Expanded Notations
Understanding Time
MathFlare Publishing

MathFlare
MATH WORKBOOK
Grade 1-2
Step by Step Guide and Essential Practice with Answers
Counting and Numbers
Addition and Subtraction
Place Value and Expanded Notations
Understanding Time
MathFlare Publishing

MathFlare
MATH WORKBOOK
Grade 3-4
Step by Step Guide and Essential Practice with Answers
Addition Subtraction
Multiplication Division
Place Value and Expanded Notations
Fractions and Geometry
MathFlare Publishing

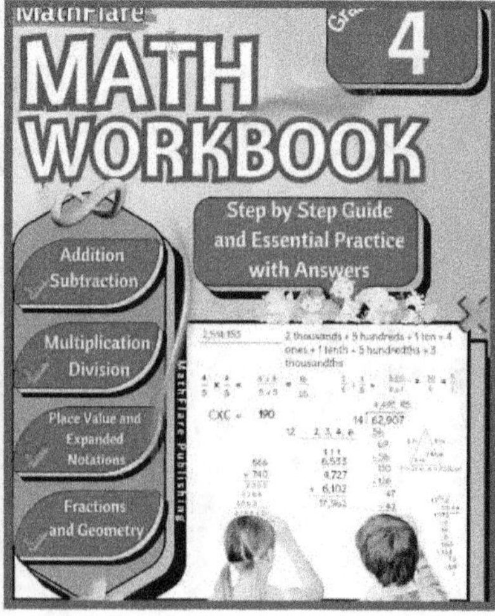
MathFlare
MATH WORKBOOK
Grade 4
Step by Step Guide and Essential Practice with Answers
Addition Subtraction
Multiplication Division
Place Value and Expanded Notations
Fractions and Geometry
MathFlare Publishing

MathFlare
MATH WORKBOOK
Grade 4-5
Step by Step Guide and Essential Practice with Answers
Multiplication Division
Place Value and Expanded Notations
Fractions and Geometry
Unit Conversion
MathFlare Publishing

MathFlare
MATH WORKBOOK
Grade 5
Step by Step Guide and Essential Practice with Answers
Multiplication Division
Place Value and Expanded Notations
Fractions and Geometry
Unit Conversion
MathFlare Publishing

MathFlare
MATH WORKBOOK
Grade 5-6
Step by Step Guide and Essential Practice with Answers
Multiplication Division
Place Value and Expanded Notations
Fractions and Geometry
Units and Statistics
MathFlare Publishing

MathFlare
MATH WORKBOOK
Grade 6
Step by Step Guide and Essential Practice with Answers
Integers and Statistics
Arithmetic and Pre-Algebra
Fractions and Geometry
Ratio and Percentage
MathFlare Publishing

MathFlare
MATH WORKBOOK
Grade 6-7
Step by Step Guide and Essential Practice with Answers
Arithmetic and Pre-Algebra
Ratio, Percent Proportion
Geometry
Statistics
MathFlare Publishing

MathFlare
MATH WORKBOOK
Grade 7
Step by Step Guide and Essential Practice with Answers
Pre-Algebra
Ratio, Percent Proportion
Geometry
Statistics
MathFlare Publishing

MathFlare
MATH WORKBOOK
Grade 7-8
Step by Step Guide and Essential Practice with Answers
Pre-Algebra
Ratio, Percent Proportion
Geometry and Cartesian Plane
Statistics
MathFlare Publishing

MathFlare
MATH WORKBOOK
Grade 8-9
Step by Step Guide and Essential Practice with Answers
Pre-Algebra
Ratio, Proportion and Percentage
Linear Equations
Geometry and Cartesian Plane
MathFlare Publishing

MathFlare
MATH WORKBOOK
Grade 8
Step by Step Guide and Essential Practice with Answers
Pre-Algebra
Percentage
Linear Equations
Geometry
MathFlare Publishing

Chapter. 01

Foundations of Arithmetic

Positive and negative integers are whole numbers that can represent quantities greater than zero and less than zero, respectively.

Positive Integers: Positive integers are whole numbers greater than zero. They are denoted by the numbers 1,2,3,4...

Negative Integers: Negative integers are whole numbers less than zero. They are denoted by placing a negative sign ("-") before the numbers, such as $-1,-2,-3,-4,...$

The positive integers are used to represent the number of objects, scores, etc. whereas the negative integers can be used to represent debt, losses, temperatures below freezing points, etc.

Let's solve some problems:

1. $6 - (-8) - 9$

- Start by simplifying within the parentheses:

$$-(-8) \text{ becomes } 8.$$

- Rewrite the expression with the simplified part:

$$6 + 8 - 9.$$

- Now perform addition and subtraction from left to right:

$$6 + 8 = 14, \text{ then } 14 - 9 = 5$$

2. $(-5) - (-3) + 10$

$$(-5) + 3 + 10$$

$$(-5) + 3 = -2, \text{ then } -2 + 10 = 8$$

Exponents

An exponent tells you how many times a number (called the base) is multiplied by itself. It is written as a superscript to the right of the base number. For example, in 2^3, 2 is the base and 3 is the exponent.

Rules:

1. **Product Rule**: When multiplying powers with the same base, add the exponents.

$$a^m \times a^n = a^{m+n}$$

For example:

$$2^3 = 2 \times 2 \times 2 = 8$$

$$3^2 \times 3^4 = 3^{2+4} = 3^6 = 3 \times 3 \times 3 \times 3 \times 3 \times 3 = 729$$

2. **Quotient Rule**: When dividing powers with the same base, subtract the exponents.

$$a^m \div a^n = a^{m-n}$$

For example:

$$5^3 \div 5^2 = 5^{3-2} = 5^1 = 5$$

3. **Power of a Power Rule**: When raising a power to another power, multiply the exponents.

$$(a^m)^n = a^{mn}$$

For example:

$$(2^2)^3 = 2^{2 \times 3} = 26 = 64$$

4. **Power of a Product Rule**: When raising a product to a power, distribute the power to each factor.

$$(ab)^n = a^n \times b^n$$

For example:

$$(2 \times 3)^2 = 2^2 \times 3^2 = 4 \times 9 = 36$$

5. **Power of a Quotient Rule**: When raising a quotient to a power, distribute the power to the numerator and denominator separately.

$$\left(\frac{a}{b}\right)^n = \frac{a^n}{b^n}$$

For example:

$$\left(\frac{4}{2}\right)^3 = \frac{4^3}{2^3} = \frac{64}{8} = 8$$

6. **Zero Exponent Rule**: Any nonzero number raised to the power of zero equals 11.

$$a^0 = 1$$

For example:

$$7^0 = 1$$

7. **Negative Exponent Rule**: A negative exponent means the reciprocal of the base raised to the positive exponent.

$$a^{-n} = \frac{1}{a^n}$$

For example:

$$2^{-3} = \frac{1}{2^3} = \frac{1}{8}$$

To evaluate expressions with exponents, we can use:

- **Repeated Multiplication**: Perform the multiplication indicated by the exponent.

- **Using the Rules of Exponents**: Apply the appropriate rule to simplify expressions involving exponents.

Square Roots

The square root of a number is a value that, when multiplied by itself, gives the original number. It's denoted by the symbol $\sqrt{}$.

For example, the square root of 9 is 3 because 3 * 3 = 9.

Cube Roots

The cube root of a number is a value that, when multiplied by itself twice, gives the original number. It's denoted by the symbol $\sqrt[3]{}$.

For example, the cube root of 8 is 2 because 2 * 2 * 2 = 8.

Factors

Factors are numbers that divide another number without leaving a remainder.

For example, the factors of 12 are 1, 2, 3, 4, 6, and 12 because these numbers can divide 12 evenly.

Factors always come in pairs, except for perfect squares.

Multiples

Multiples are the result of multiplying a number by an integer.

For example, the multiples of 3 are 3, 6, 9, 12, 15, and so on because these numbers are obtained by multiplying 3 by 1, 2, 3, 4, 5, and so on.

Every number has an infinite number of multiples.

Every factor of a number is a divisor of that number, and every multiple of a number is divisible by that number.

Let's solve some problems:

Factors of **44**

2, 4, 11, 22

Multiples of **77**

77, 154, 231, 308, 385

Positive and Negative Integers

Evaluate.

1) $4 - (-10) - 5 =$

2) $5 - 3 + 4 =$

3) $8 - 9 + (-3) =$

4) $4 + (-8) =$

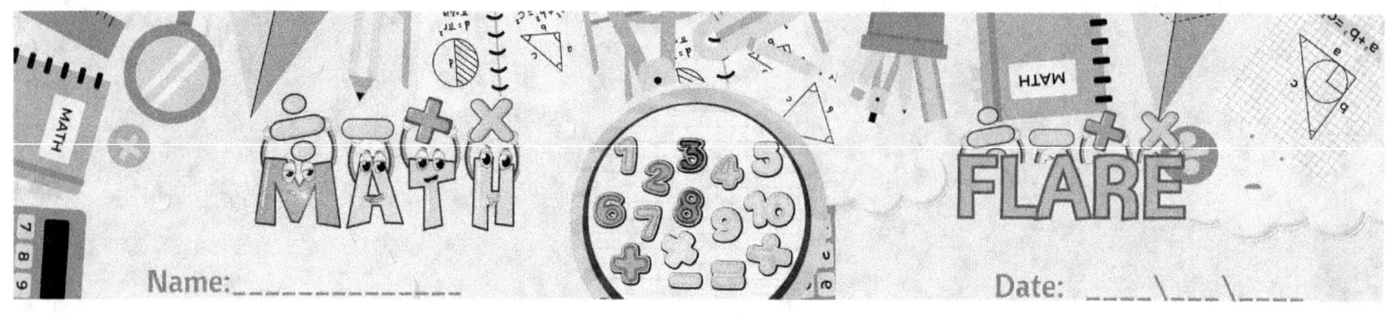

5) $(-3) - (-3) + 7 =$

6) $(-10) + (-4) + 6 =$

7) $(-4) + 2 =$

8) $(-9) + 1 =$

9) $10 + 6 - 7 =$

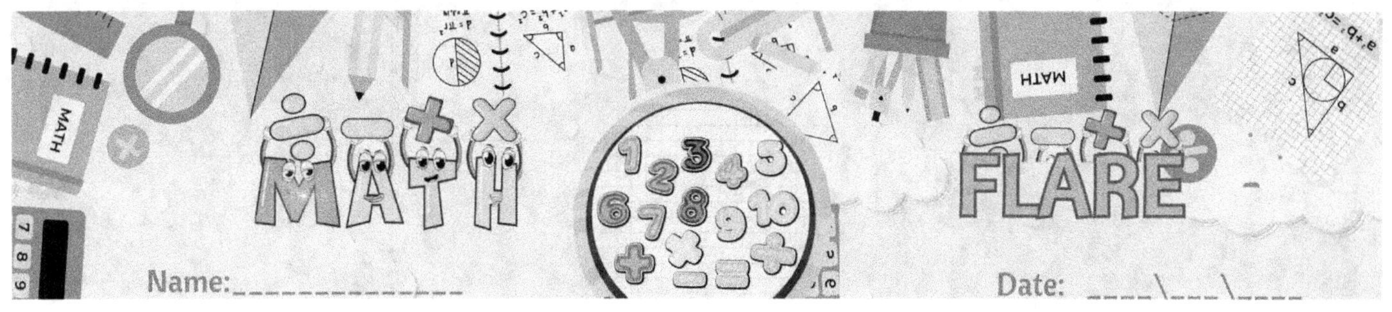

10) $(-10) - 9 =$

11) $10 + 6 - 6 =$

12) $(-3) + (-2) + (-1) =$

13) $(-5) - (-2) - (-7) =$

14) $7 - 6 + 6 =$

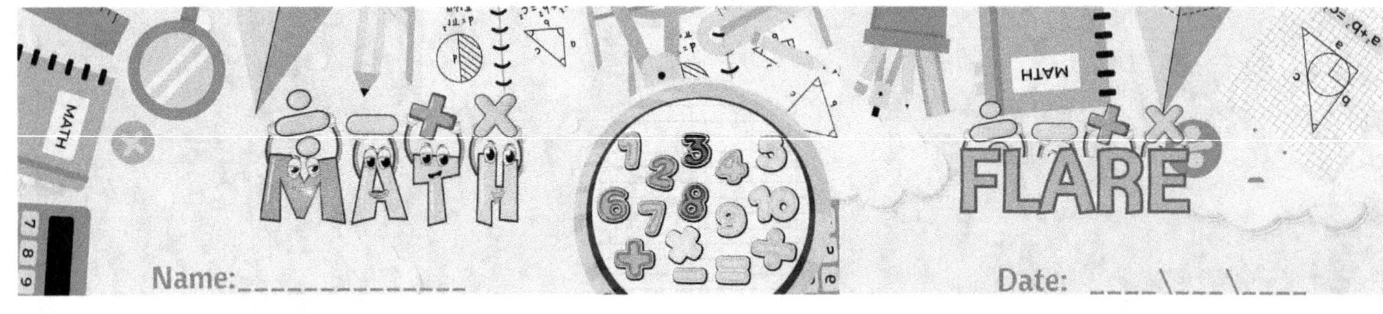

15) $1 + 3 - 7 =$

16) $(-7) + (-5) + 1 =$

17) $8 + 5 - 9 =$

18) $(-5) + 7 + (-6) =$

19) $7 + (-4) + 10 =$

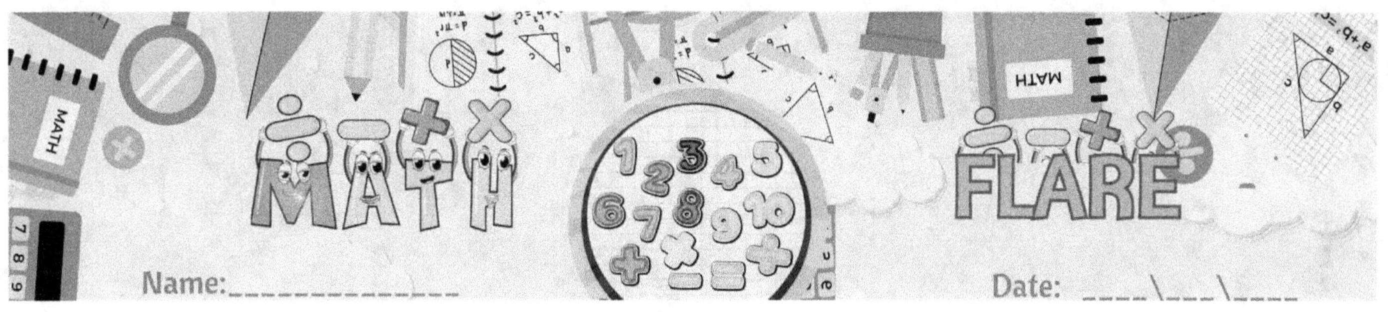

20) $6 - 3 + 5 =$

21) $5 + (-4) =$

22) $(-4) + (-3) + (-3) =$

23) $10 - 2 + 8 =$

24) $8 + (-2) - 10 =$

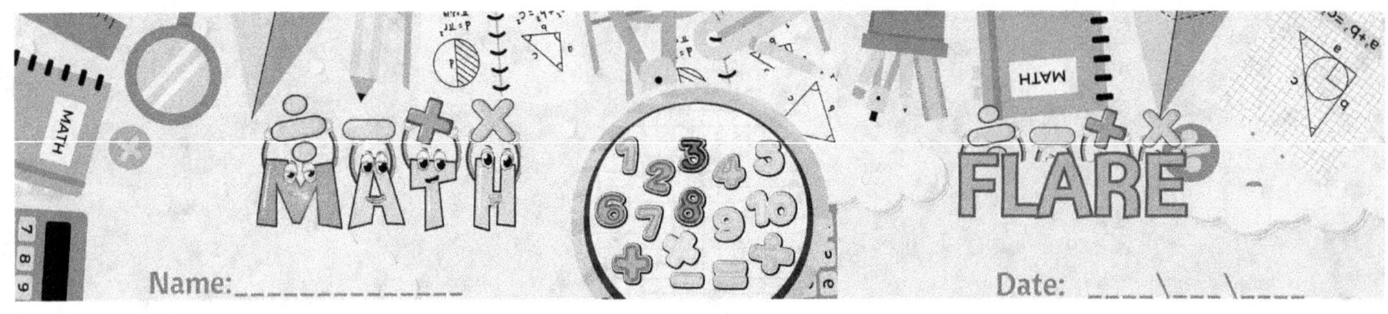

25) $(-3) - (-9) + 1 =$

26) $3 - 10 - 2 =$

27) $(-5) - 5 + (-6) =$

28) $10 - 5 + 1 =$

29) $5 + 10 - 1 =$

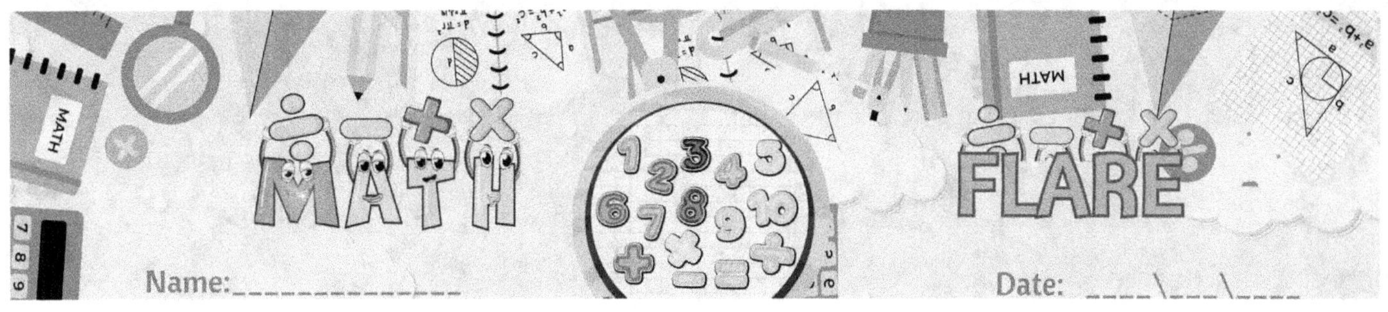

30) $6 + (-9) =$

31) $1 - 9 + 10 =$

32) $(-3) - (-3) + 8 =$

33) $(-1) - (-8) - (-10) =$

34) $(-4) + (-4) + 5 =$

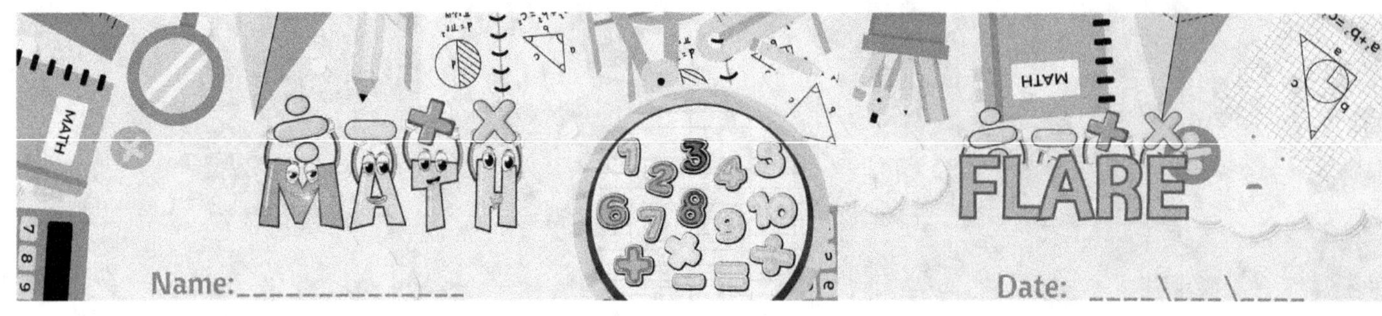

35) $9 - 1 + 8 =$

36) $(-7) + (-6) - 4 =$

37) $(-8) + 7 + (-1) =$

38) $1 - (-5) =$

39) $8 + (-1) - 9 =$

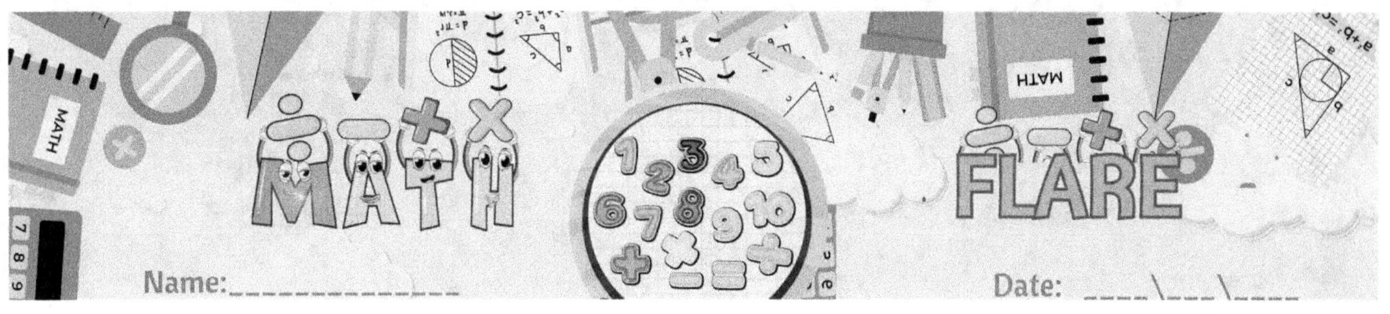

40) $9 - 1 + (-3) =$

41) $(-9) + (-4) =$

42) $3 + (-5) =$

43) $3 + 7 - 9 =$

44) $(-3) - 8 + (-1) =$

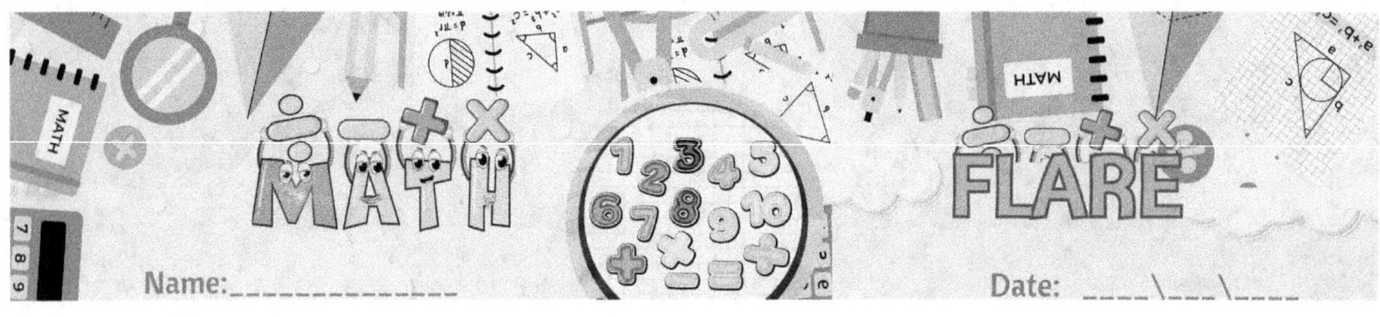

45) $(-1) - (-1) - (-6) =$

46) $10 + (-8) + 2 =$

47) $(-10) + 7 =$

48) $10 + 8 - 4 =$

49) $(-10) - (-6) + 3 =$

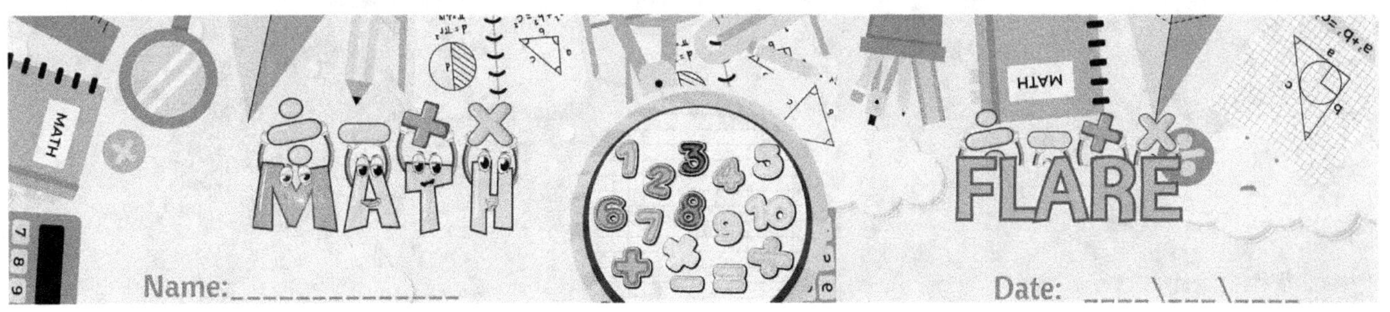

Exponents

Convert the values.

1) $3^4 =$ _______________

2) $17^{-2} =$ _______________

3) $4^{-3} =$ _______________

4) $10^2 =$ _______________

5) $9^3 =$ _______________

6) $4^{-2} =$ _______________

7) $14^{-2} =$ _______________

8) $5^{-3} =$ _______________

9) $13^4 =$ _______________

10) $15^3 =$ _______________

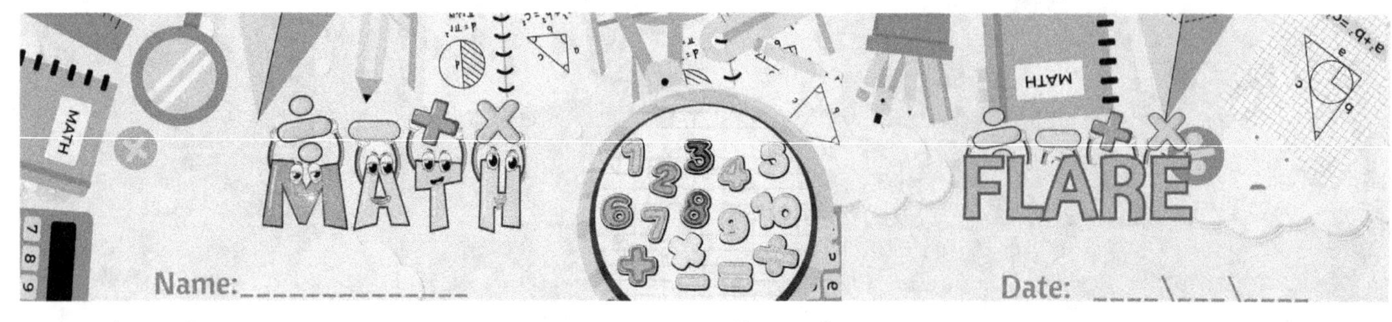

11) 1^{-3} = _______________

12) 3^{-2} = _______________

13) 10^{4} = _______________

14) 7^{2} = _______________

15) 3^{-3} = _______________

16) 8^{4} = _______________

17) 2^{-3} = _______________

18) 2^{4} = _______________

19) 15^{4} = _______________

20) 4^{3} = _______________

21) $2^2 =$ ___________________________

22) $19^3 =$ ___________________________

23) $12^3 =$ ___________________________

24) $6^2 =$ ___________________________

25) $17^3 =$ ___________________________

26) $3^3 =$ ___________________________

27) $20^{-3} =$ ___________________________

28) $20^2 =$ ___________________________

29) $8^{-3} =$ ___________________________

30) $17^4 =$ ___________________________

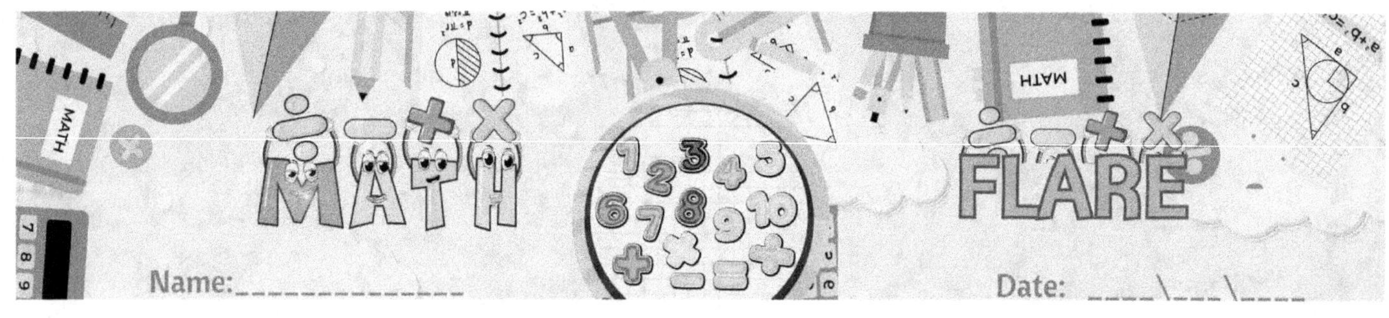

31) $6^4 =$ ________________

32) $14^2 =$ ________________

33) $1^2 =$ ________________

34) $14^{-3} =$ ________________

35) $10^{-3} =$ ________________

36) $15^{-2} =$ ________________

37) $16^{-2} =$ ________________

38) $15^2 =$ ________________

39) $18^{-2} =$ ________________

40) $6^{-2} =$ ________________

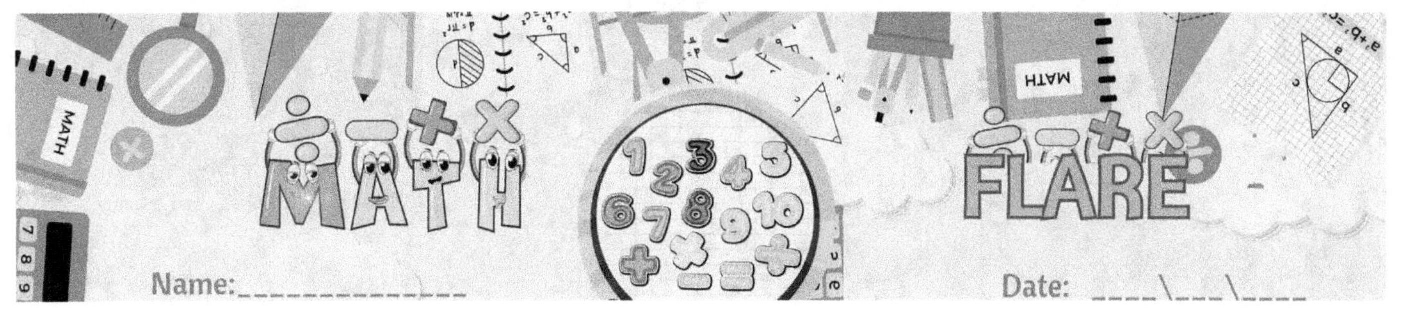

41) $1^4 =$ _______________

42) $9^4 =$ _______________

43) $12^{-3} =$ _______________

44) $17^{-3} =$ _______________

45) $19^4 =$ _______________

46) $16^{-3} =$ _______________

47) $4^4 =$ _______________

48) $18^4 =$ _______________

49) $14^4 =$ _______________

50) $2^{-2} =$ _______________

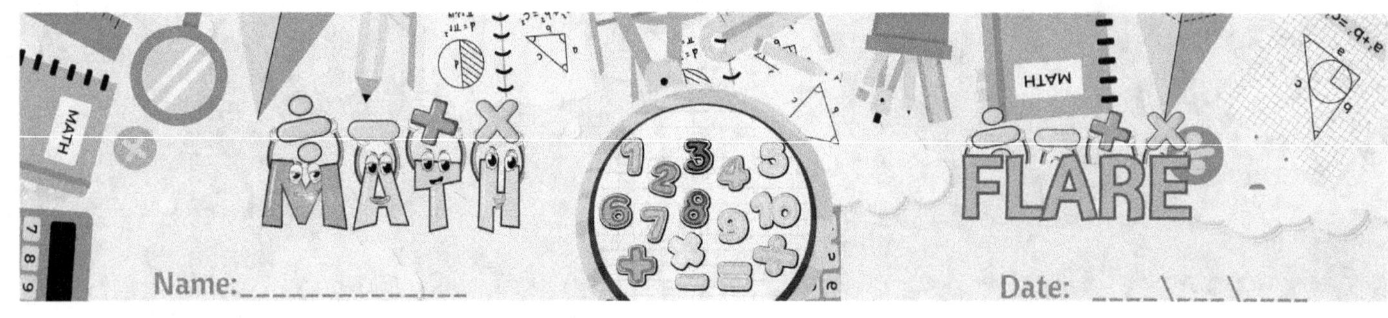

51) $20^{-2} =$ ________________

52) $16^{4} =$ ________________

53) $5^{3} =$ ________________

54) $11^{3} =$ ________________

55) $18^{-3} =$ ________________

56) $4^{2} =$ ________________

57) $18^{3} =$ ________________

58) $20^{3} =$ ________________

59) $15^{-3} =$ ________________

60) $12^{2} =$ ________________

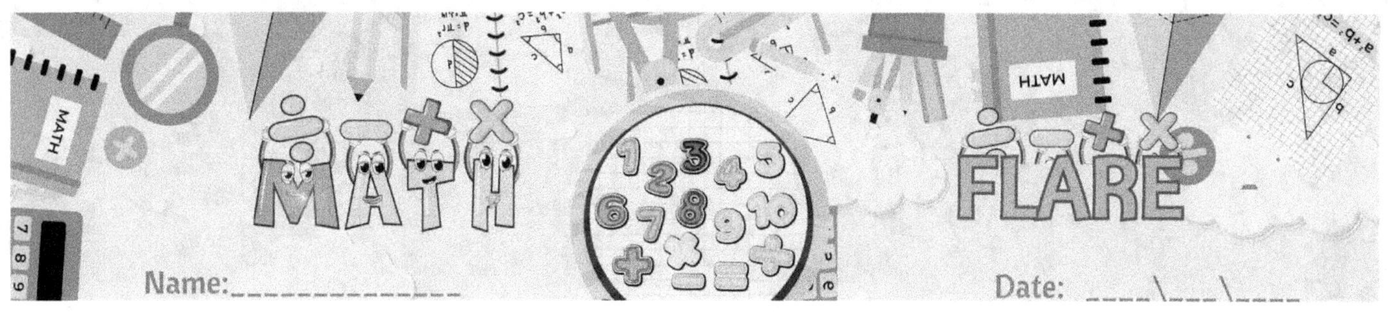

61) $8^3 =$ ___________________

62) $7^{-2} =$ ___________________

63) $1^3 =$ ___________________

64) $13^{-2} =$ ___________________

65) $7^4 =$ ___________________

66) $9^{-3} =$ ___________________

67) $7^3 =$ ___________________

68) $3^2 =$ ___________________

69) $14^3 =$ ___________________

70) $5^4 =$ ___________________

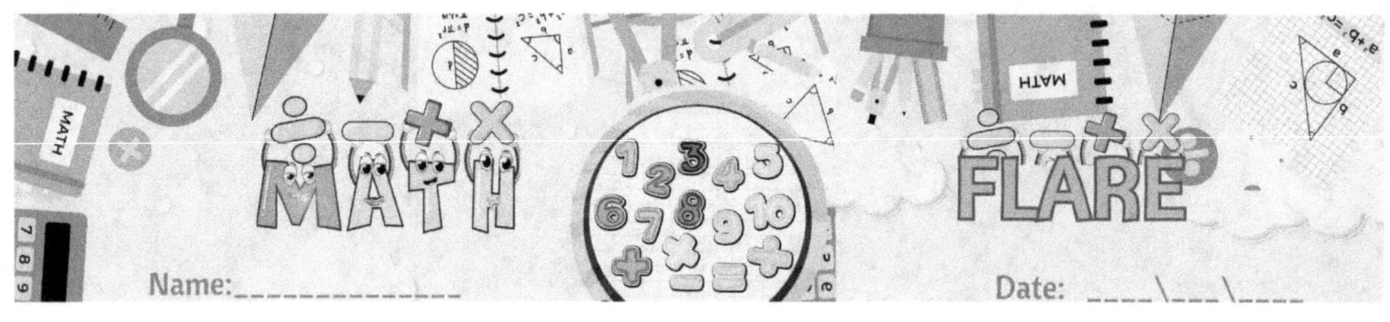

Name:_______________   Date: _______________

71) 7^{-3} = __________________

72) 19^{2} = __________________

73) 17^{2} = __________________

74) 11^{2} = __________________

75) 6^{-3} = __________________

76) 5^{-2} = __________________

77) 8^{-2} = __________________

78) 2^{3} = __________________

79) 11^{4} = __________________

80) 19^{-3} = __________________

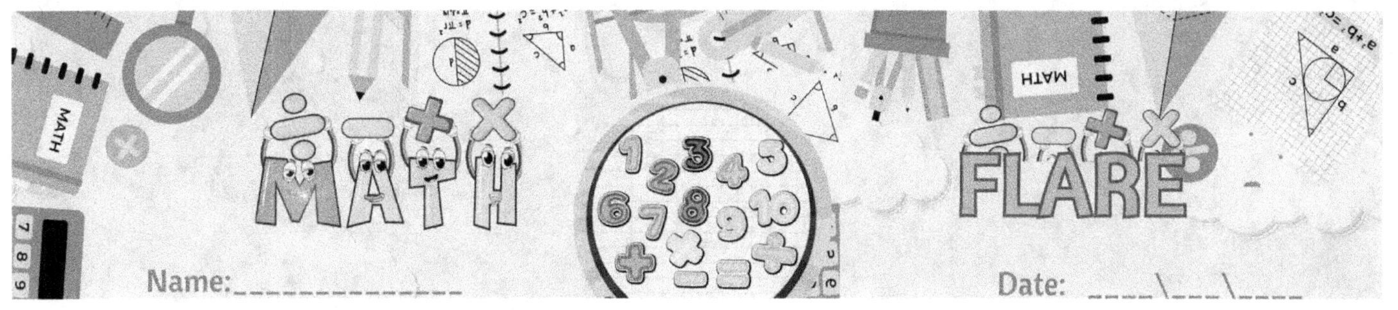

Square and Cube Roots

Calculate the root of each value.

1) $\sqrt{1} =$ _______________

2) $\sqrt{9} =$ _______________

3) $\sqrt{1,156} =$ _______________

4) $\sqrt{100} =$ _______________

5) $\sqrt[3]{729} =$ _______________

6) $\sqrt{7,396} =$ _______________

7) $\sqrt[3]{8,000} =$ _______________

8) $\sqrt[3]{27} =$ _______________

9) $\sqrt{625} =$ _______________

10) $\sqrt{484} =$ _______________

11) $\sqrt{169} =$ _______________

12) $\sqrt[3]{8} =$ _______________

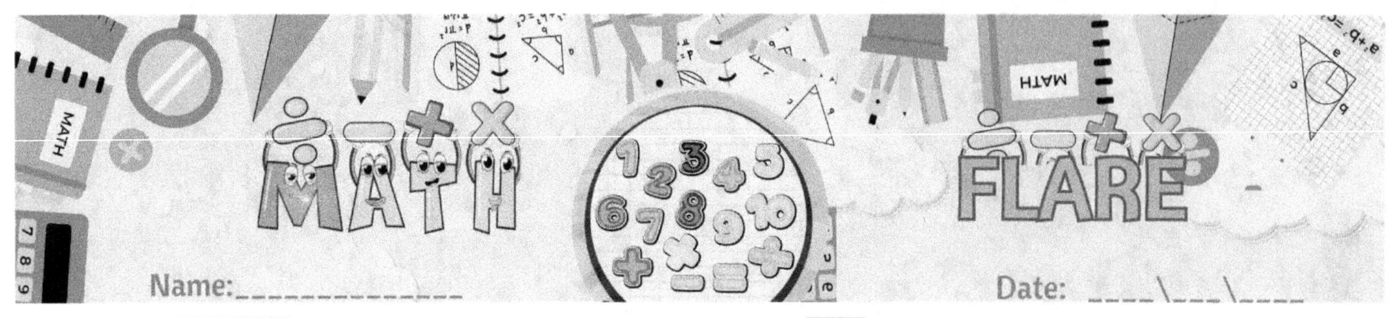

13) $\sqrt[3]{6,859}$ = _______________

14) $\sqrt{64}$ = _______________

15) $\sqrt[3]{10,648}$ = _______________

16) $\sqrt{16}$ = _______________

17) $\sqrt{729}$ = _______________

18) $\sqrt{81}$ = _______________

19) $\sqrt[3]{125}$ = _______________

20) $\sqrt[3]{343}$ = _______________

21) $\sqrt{1,444}$ = _______________

22) $\sqrt{4,489}$ = _______________

23) $\sqrt{2,304}$ = _______________

24) $\sqrt{2,401}$ = _______________

25) $\sqrt[3]{1,000}$ = _______________

26) $\sqrt[3]{1}$ = _______________

27) $\sqrt{441}$ = _______________

28) $\sqrt{4}$ = _______________

29) $\sqrt[3]{216}$ = _______________

30) $\sqrt[3]{1,331}$ = _______________

31) $\sqrt{6,400}$ = _______________

32) $\sqrt{36}$ = _______________

33) $\sqrt{49}$ = _______________

34) $\sqrt[3]{64}$ = _______________

35) $\sqrt[3]{1,728}$ = _______________

36) $\sqrt{4,096}$ = _______________

37) $\sqrt{529}$ = _______________

38) $\sqrt{256}$ = _______________

39) $\sqrt{196}$ = _______________

40) $\sqrt{25}$ = _______________

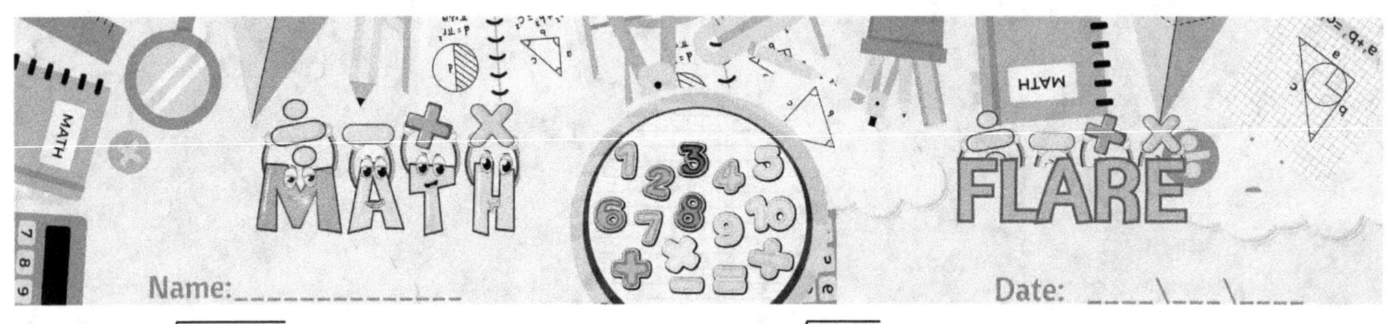

41) $\sqrt{7,569}$ = _______________

42) $\sqrt[3]{512}$ = _______________

43) $\sqrt{289}$ = _______________

44) $\sqrt{1,024}$ = _______________

45) $\sqrt{3,025}$ = _______________

46) $\sqrt[3]{3,375}$ = _______________

47) $\sqrt{841}$ = _______________

48) $\sqrt{4,761}$ = _______________

49) $\sqrt{5,184}$ = _______________

50) $\sqrt{324}$ = _______________

51) $\sqrt[3]{2,197}$ = _______________

52) $\sqrt{9,409}$ = _______________

53) $\sqrt{7,225}$ = _______________

54) $\sqrt{400}$ = _______________

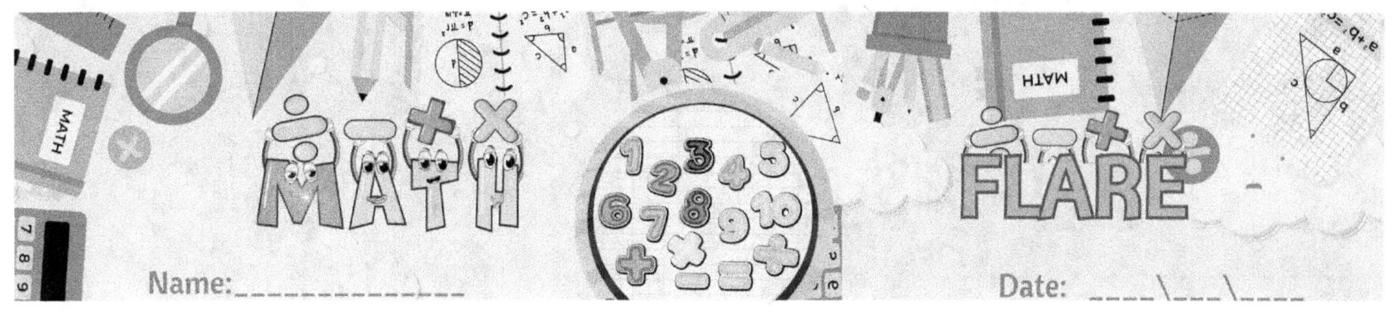

55) $\sqrt[3]{2,744}$ = _______________

56) $\sqrt{144}$ = _______________

57) $\sqrt{5,929}$ = _______________

58) $\sqrt{4,624}$ = _______________

59) $\sqrt{2,116}$ = _______________

60) $\sqrt{1,764}$ = _______________

61) $\sqrt{676}$ = _______________

62) $\sqrt{3,481}$ = _______________

63) $\sqrt{8,281}$ = _______________

64) $\sqrt{961}$ = _______________

65) $\sqrt{5,776}$ = _______________

66) $\sqrt{1,521}$ = _______________

67) $\sqrt[3]{5,832}$ = _______________

68) $\sqrt{7,056}$ = _______________

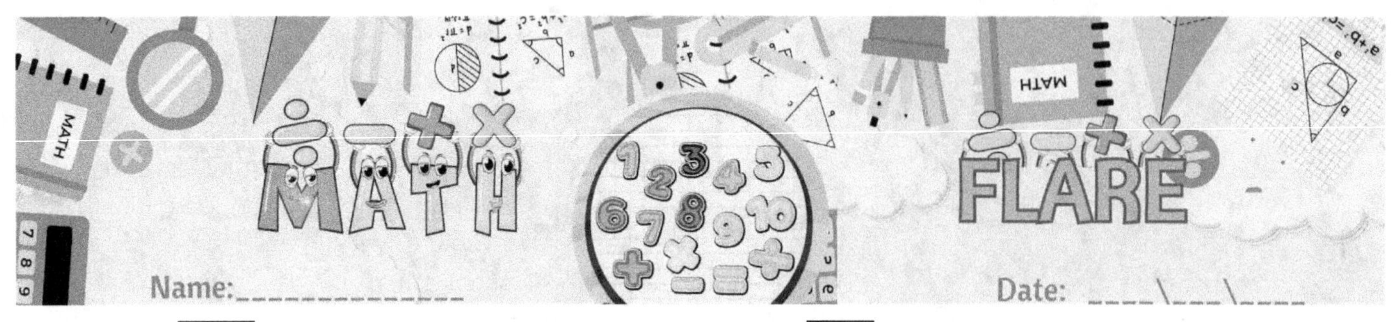

69) $\sqrt{784}$ = _______________

70) $\sqrt{121}$ = _______________

71) $\sqrt[3]{9{,}261}$ = _______________

72) $\sqrt{1{,}936}$ = _______________

73) $\sqrt{1{,}089}$ = _______________

74) $\sqrt{3{,}364}$ = _______________

75) $\sqrt[3]{4{,}913}$ = _______________

76) $\sqrt{361}$ = _______________

77) $\sqrt{576}$ = _______________

78) $\sqrt{8{,}100}$ = _______________

79) $\sqrt{1{,}225}$ = _______________

80) $\sqrt{8{,}464}$ = _______________

81) $\sqrt{4{,}356}$ = _______________

82) $\sqrt{6{,}724}$ = _______________

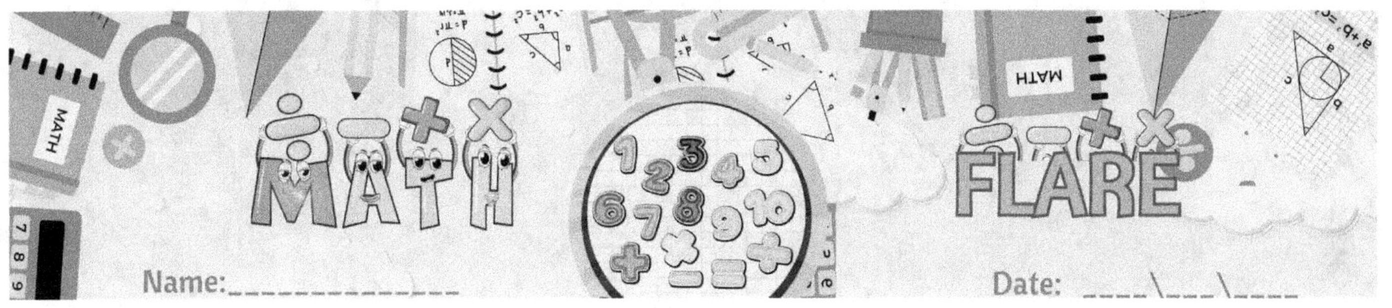

Factors

1) 1   None

2) 64   2, 4, 8, 16, 32

3) 7

4) 54

5) 10

6) 4

7) 57

8) 82 _______________________________________

9) 9 _______________________________________

10) 33 _______________________________________

11) 37 _______________________________________

12) 60 _______________________________________

13) 74 _______________________________________

14) 56 _______________________________________

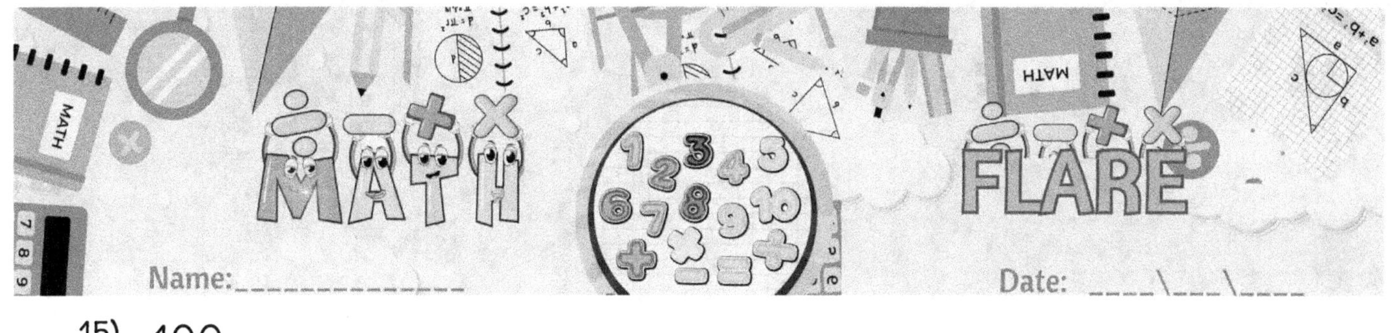

15) 100 _______________________________

16) 36 _______________________________

17) 62 _______________________________

18) 3 _______________________________

19) 27 _______________________________

20) 15 _______________________________

21) 49 _______________________________

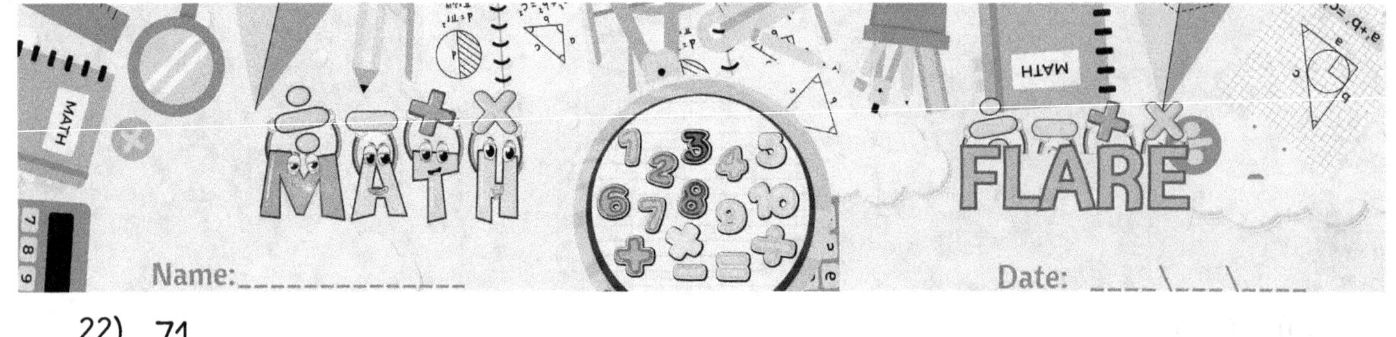

22) 71 ____

23) 95 ____

24) 5 ____

25) 73 ____

26) 2 ____

27) 19 ____

28) 79 ____

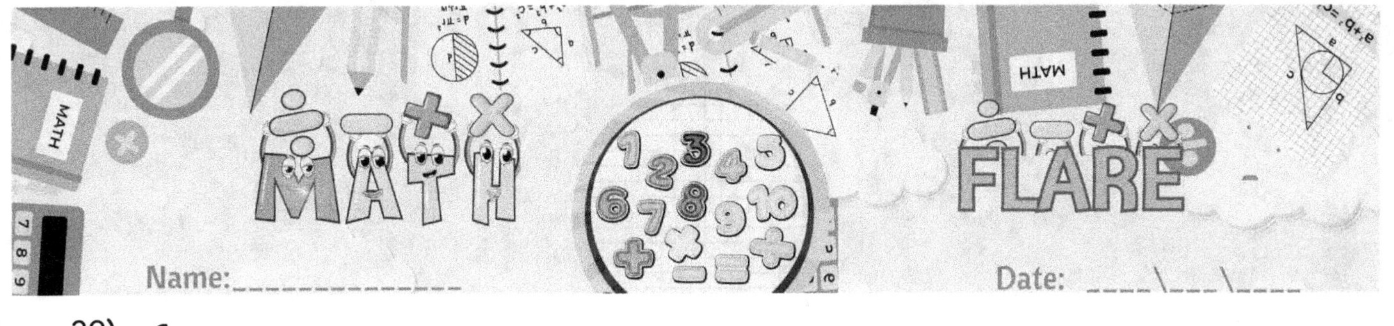

29) 6 ______________________________

30) 99 ______________________________

31) 92 ______________________________

32) 14 ______________________________

33) 8 ______________________________

34) 34 ______________________________

35) 17 ______________________________

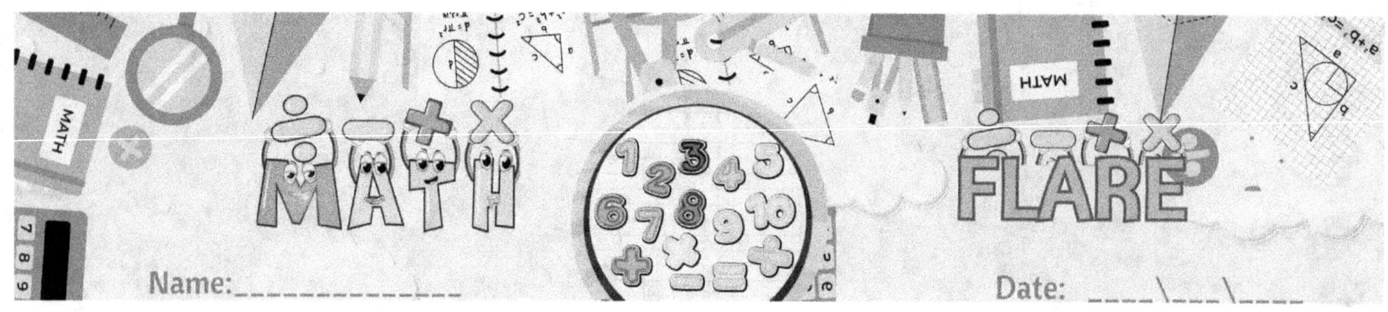

Multiples

1) 50   50, 100, 150, 200, 250 ___________________________________

2) 18   ___________________________________

3) 68   ___________________________________

4) 72   ___________________________________

5) 64   ___________________________________

6) 1   ___________________________________

7) 31   ___________________________________

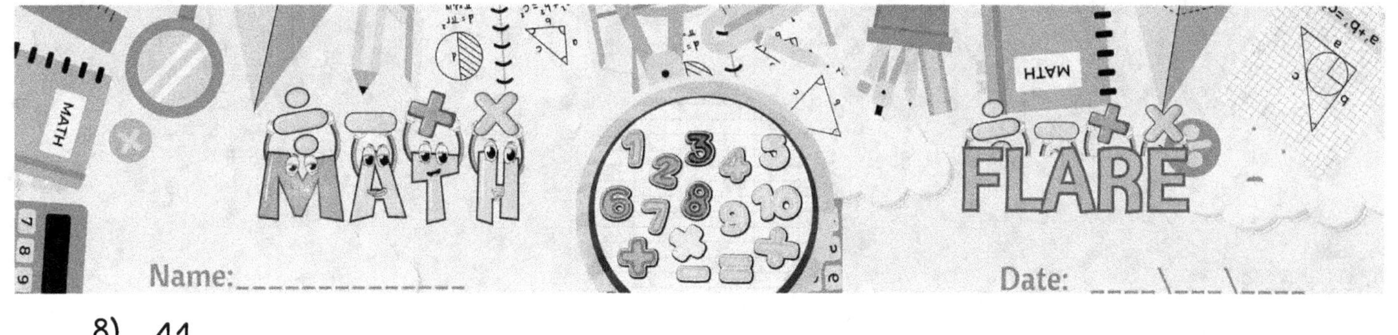

8) 41 ______________________________

9) 98 ______________________________

10) 95 ______________________________

11) 78 ______________________________

12) 12 ______________________________

13) 14 ______________________________

14) 83 ______________________________

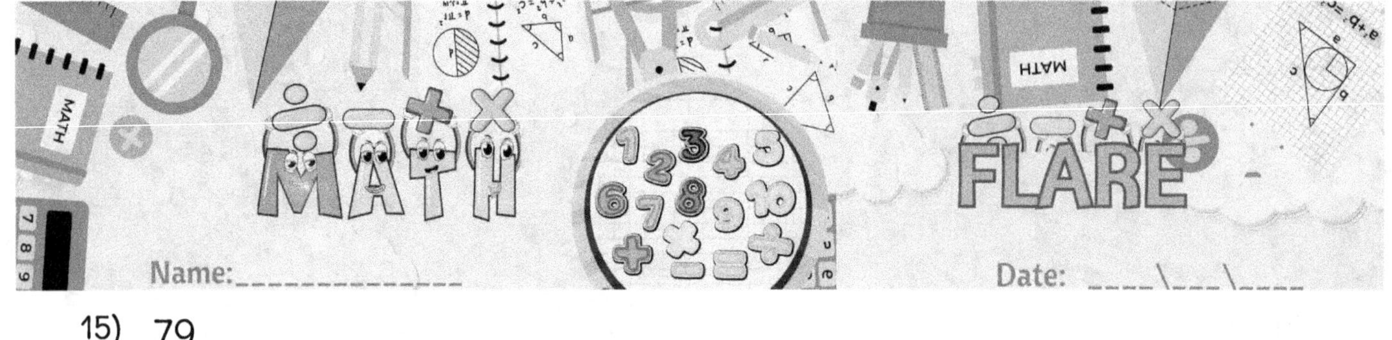

15) 79 ____

16) 5 ____

17) 39 ____

18) 38 ____

19) 42 ____

20) 2 ____

21) 86 ____

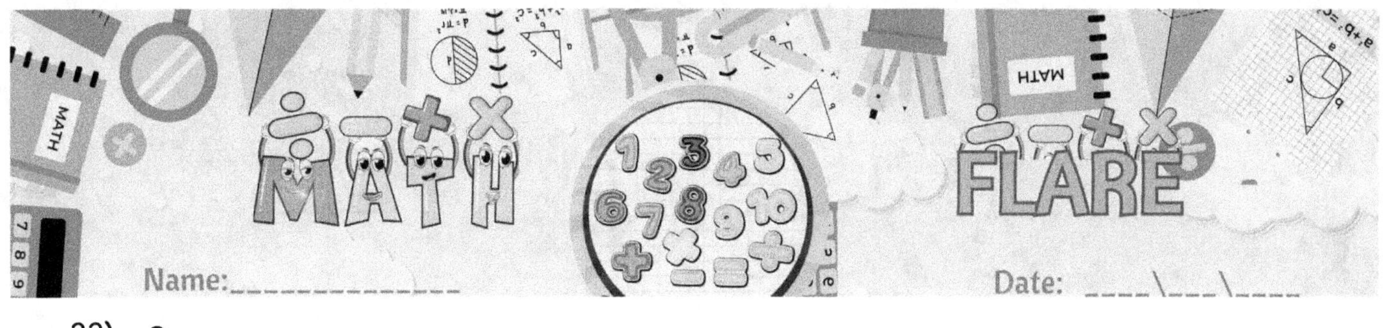

22) 8 ___________________________________

23) 57 ___________________________________

24) 49 ___________________________________

25) 19 ___________________________________

26) 26 ___________________________________

27) 6 ___________________________________

28) 4 ___________________________________

29) 3 _______________________________________

30) 44 ______________________________________

31) 52 ______________________________________

32) 25 ______________________________________

33) 99 ______________________________________

34) 84 ______________________________________

35) 88 ______________________________________

Chapter. 02

Pre-Algebra

Order of Operations (PEMDAS)

The order of operations, often remembered by the acronym PEMDAS, stands for:

- **Parentheses**: Perform operations inside parentheses first.
- **Exponents**: Evaluate exponents (powers and roots) next.
- **Multiplication and Division**: Perform multiplication and division from left to right.
- **Addition and Subtraction**: Perform addition and subtraction from left to right.

The order of operations helps to clarify which operations should be performed first in a mathematical expression to ensure consistent and accurate results.

- **Parentheses**: Evaluate expressions within parentheses first. If there are nested parentheses, start with the innermost ones and work your way out.

  1. Example: $2 \times (3 + 4) = 2 \times 7 = 14$

- **Exponents**: Evaluate expressions with exponents (powers and roots) next.

  1. Example: $2^3 + 4 = 8 + 4 = 12$

- **Multiplication and Division**: Perform multiplication and division from left to right.

  1. Example: $2 \times 3 + 4 = 6 + 4 = 10$

  2. Example: $6 \div 2 \times 3 = 3 \times 3 = 9$

- **Addition and Subtraction**: Perform addition and subtraction from left to right.

  1. Example: $2 + 3 \times 4 = 2 + 12 = 14$

  2. Example: $10 - 4 \div 2 = 10 - 2 = 8$

Solving Equations (One Step)

Solving one-step equations involves performing a single operation to isolate the variable and find its value.

Let's solve an equation step by step: $16 + x = 31$

1. **Identify the Goal**:

    The goal is to isolate the variable x on one side of the equation.

2. **Simplify the Equation**: Combine like terms on both sides of the equation, if necessary.

    The equation is already simplified.

3. **Undo Addition or Subtraction**: If there's addition or subtraction involving the variable, undo it by performing the opposite operation on both sides of the equation.

    Since x is being added to 16, we'll undo this operation by subtracting 16 from both sides of the equation:

    $$16 + x - 16 = 31 - 16$$

4. **Isolate the Variable**: Ensure that the variable is alone on one side of the equation.

    $$x = 15$$

5. **Check Your Solution**: Substitute the value of x back into the original equation to verify that it satisfies the equation.

    $$16 + 15 = 31$$

    $$31 = 31$$

    The equation is balanced, so the solution.

Evaluate Expressions

Evaluating expressions involves substituting given values for variables in an expression and then performing the indicated operations to find the result.

For example: Let's evaluate $4x - 10$, when $x = 3$:

Step 1: Substitute the given value for the variable:

Replace every occurrence of x in the expression $4x - 10$ with the given value, which is 3:

$$= 4(3) - 10$$

Step 2: Perform the operations:

Perform the indicated operations according to the order of operations (PEMDAS - Parentheses, Exponents, Multiplication and Division, Addition and Subtraction):

$$= 4 \times 3 - 10$$

Step 3: Simplify:

Calculate the result:

$$12 - 10 = 2$$

Solving Inequalities

Inequalities are mathematical expressions that compare the relative sizes of two values. They are used to express relationships where one quantity is:

- "$<$" (less than),
- "$>$" (greater than),
- "$<=$" (less than or equal to),
- "$>=$" (greater than or equal to),
- and "$\neq$" (not equal to) another quantity.

MathFlare - Math Workbook 6th and 7th Grade

For example:

$$y + {-10} \leq -8$$

To isolate y, we need to get rid of the constant term -10. Since -10 is being subtracted from y, we can undo this operation by adding 10 to both sides of the inequality:

$$y - 10 + 10 \leq -8 + 10$$

$$y \leq 2$$

To check the solution:

$$2 - 10 \leq -8$$

$$-8 = -8$$

The inequality is true when $y = 2$

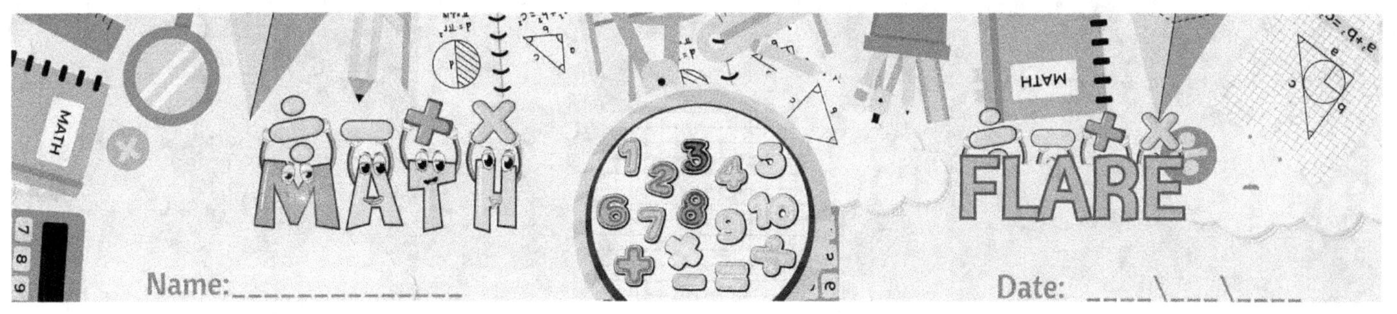

Name:_______________   Date: _______________

Order of Operations (PEMDAS)
Evaluate Expressions.

1) $5 \times 8 + 3 =$ 43

2) $(1 + 4) \div 4 =$

3) $6 \times 2 + 7 =$

4) $7 \times 10 \times 4 =$

5) $[9 - (9 - 2)] \times 9 =$

6) $2 + (1 - (5 + 7)) =$

7) $1(6 + 6) =$

8) $2 \times 8 + 7 =$

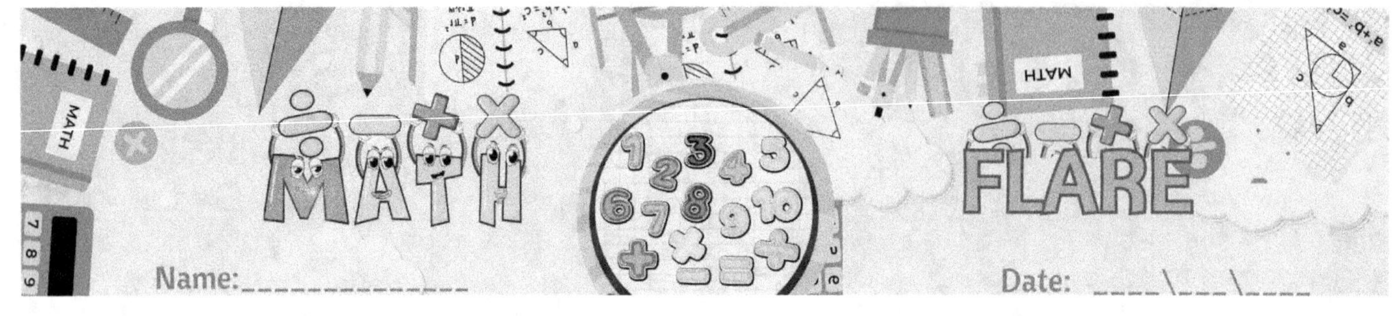

9) $(7 \times 6) - (1 + 7) =$

10) $4 + 9^2 + 9 + 5^2 =$

11) $(9 + 7)^2 =$

12) $1 + (6 - (1 + 10)) =$

13) $(7 \times 2) - (2 + 3) =$

14) $9 \times 1 + 8 =$

15) $7(8 + 8) =$

16) $[10 - (8 + 8)] - 2 =$

17) $(4^2) \times (10^2) + 2 =$

18) $1 \times 3 \times 8 =$

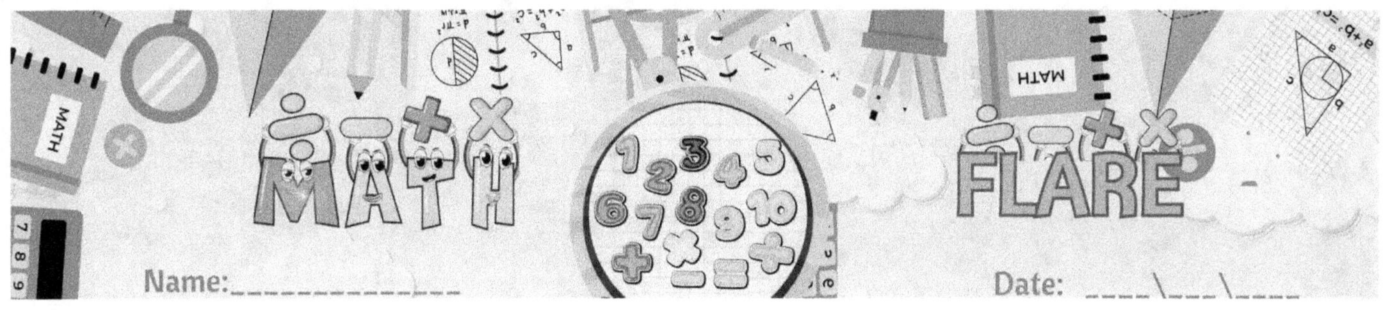

19) $7 \times 10 + 1 =$

20) $10 \times (4 + 2) =$

21) $(6 + 4)^2 =$

22) $10 + (5 + (8 \times 6)) =$

23) $(10 + 5)(10 + 10) =$

24) $(4^2) \times (4^2) + 4 =$

25) $7 + (10 - (1 + 9)) =$

26) $(3^2) \times (8^2) + 6 =$

27) $[1 - (8 + 2)] - 9 =$

28) $(6 + 10)(3 + 4) =$

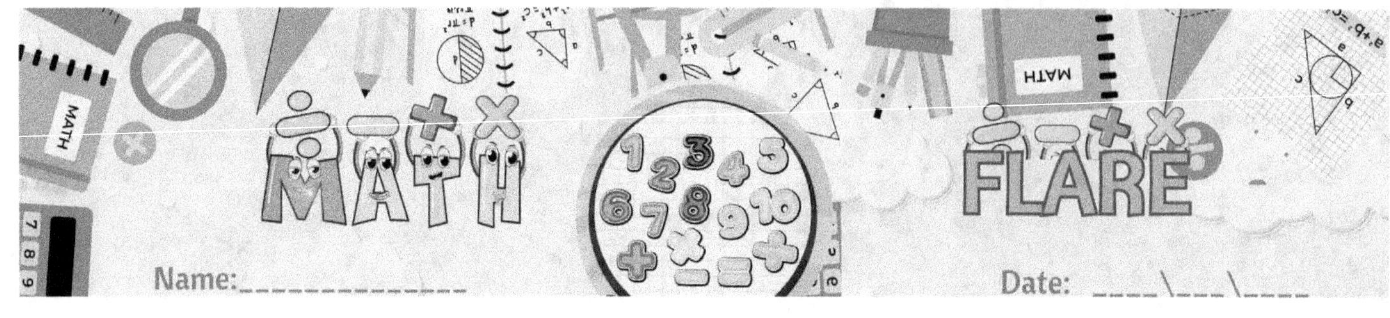

29) $3 + 8 - 1 + 2 =$

30) $[10 - (7 + 6)] - 4 =$

31) $7(3 + 10) =$

32) $(4 + 9)^2 + (4 + 2)^2 =$

33) $4 + 6 + 8 + 8 =$

34) $6 + (9 + (6 \times 2)) =$

35) $9 \times (3 + 8) =$

36) $2 + (8 - (3 + 1)) =$

37) $(10 + 8)^2 =$

38) $[4 + (6 - 2)] \times 3 =$

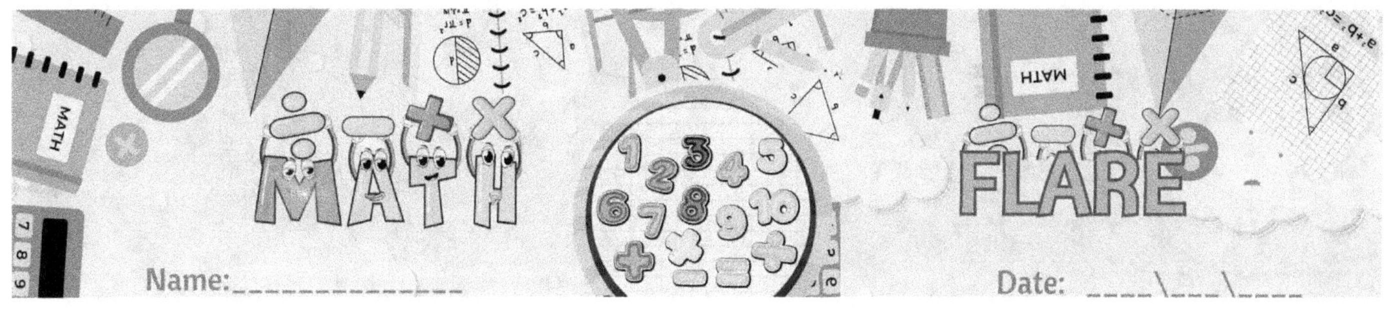

39) $[9 - (2 + 5)] \div 7 =$

40) $2 + 6 + 4 + 6 =$

41) $[3 - (4 - 8)] \times 8 =$

42) $(7 + 8)^2 + (4 + 8)^2 =$

43) $3(7 + 6) =$

44) $(7 + 6)^2 =$

45) $3 \times 10 =$

46) $2 + 6 + 9 =$

47) $2 + 7 + 4 =$

48) $[2 - (1 + 3)] - 2 =$

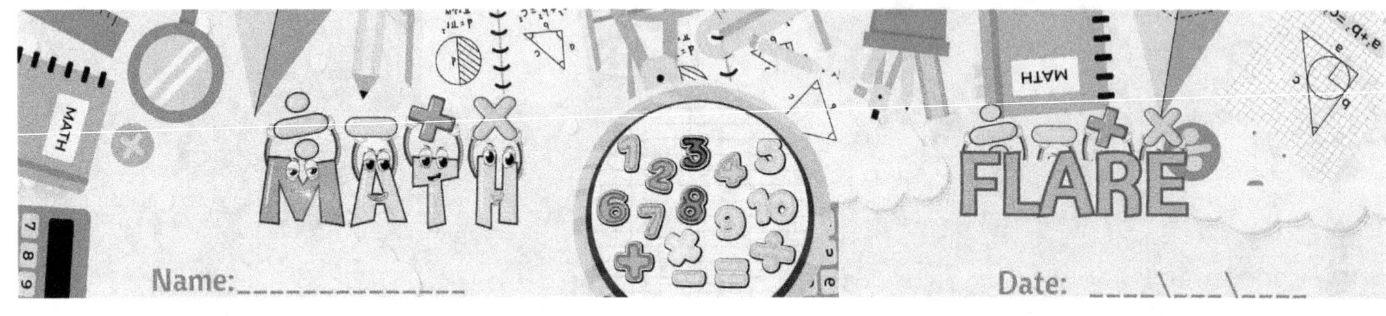

49) $10 \times 6 \times 4 =$

50) $(4 + 1)(5 + 3) =$

51) $(3^2) \times (6^2) + 6 =$

52) $(9^2) \times (10^2) + 5 =$

53) $(1 + 5)^2 + (8 + 2)^2 =$

54) $(6 \times 7) - (10 + 5) =$

55) $(7 + 7)^2 + (3 + 3)^2 =$

56) $2 \times (3 + 5) =$

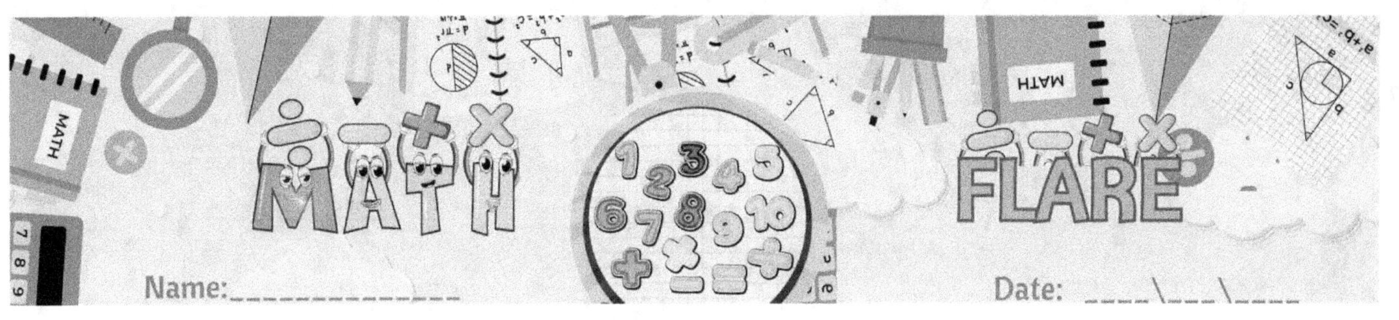

Solving Equations: (One Step)

Solve the equations for the variable.

1) $11 = x \div 19$

$x = 209$

2) $272 = 16 \times x$

3) $7 - x = 3$

4) $18 = x \div 12$

5) $13 = 19 - x$

6) $7 = x \times 7$

7) $20 = x + 18$

8) $x + 8 = 21$

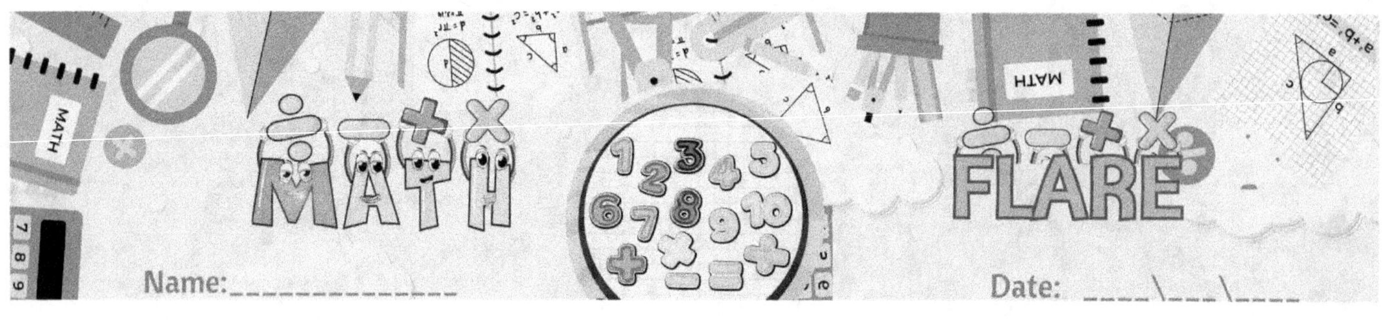

9) $x \times 8 = 120$

10) $2 + x = 17$

11) $3 = x - 9$

12) $1 + x = 16$

13) $x - 2 = 15$

14) $19 - x = 9$

15) $10 = x \div 12$

16) $x \times 13 = 260$

17) $140 = 7 \times x$

18) $14 + x = 15$

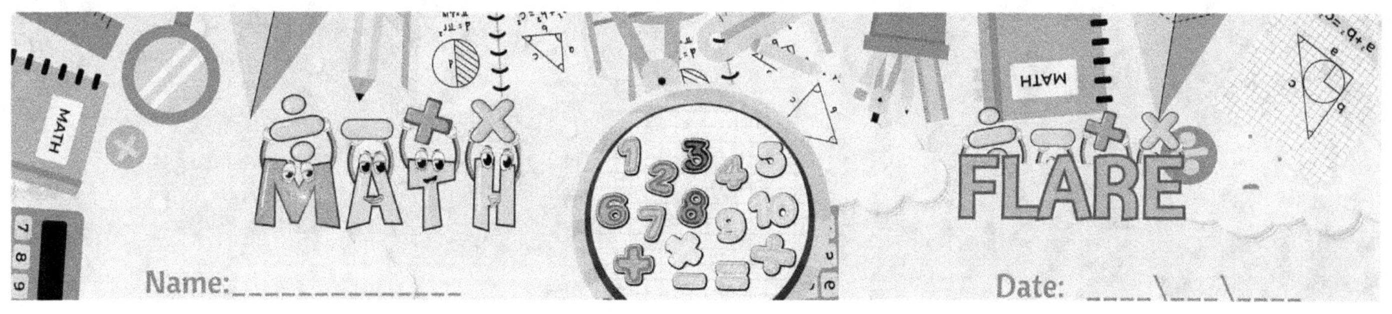

19) $12 - x = 4$

20) $x - 5 = 11$

21) $x - 15 = 4$

22) $6 = x \div 12$

23) $16 \times x = 256$

24) $x \times 2 = 8$

25) $19 + x = 28$

26) $12 = x - 4$

27) $x \div 18 = 4$

28) $12 \times x = 48$

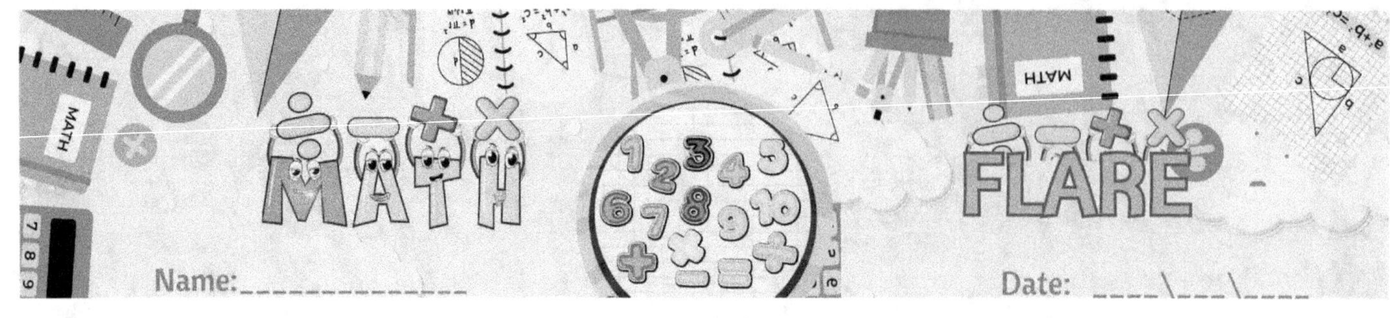

29) $8 \times x = 32$

30) $17 = 16 + x$

31) $8 = x - 2$

32) $x + 11 = 31$

33) $6 = x \div 16$

34) $x - 13 = 5$

35) $x + 18 = 35$

36) $6 = 3 + x$

37) $8 + x = 18$

38) $29 = x + 12$

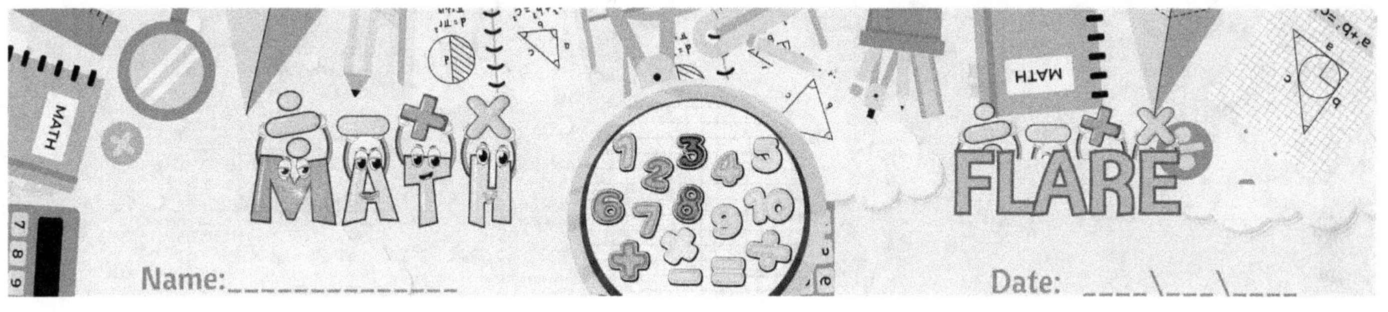

39) $1 = 3 - x$

40) $19 = 342 \div x$

41) $x + 5 = 13$

42) $x \div 5 = 14$

43) $x \div 3 = 17$

44) $19 = x \times 1$

45) $1 = x - 13$

46) $23 = x + 6$

47) $4 = 5 - x$

48) $0 = x - 19$

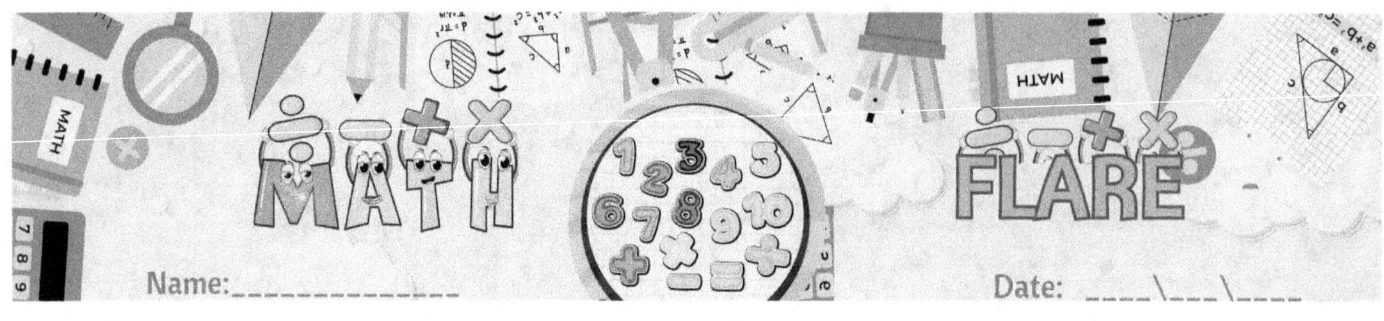

49) $2 + x = 20$

50) $x \div 2 = 16$

51) $x - 3 = 3$

52) $x - 10 = 8$

53) $24 = 3 \times x$

54) $160 = 16 \times x$

55) $23 = 10 + x$

56) $x \times 18 = 270$

57) $13 = x \div 5$

58) $6 = x - 13$

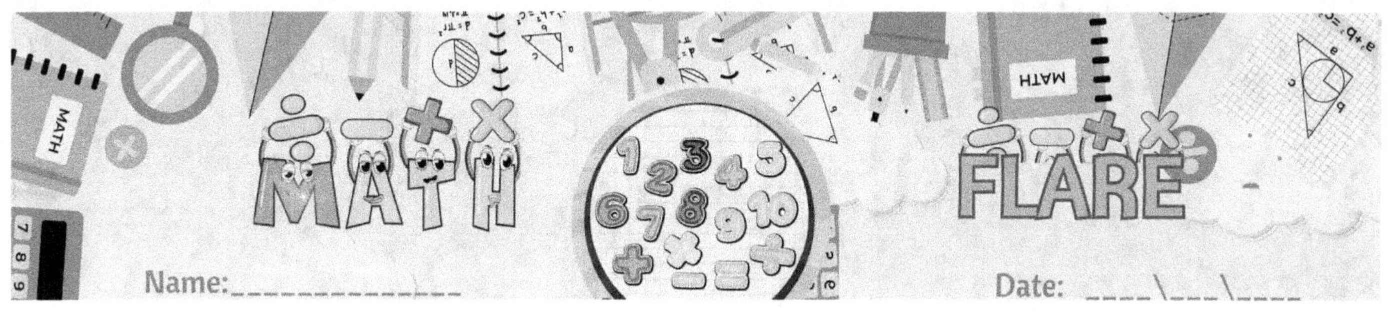

59) $10 = x - 2$

60) $6 = 12 \div x$

61) $2 = x \div 4$

62) $x \times 4 = 76$

63) $6 + x = 18$

64) $18 - x = 7$

65) $16 - x = 10$

66) $x + 11 = 30$

67) $18 = x + 3$

68) $x \times 20 = 380$

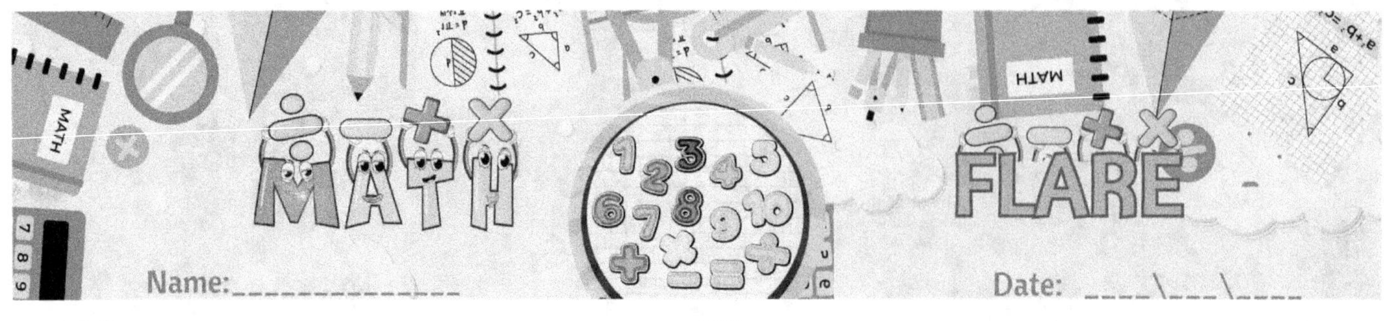

69) $x \times 10 = 20$

70) $5 = x \div 15$

71) $9 + x = 28$

72) $132 \div x = 12$

73) $64 = x \times 8$

74) $5 = 7 - x$

75) $3 = 10 - x$

76) $x \div 7 = 8$

77) $1 = x - 5$

78) $26 = x + 10$

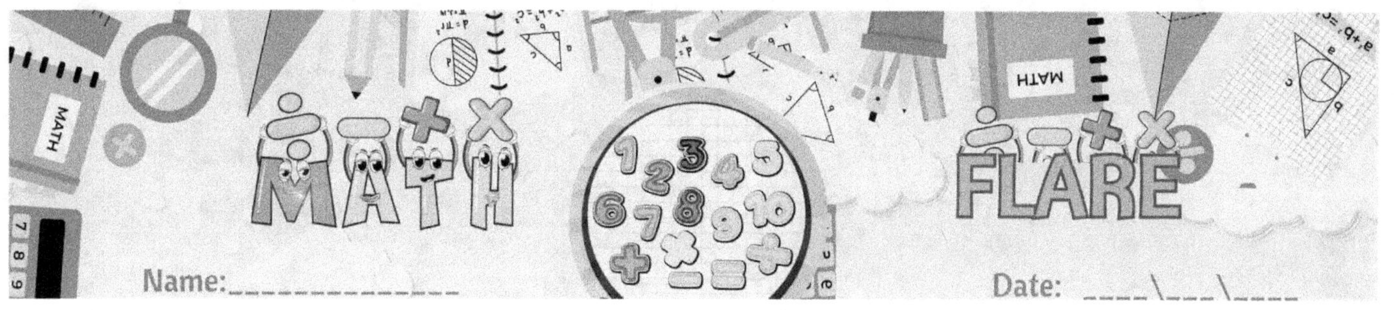

79) $x + 3 = 4$

80) $78 \div x = 13$

81) $7 - x = 4$

82) $1 = 4 - x$

83) $x \div 20 = 1$

84) $x \times 17 = 17$

85) $12 = x \div 12$

86) $5 = 12 - x$

87) $8 = x + 2$

88) $13 = x \times 13$

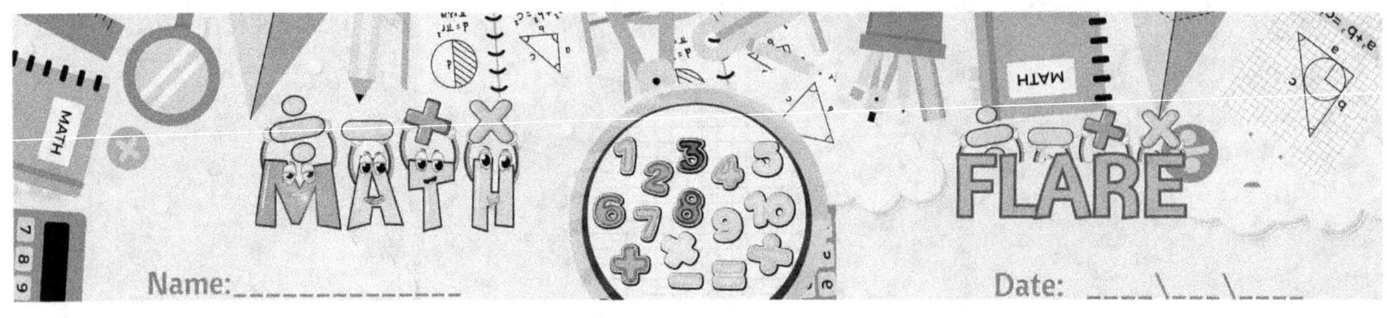

89) $16 = 80 \div x$

90) $x \times 16 = 32$

91) $31 = 15 + x$

92) $x \times 2 = 14$

93) $x \times 2 = 16$

94) $1 + x = 9$

95) $17 \times x = 340$

96) $x + 5 = 6$

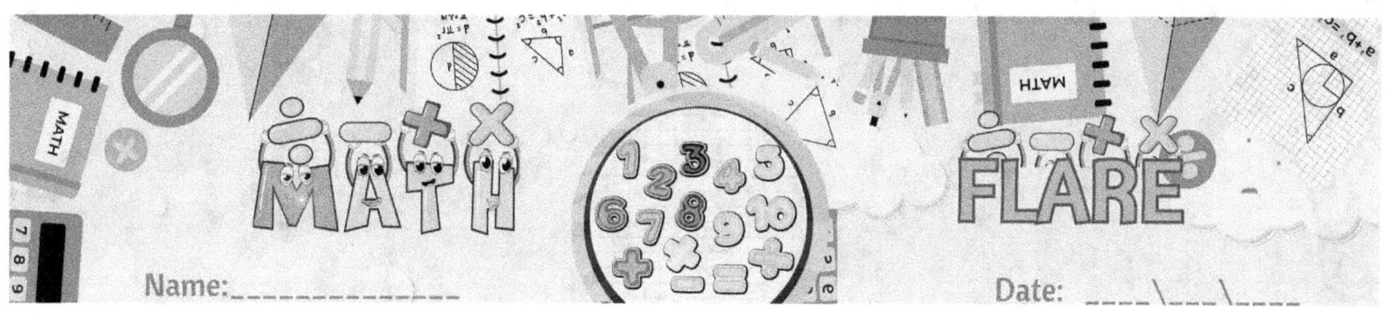

Evaluate Expressions

Evaluate the expression when: x = 3

1) $4x - 10 =$

2) $x + x =$

3) $\dfrac{39}{x} =$

4) $6(2 - x) =$

5) $(9x + 1) + (4x - 6) =$

6) $8(5x) =$

7) $5 + (8x + 8) - 6 + (7x) =$

8) $5x^3 + 7x^1 =$

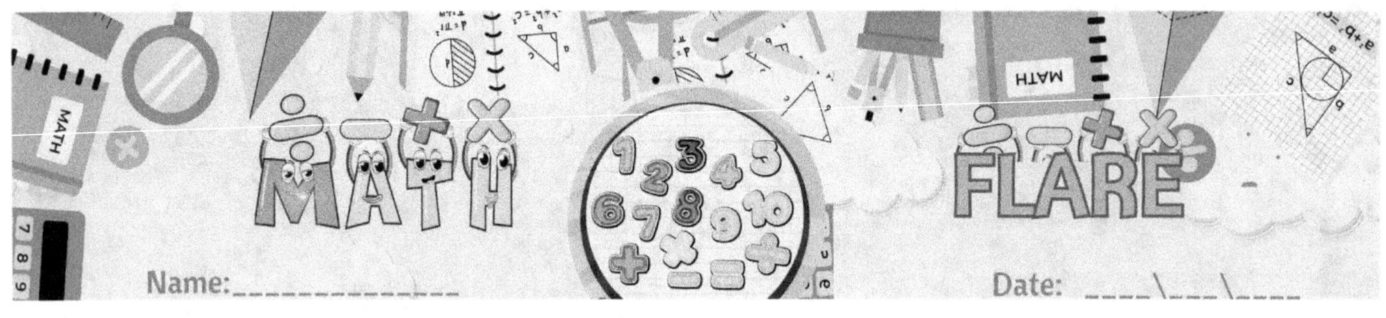

Evaluate Expressions

Evaluate the expression when: x = 6

1) $2x - 6 =$

2) $\dfrac{x}{1} + 10 =$

3) $3x + 6 + (7x - 7) =$

4) $(8 + 3x) + (7x - 1) - (10 + 4x) =$

5) $5x + 6 - 9x =$

6) $8x + x + 6x =$

7) $9x + 9x + 2x =$

8) $9x + 8 =$

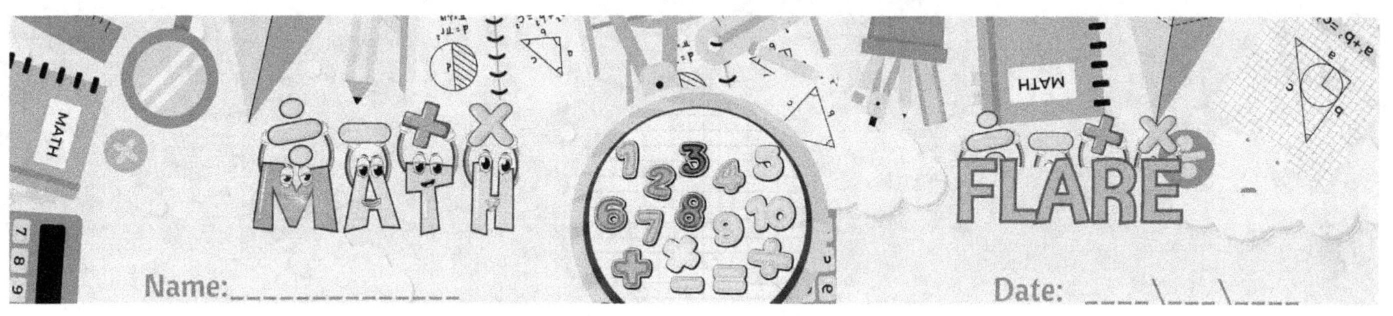

Evaluate Expressions

Evaluate the expression when: x = 4

1) $9x - 5 + 2x =$

2) $3x + 8 + (9x - 1) =$

3) $x^3 + x - 8 =$

4) $\dfrac{x}{4} + 4 =$

5) $\dfrac{x}{4} + 9 =$

6) $x + 7 =$

7) $1 + 3x =$

8) $x - x =$

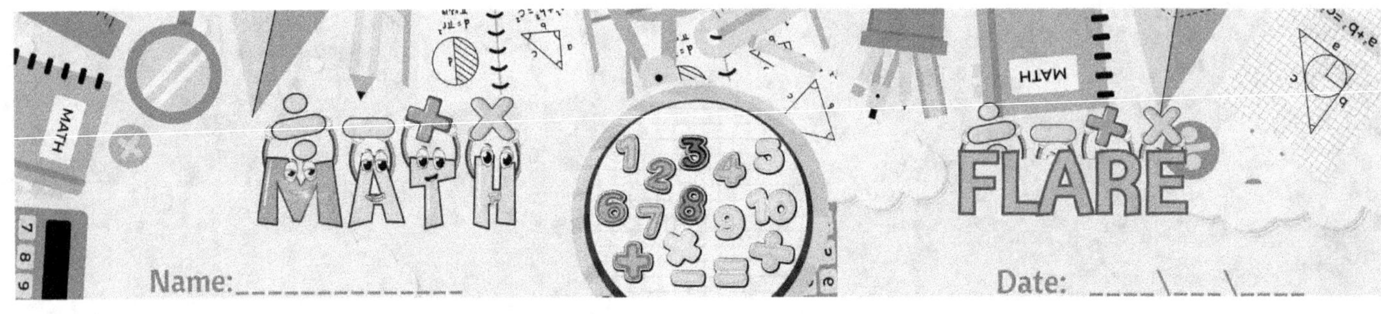

Evaluate Expressions

Evaluate the expression when: x = 7

1) $5(7 - x) =$

2) $x + 8 + 8x =$

3) $x + 9 =$

4) $5 + (6x + 3) - 10 + (2x) =$

5) $4(2 - x) =$

6) $x(1 + x) =$

7) $2(7 - x) =$

8) $x^1 + x - 2 =$

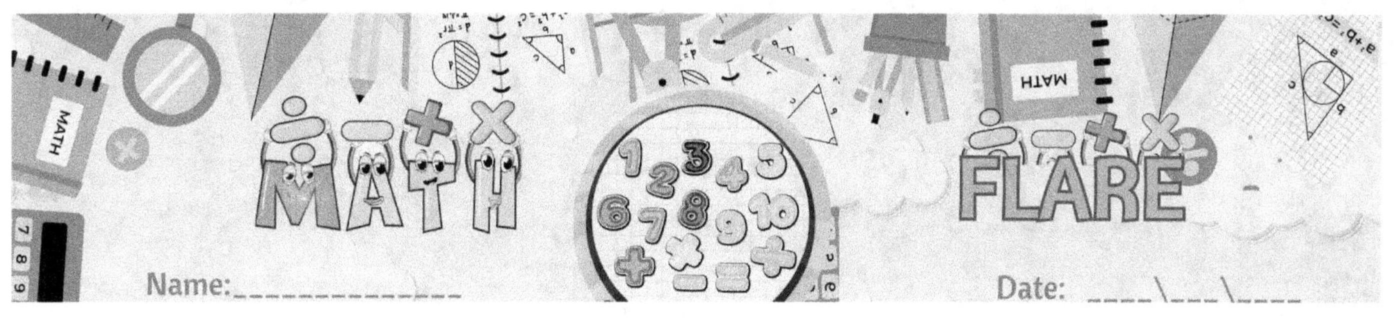

Evaluate Expressions

Evaluate the expression when: x = 4

1) $\dfrac{8 + 12}{x + 7} =$

2) $1 + (7x + 10) =$

3) $10x^3 + 7x^2 =$

4) $9x - x =$

5) $3 + (9x + 2) =$

6) $10 \div x =$

7) $3x + 9x - 9 =$

8) $4x - x =$

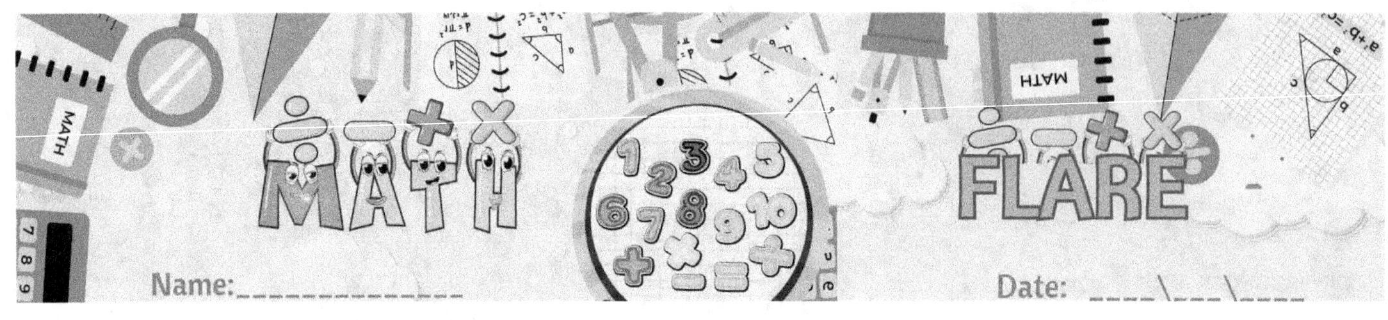

Evaluate Expressions

Evaluate the expression when: x = 3

1) $4 \div x =$

2) $3 \div x + 7 =$

3) $\dfrac{24}{x} =$

4) $\dfrac{4 + x}{x + 6} =$

5) $\dfrac{x}{1} =$

6) $8 + 4x =$

7) $7x - x =$

8) $3 + (2x + 8) =$

Evaluate Expressions

Evaluate the expression when: x = 4

1) $2x + 7 + (6x - 7) =$

2) $x(9 + x) =$

3) $7 + \dfrac{x}{1} =$

4) $1(4 - x) =$

5) $(4x)^1 =$

6) $6(7 - x) =$

7) $\dfrac{6 + x}{x + 7} =$

8) $3x + 6 =$

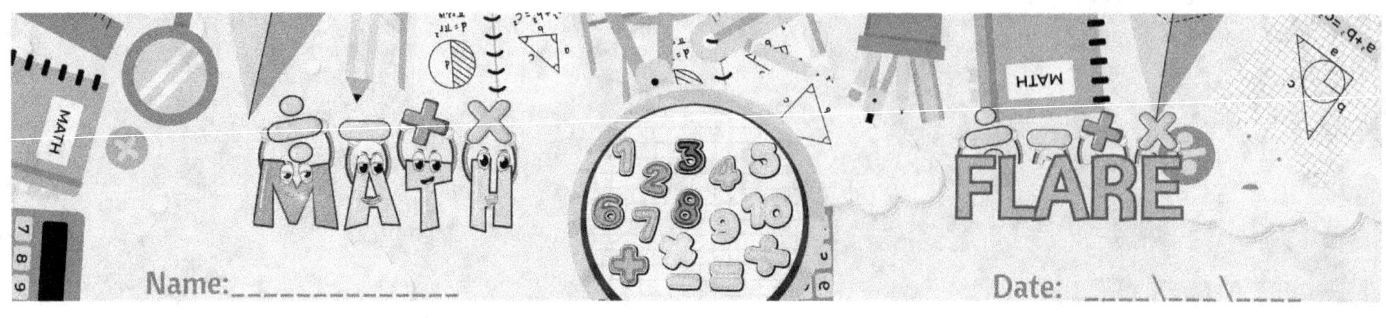

Evaluate Expressions

Evaluate the expression when: $x = 6$

1) $2(9x) =$

2) $x + 2 =$

3) $(8 + 8x) + (2x - 8) - (3 + 10x) =$

4) $(9x)^3 =$

5) $2 + 8x =$

6) $(8x)^2 =$

7) $x + 9 + 6x =$

8) $9 + \dfrac{x}{6} =$

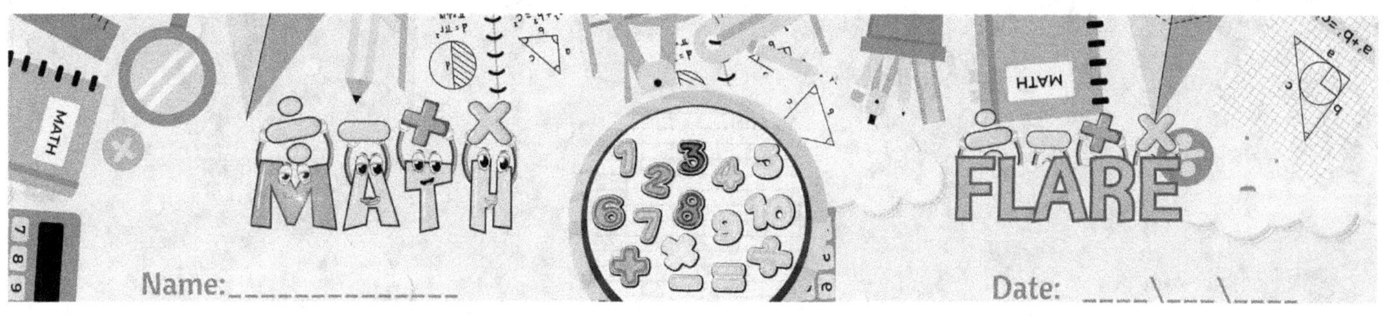

Evaluate Expressions

Evaluate the expression when: x = 3

1) $6(8x) =$

2) $x + 8 =$

3) $2x + 2 - 8x =$

4) $9 \div x + 7 =$

5) $(8x + 6) + (10x + 6) =$

6) $4(7 + x) =$

7) $(3x)^3 =$

8) $9x + 4x + 7x =$

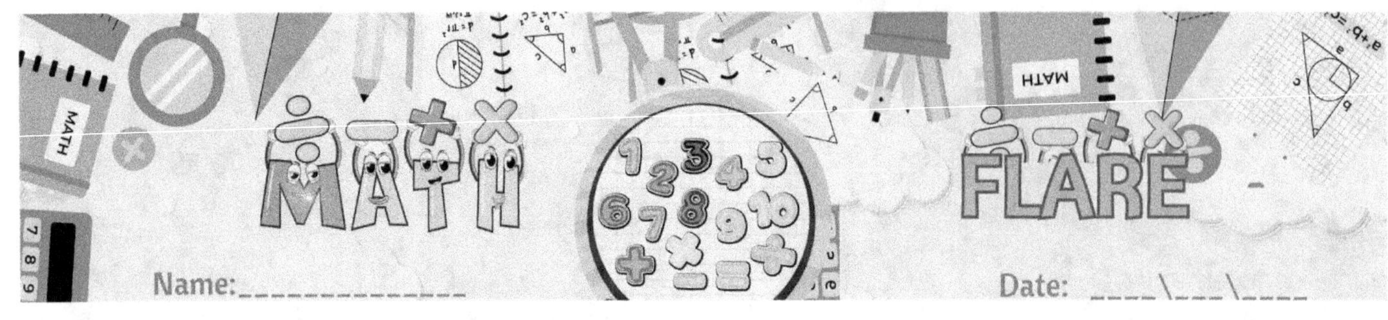

Evaluate Expressions

Evaluate the expression when: x = 6

1) $(x + 10) \div 3 =$

2) $3x + 10 =$

3) $\dfrac{2 + x}{x + 8} =$

4) $\dfrac{x}{6} =$

5) $4 - x =$

6) $x + 2 =$

7) $\dfrac{4 + 12}{x + 10} =$

8) $(2x + 8) + (2x + 4) =$

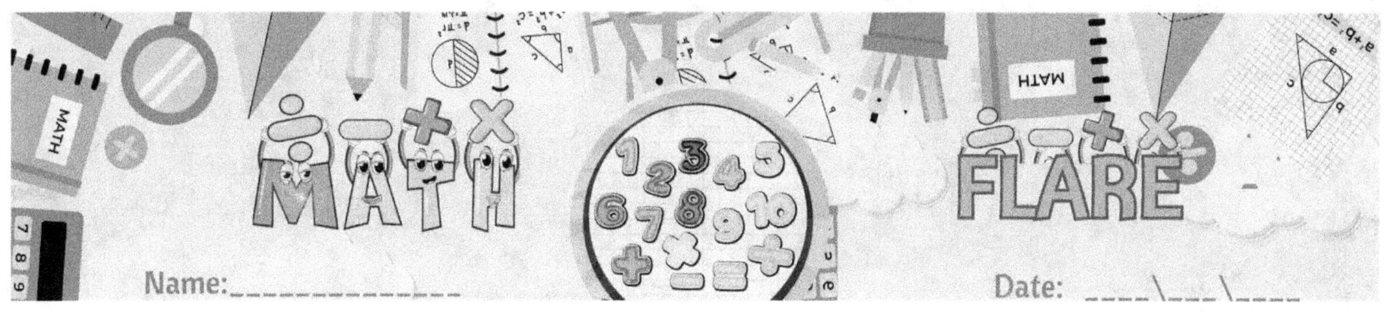

Solving Inequalities

1) $y + -10 \leq -8$

2) $9 \leq 8 - y$

3) $z + 1 < 2$

4) $2 > z - -1$

5) $-2 \leq -5 - k$

6) $-2 < x + 3$

7) $-6 < k + 3$

8) $3 - k > 4$

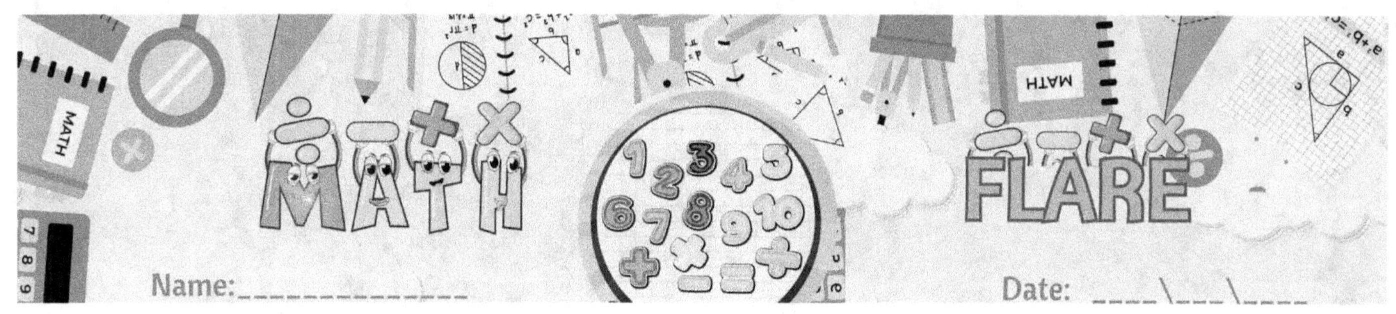

9) $x - 5 \leq 6$

10) $-3 + z > -2$

11) $6 - m \leq 8$

12) $6 + x < 7$

13)

$$7 > z + 1$$

14)

$$8 \geq -3 - y$$

15)

$$y - -8 < -2$$

16)

$$7 \geq y + -5$$

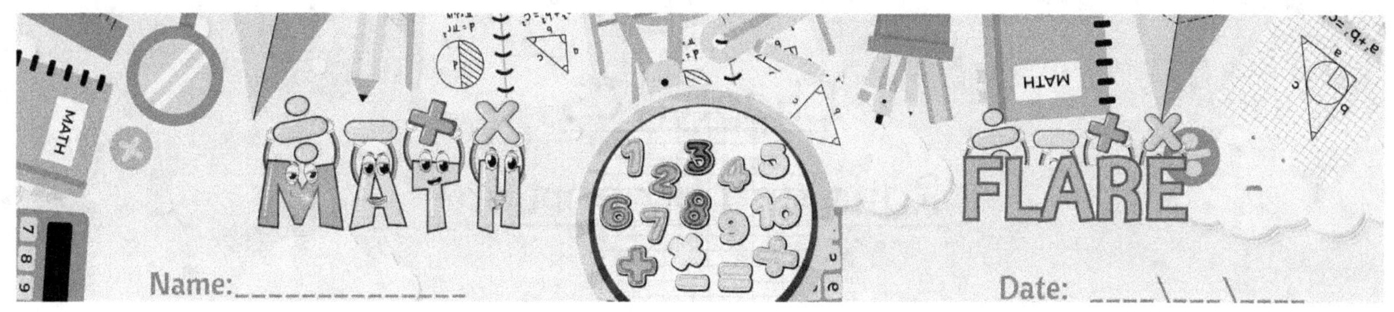

17)
$z + -5 \geq -2$

18)
$6 \leq 5 - k$

19)
$z + 8 > -4$

20)
$0 \geq m - -1$

Chapter. 03

Ratio and Proportion

A proportional relationship between two quantities exists when they have a constant ratio or when one is a multiple of the other. In other words, if we increase one quantity, the other quantity will increase or decrease by the same factor. For example, if we double one quantity, the other quantity will also double.

Let's solve a problem:

$$\frac{x}{9} = \frac{8}{18}$$

Step 1: Cross Multiply: Cross multiply by multiplying the numerator of one fraction by the denominator of the other, and vice versa:

$$x \times 18 = 9 \times 8$$

Step 2: Solve for the Unknown: Perform the multiplication on both sides of the equation:

$$18x = 72$$

Step 3: Divide Both Sides by the Coefficient of the Unknown: To isolate x, divide both sides of the equation by the coefficient of x, which is 18:

$$\frac{18x}{18} = \frac{72}{18}$$

$$x = 4$$

Step 4: Verify Check your solution by substituting x = 4 back into the original equation:

$$\frac{4}{9} = \frac{8}{18}$$

Since both sides are equal, the solution x = 4 is correct.

Ratio and Proportion Word Problems

We can use the concept of proportionality in solving many word problems, for example:

If a car travels 620 miles in six hours, how far can it travel in 12 hours?

Since the car travels a certain distance in a certain amount of time, we can assume that the distance traveled is directly proportional to the time taken.

Let d be the distance the car can travel in 12 hours.

We can set up a proportion:

$$\frac{Distance1}{Time1} = \frac{Distance2}{Time2}$$

Substituting the given values:

$$\frac{620 \text{ miles}}{6 \text{ hours}} = \frac{d}{12 \text{ hours}}$$

Now, let's solve for d.

$$d = \frac{620 \times 12}{6} = \frac{7440}{6} = 1240$$

So, the car can travel 1240 miles in 12 hours.

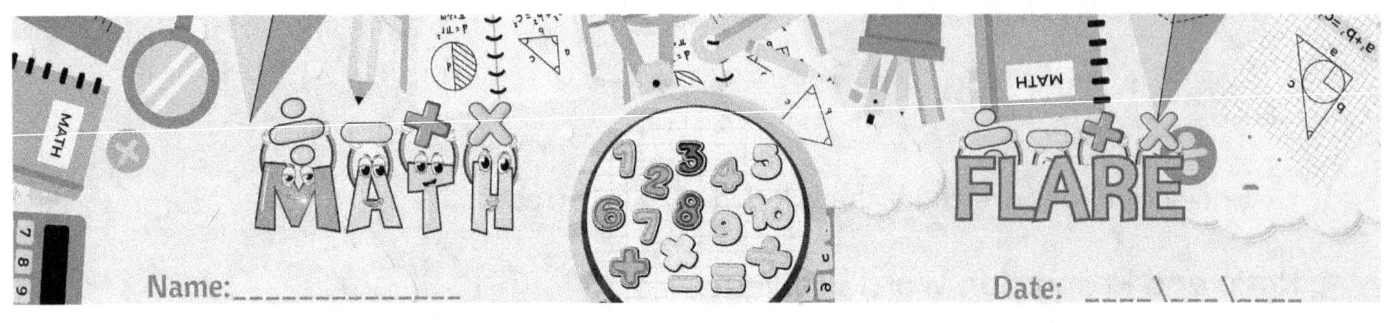

Proportional Relationship

Solve each Ratio and Proportion.

1) $\dfrac{}{9} = \dfrac{5}{45}$

2) $\dfrac{2}{10} = \dfrac{}{60}$

3) $\dfrac{4}{5} = \dfrac{40}{}$

4) $\dfrac{}{11} = \dfrac{25}{55}$

5) $\dfrac{5}{} = \dfrac{45}{72}$

6) $\dfrac{6}{7} = \dfrac{}{56}$

7) $\dfrac{1}{2} = \dfrac{}{18}$

8) $\dfrac{2}{} = \dfrac{18}{36}$

9) $\dfrac{1}{} = \dfrac{10}{30}$

10) $\dfrac{5}{12} = \dfrac{}{60}$

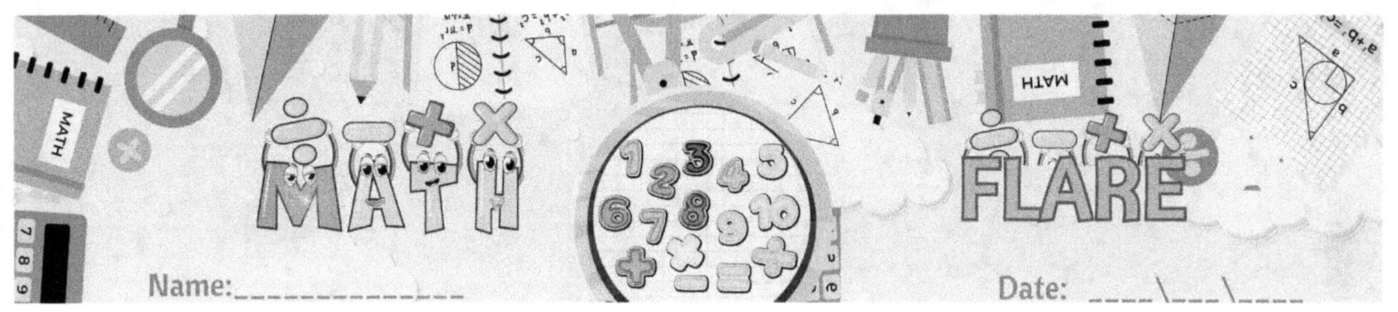

11) $\dfrac{3}{8} = \dfrac{9}{}$

12) $\dfrac{1}{5} = \dfrac{}{50}$

13) $\dfrac{5}{7} = \dfrac{35}{}$

14) $\dfrac{7}{} = \dfrac{14}{18}$

15) $\dfrac{1}{} = \dfrac{5}{15}$

16) $\dfrac{}{6} = \dfrac{32}{48}$

17) $\dfrac{2}{4} = \dfrac{4}{}$

18) $\dfrac{4}{10} = \dfrac{}{80}$

19) $\dfrac{1}{2} = \dfrac{}{8}$

20) $\dfrac{1}{} = \dfrac{10}{110}$

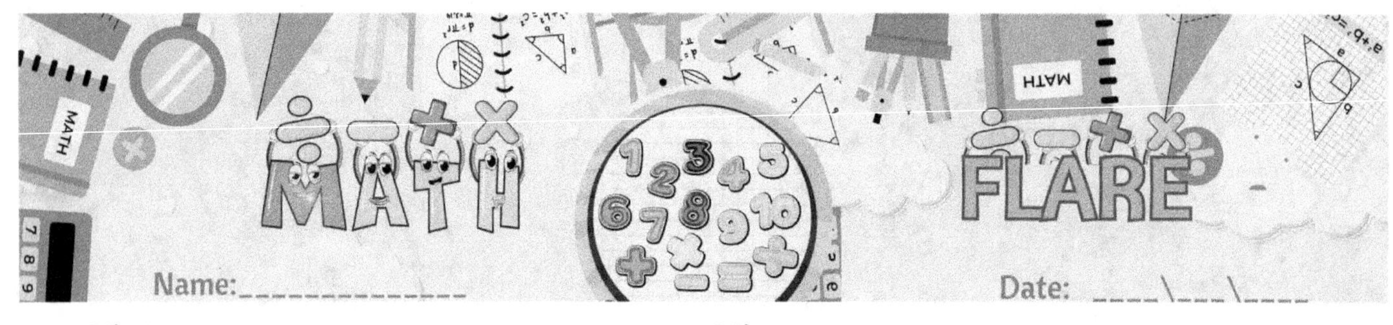

21) $\dfrac{7}{} = \dfrac{70}{110}$

22) $\dfrac{1}{2} = \dfrac{}{20}$

23) $\dfrac{2}{4} = \dfrac{10}{}$

24) $\dfrac{}{6} = \dfrac{10}{60}$

25) $\dfrac{1}{3} = \dfrac{}{21}$

26) $\dfrac{3}{7} = \dfrac{}{42}$

27) $\dfrac{}{8} = \dfrac{30}{80}$

28) $\dfrac{7}{12} = \dfrac{35}{}$

29) $\dfrac{6}{9} = \dfrac{48}{}$

30) $\dfrac{8}{10} = \dfrac{16}{}$

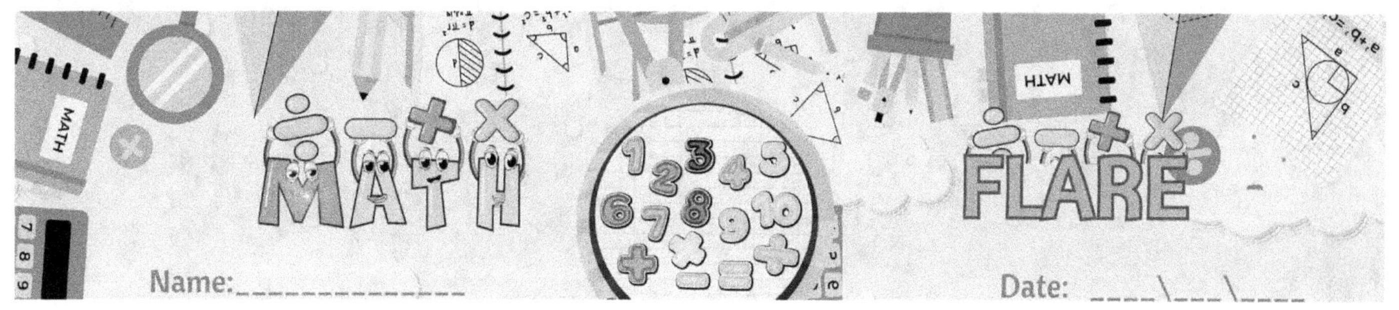

31) $\dfrac{1}{5} = \dfrac{}{40}$

32) $\dfrac{6}{} = \dfrac{18}{33}$

33) $\dfrac{2}{} = \dfrac{10}{15}$

34) $\dfrac{}{2} = \dfrac{2}{4}$

35) $\dfrac{4}{6} = \dfrac{28}{}$

36) $\dfrac{}{10} = \dfrac{70}{100}$

37) $\dfrac{1}{12} = \dfrac{}{120}$

38) $\dfrac{3}{5} = \dfrac{12}{}$

39) $\dfrac{2}{4} = \dfrac{}{32}$

40) $\dfrac{5}{} = \dfrac{15}{24}$

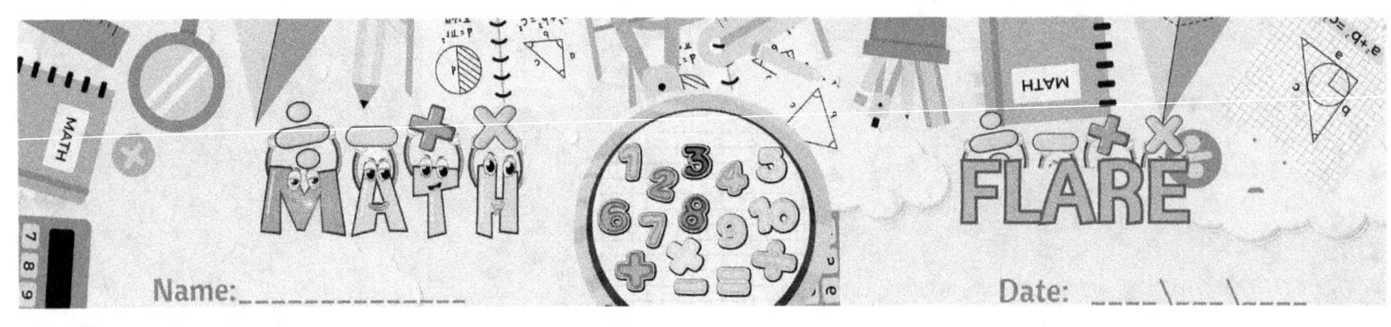

41) $\dfrac{6}{9} = \dfrac{}{18}$

42) $\dfrac{}{7} = \dfrac{4}{14}$

43) $\dfrac{1}{4} = \dfrac{}{40}$

44) $\dfrac{8}{} = \dfrac{40}{60}$

45) $\dfrac{4}{5} = \dfrac{}{25}$

46) $\dfrac{2}{9} = \dfrac{16}{}$

47) $\dfrac{3}{6} = \dfrac{}{36}$

48) $\dfrac{1}{} = \dfrac{8}{64}$

49) $\dfrac{1}{3} = \dfrac{}{12}$

50) $\dfrac{}{7} = \dfrac{16}{56}$

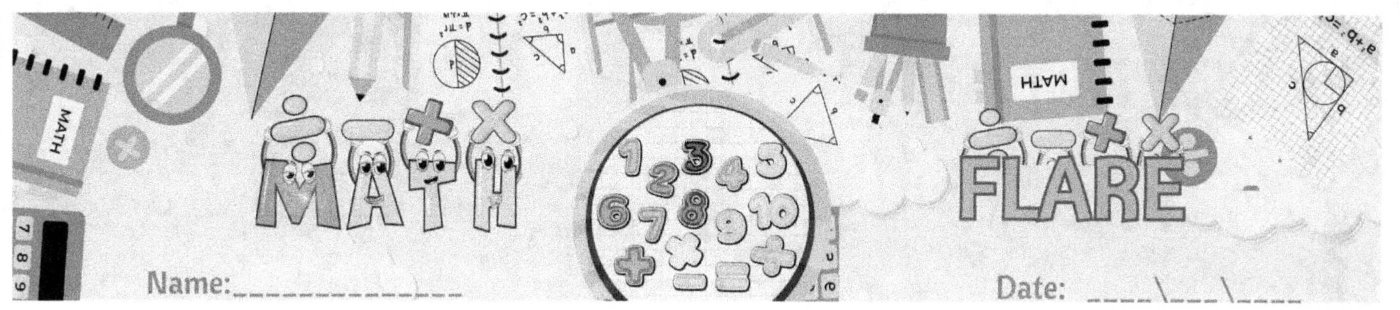

51) $\dfrac{1}{11} = \dfrac{}{99}$

52) $\dfrac{1}{} = \dfrac{6}{12}$

53) $\dfrac{4}{10} = \dfrac{40}{}$

54) $\dfrac{5}{6} = \dfrac{25}{}$

55) $\dfrac{6}{} = \dfrac{12}{16}$

56) $\dfrac{3}{10} = \dfrac{}{60}$

57) $\dfrac{5}{9} = \dfrac{10}{}$

58) $\dfrac{}{11} = \dfrac{27}{99}$

59) $\dfrac{1}{} = \dfrac{4}{20}$

60) $\dfrac{4}{7} = \dfrac{}{63}$

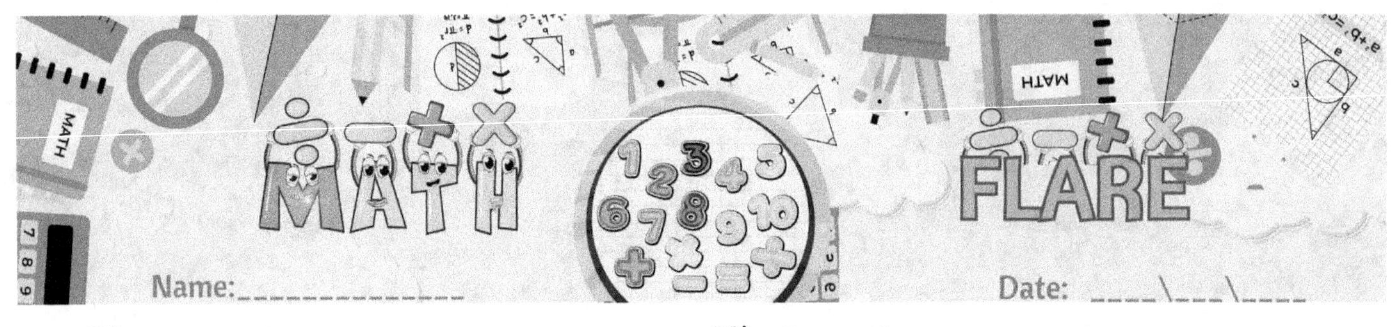

61) $\dfrac{2}{3} = \dfrac{12}{}$

62) $\dfrac{3}{} = \dfrac{6}{8}$

63) $\dfrac{4}{12} = \dfrac{40}{}$

64) $\dfrac{3}{11} = \dfrac{}{88}$

65) $\dfrac{8}{10} = \dfrac{80}{}$

66) $\dfrac{1}{} = \dfrac{6}{18}$

67) $\dfrac{}{7} = \dfrac{24}{42}$

68) $\dfrac{1}{4} = \dfrac{}{20}$

69) $\dfrac{6}{} = \dfrac{30}{40}$

70) $\dfrac{6}{9} = \dfrac{}{81}$

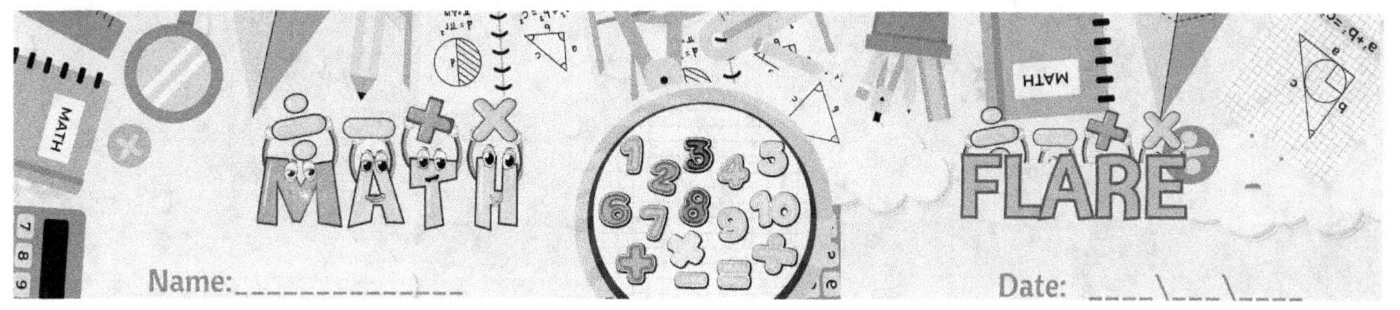

71) $\dfrac{11}{12} = \dfrac{}{96}$

72) $\dfrac{}{6} = \dfrac{6}{18}$

73) $\dfrac{2}{5} = \dfrac{18}{}$

74) $\dfrac{3}{} = \dfrac{30}{60}$

75) $\dfrac{2}{} = \dfrac{4}{6}$

76) $\dfrac{1}{8} = \dfrac{9}{}$

77) $\dfrac{}{9} = \dfrac{6}{27}$

78) $\dfrac{}{11} = \dfrac{50}{110}$

79) $\dfrac{4}{5} = \dfrac{12}{}$

80) $\dfrac{2}{4} = \dfrac{}{12}$

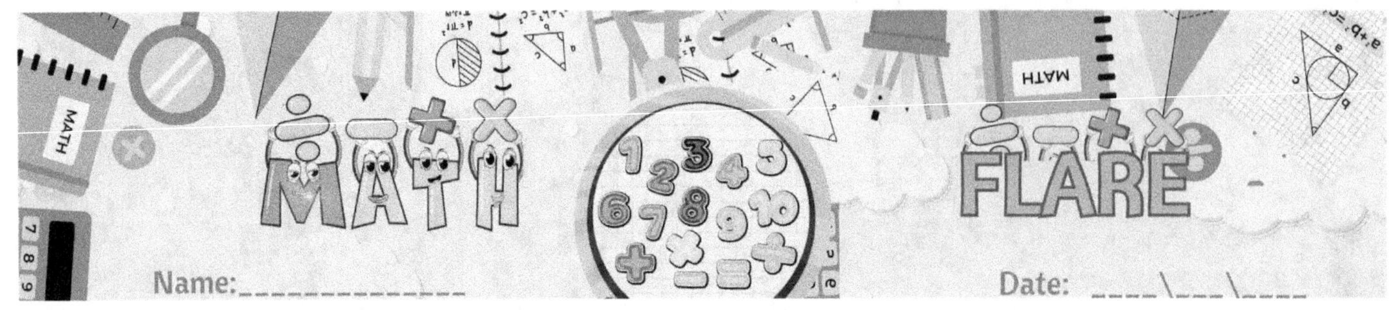

Ratio and Proportion Word Problems

1) A rectangular pool has an area of 347 square meters and a width of 13 meters. What is the length of the pool?

2) In a bag of candies, the ratio of chocolate candies to fruit candies is one:six. If there are 17 fruit candies, how many chocolate candies are there?

3) If two chefs can bake 100 cakes in 16 hours, how many chefs are needed to bake the same number of cakes in 10 hours?

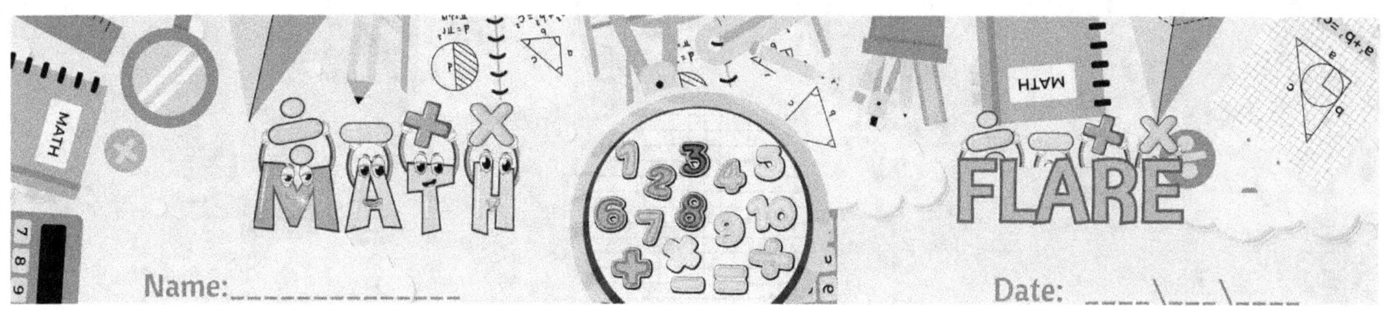

4) A company has a ratio of five managers for every 28 employees. If the company has 127 employees, how many managers are there?

5) A class has a ratio of two girls to every eight boys. If there are 24 boys, how many girls are there?

6) A road is 111 miles long and it takes a car three hour to travel the entire length. What is the speed of the car in miles per hour?

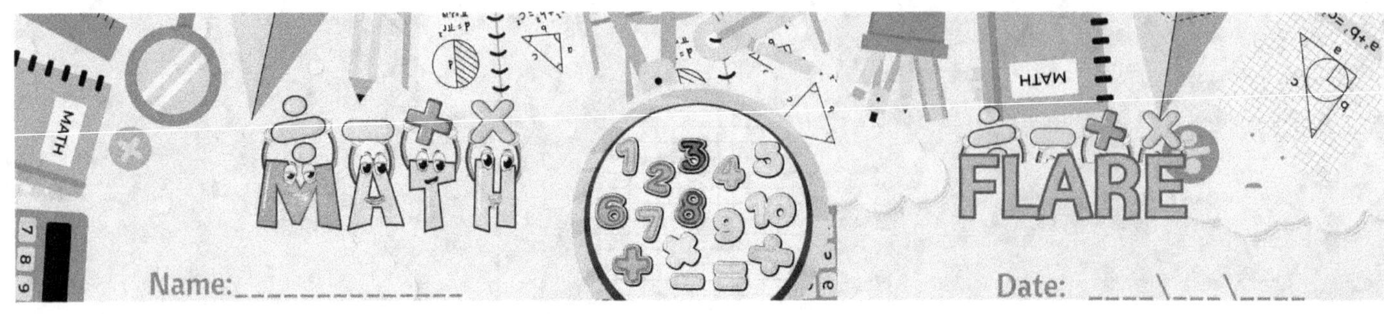

7) A recipe calls for five cups of sugar for every eight cups of flour. If you have 17 cups of flour, how much sugar is needed?

8) A room has an area of 152 square meters and a length of 13 meters. What is the width of the room?

9) A charity received a donation of $3,321 from a company. If the donation was divided among five charities in the ratio 2:3:4:5:6, how much did the fourth charity receive?

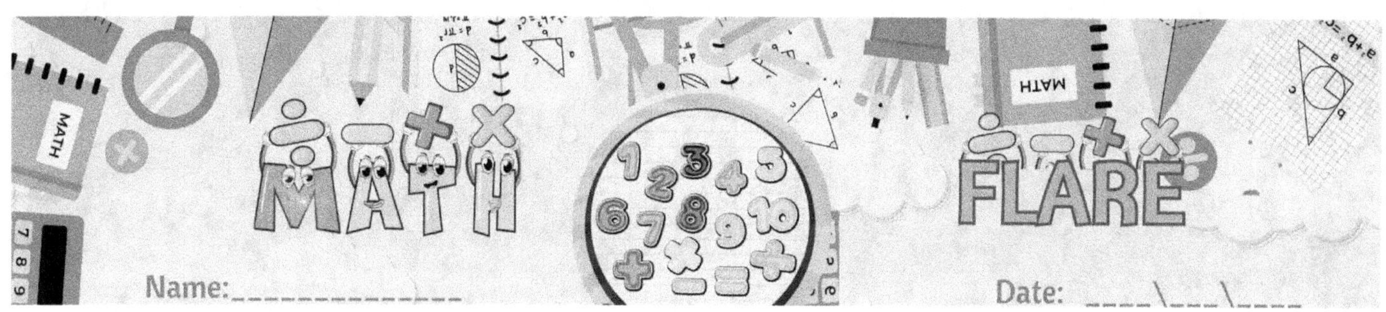

10) A farmer has a ratio of four sheep to every six cows in his pasture. If there are 43 cows in the pasture, how many sheep are there?

11) If a recipe calls for five eggs for every seven cups of flour, how many eggs are needed for 11 cups of flour?

12) A bus travels at a speed of 66 miles per hour. How long will it take to travel 155 miles?

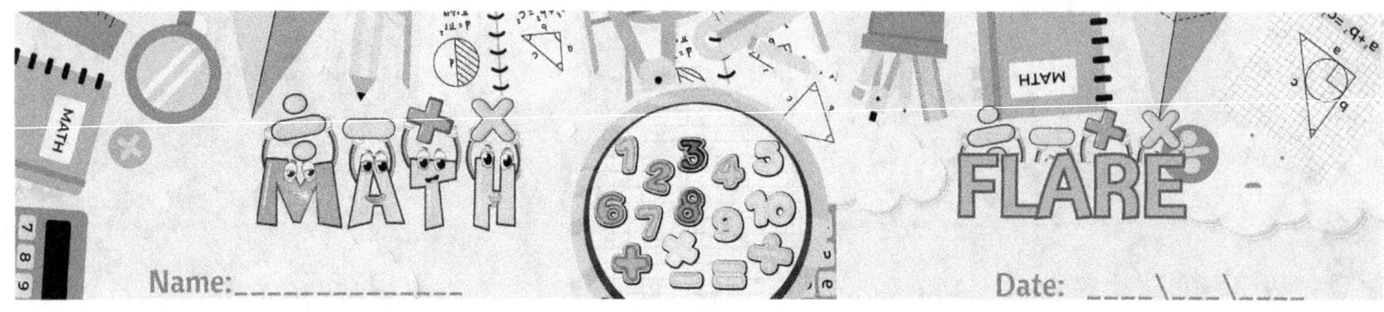

13) If three painters can paint a house in 14 days, how many painters are needed to paint the same house in six days?

14) If a team of eight construction workers can build a road in eight days, how many workers are required to complete the road in eight days?

15) If nine workers can build a wall in 14 hours, how many workers are needed to build the wall in four hours?

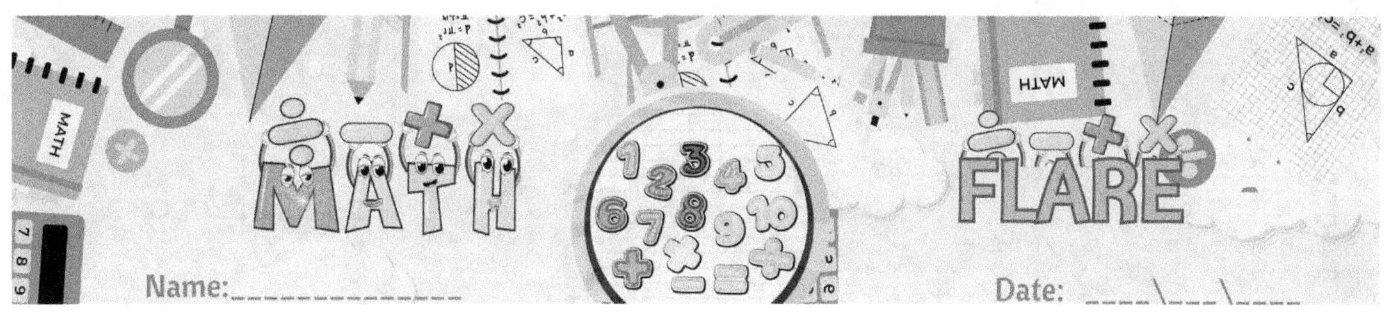

16) If a recipe calls for five eggs for every four cups of flour, how many eggs are needed for 11 cups of flour?

17) If it takes nine students 20 hours to complete a science project, how many students are needed to finish the project in five hours?

18) A school has a ratio of two teachers for every 23 students. If the school has 114 students, how many teachers are there?

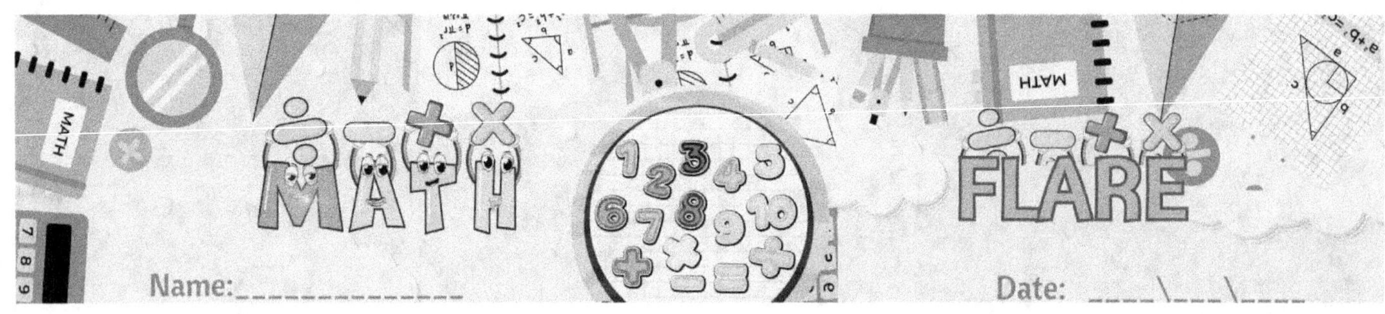

19) If a recipe calls for three cups of sugar for every six cups of flour, how many cups of sugar are needed for 25 cups of flour?

20) A company has a ratio of four female employees to every six male employees. If there are 28 male employees, how many female employees are there?

21) If a map scale is 1 inch to eight miles, how far apart are two cities that are six inches apart on the map?

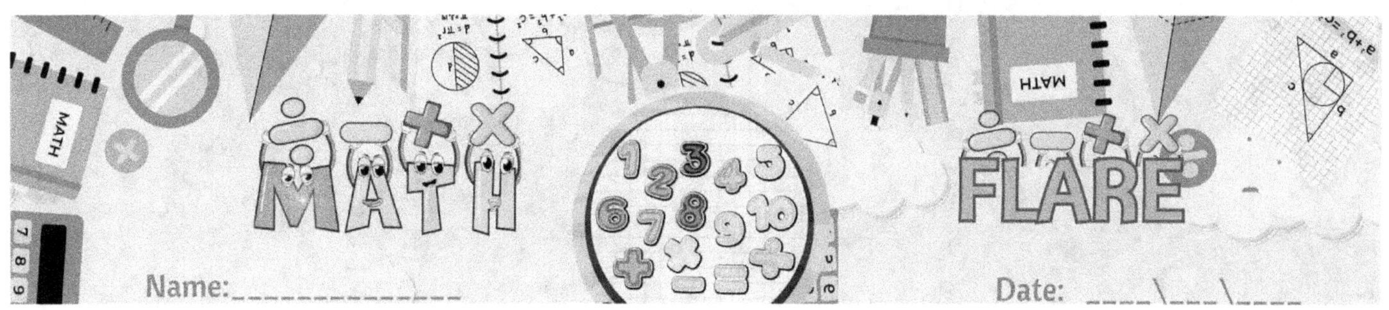

22) If a car travels 205 miles using 15 gallons of gas, how far can it travel using 16 gallons of gas?

23) A charity received a donation of $2,485 from a company. If the donation was divided among five charities in the ratio 2:3:4:5:6, how much did the fifth charity receive?

24) A zoo has a ratio of five monkeys to every 10 lions. If there are 41 lions in the zoo, how many monkeys are there?

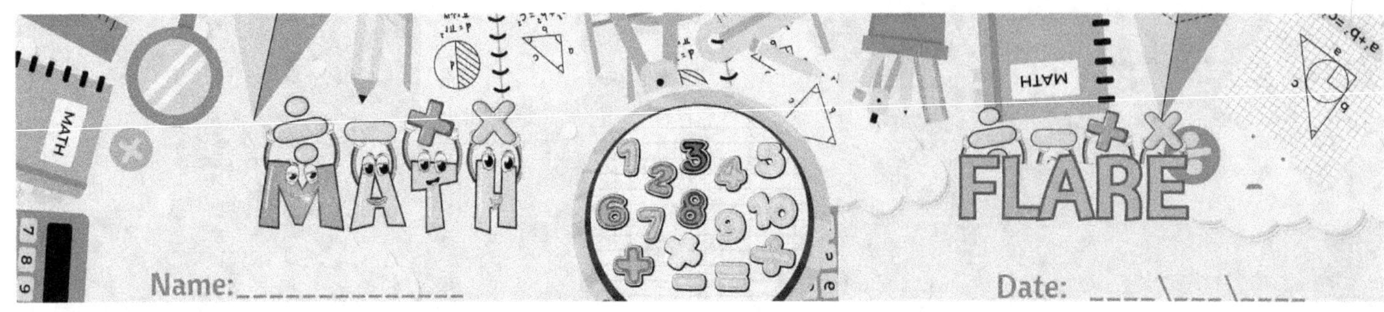

25) If a recipe calls for one teaspoon of salt for every seven cups of flour, how much salt is needed for 12 cups of flour?

26) If a square has an area of 116 square meters, what is the length of each side of the square?

27) A school has a ratio of three female teachers to every seven male teachers. If there are 30 male teachers, how many female teachers are there?

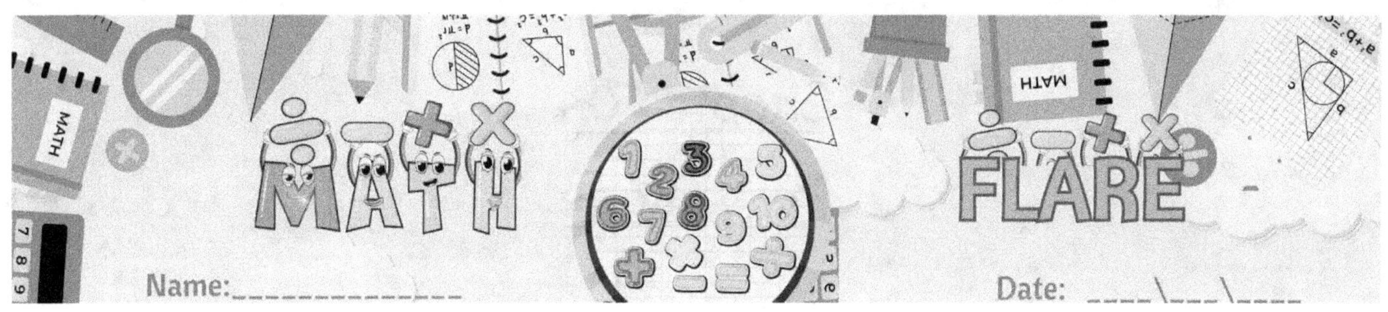

28) A train travels 107 miles in four hours. How far can it travel in nine hours?

29) If a car travels 279 miles in seven hours, how far can it travel in eight hours?

30) If eight workers can complete a job in 20 days, how many workers are needed to complete the job in seven days?

Chapter. 04

Percentage

Percentage is a way of expressing a number as a fraction of 100. It is commonly used to represent proportions, rates, and comparisons. The symbol "%" is used to denote percentages.

To calculate a percentage, we multiply the given number by the appropriate fraction or decimal equivalent.

How to calculate a percentage:

Convert Percentage to Decimal: If the percentage is given as a percentage value (e.g., 25%), convert it to its decimal equivalent by dividing by 100.

$$\text{For example, 25\% as a decimal is } \frac{25}{100} = 0.25$$

Multiply: Multiply the decimal equivalent of the percentage by the given number. This gives us the portion of the number that represents the percentage.

$$100 \times 0.25 = 25\%$$

Result: The result is the calculated percentage value.

For example, to calculate 25% of 80:

Convert 25% to a decimal: 25% = 0.25.

Multiply 0.25 by 80: 0.25 × 80 = 20. The result is 20.

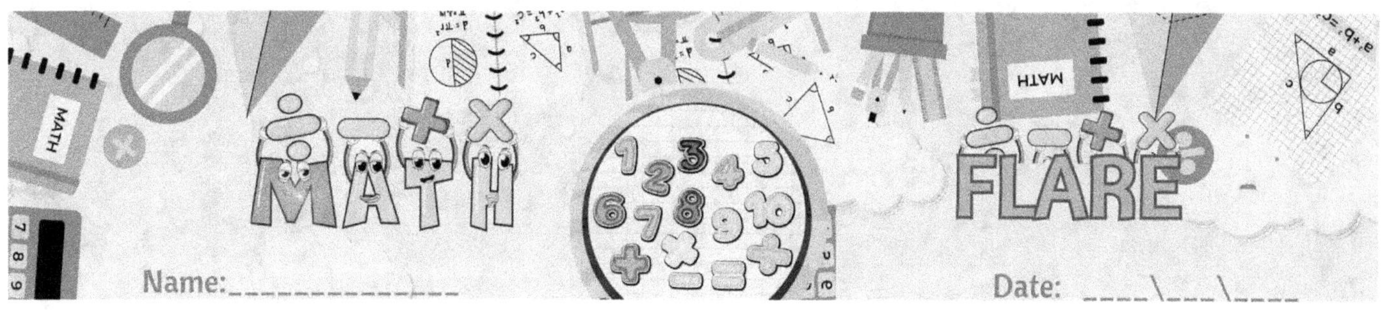

Percentage

Find the percentage of given numbers and percent values.

1) 4% of 200 = ☐

2) 2% of 800 = ☐

3) ☐ of 500 = 100

4) 40% of ☐ = 80

5) 6% of 800 = ☐

6) 8% of ☐ = 24

7) ☐ of 300 = 300

8) ☐ of 600 = 360

9) 30% of ☐ = 210

10) 200% of ☐ = 20

11) ☐ of 900 = 675

12) 7% of ☐ = 21

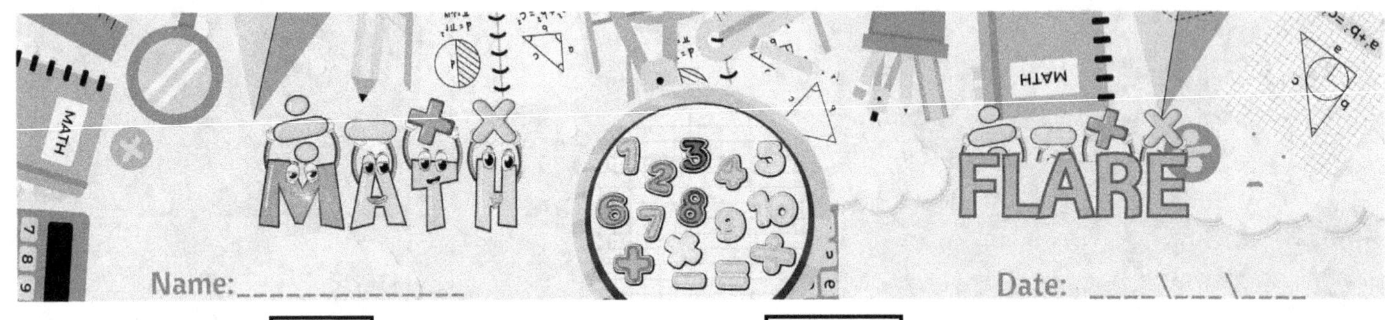

13) 5% of ☐ = 2.5

14) ☐ of 200 = 2

15) 10% of 700 = ☐

16) 35% of 700 = ☐

17) 80% of 600 = ☐

18) 70% of ☐ = 140

19) 90% of ☐ = 18

20) 9% of ☐ = 81

21) 15% of 200 = ☐

22) ☐ of 500 = 125

23) ☐ of 100 = 75

24) ☐ of 300 = 15

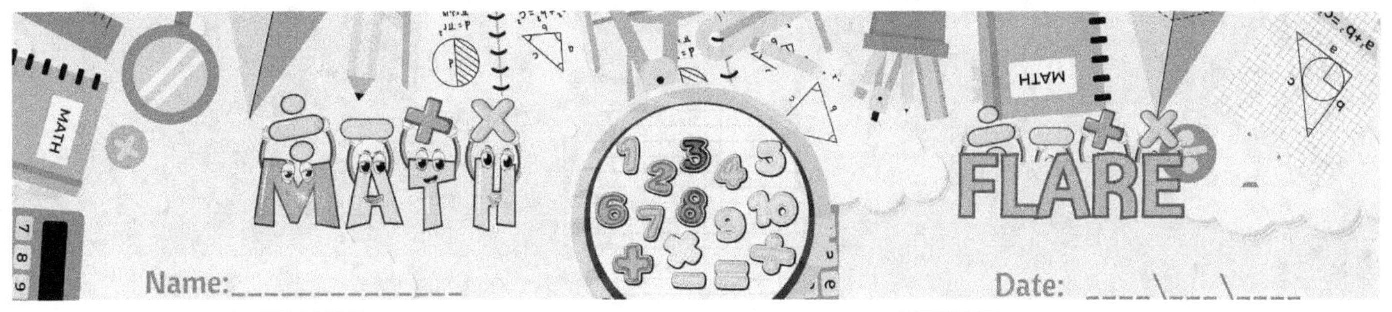

25) 7% of ☐ = 7

26) 4% of ☐ = 32

27) 10% of 300 = ☐

28) 70% of ☐ = 630

29) 80% of ☐ = 80

30) ☐ of 100 = 6

31) ☐ of 500 = 500

32) 90% of ☐ = 720

33) 40% of 50 = ☐

34) 300% of ☐ = 2700

35) ☐ of 200 = 18

36) ☐ of 200 = 16

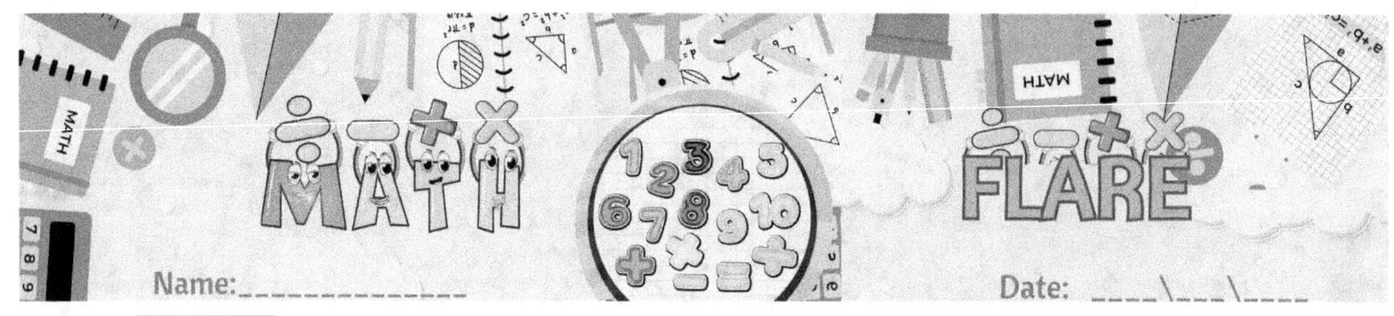

37) [ ] of 400 = 8

38) 30% of 20 = [ ]

39) 25% of 100 = [ ]

40) 1% of 900 = [ ]

41) 35% of [ ] = 315

42) 3% of 600 = [ ]

43) 15% of 100 = [ ]

44) 50% of 900 = [ ]

45) 200% of 200 = [ ]

46) 60% of 500 = [ ]

47) 20% of [ ] = 40

48) 7% of 800 = [ ]

Name: _______________   Date: ____________

Convert Percent and Decimals

1) 34 % = _______________

2) 0.86 = _______________

3) 3 % = _______________

4) 0.24 = _______________

5) 96 % = _______________

6) 0.81 = _______________

7) 78 % = _______________

8) 99 % = _______________

9) 48 % = _______________

10) 0.64 = _______________

11) 59 % = _______________

12) 0.7 = _______________

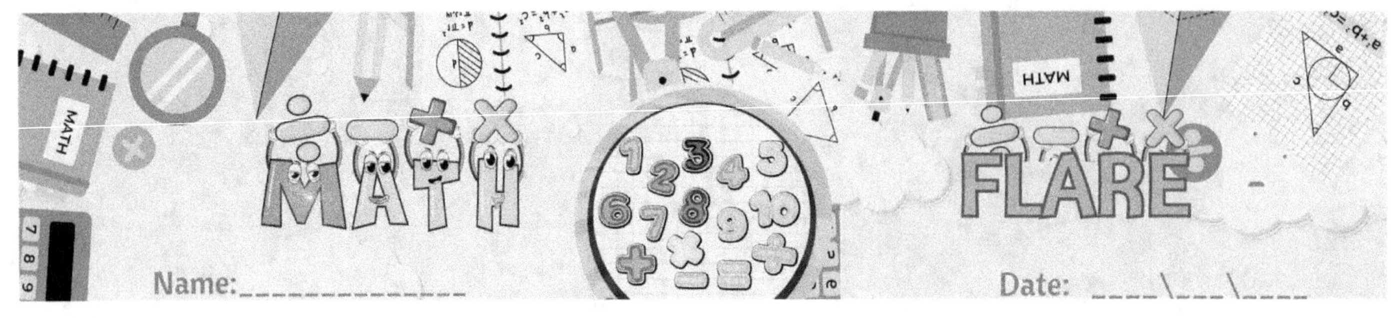

13) 80 % = ________________

14) 46 % = ________________

15) 11 % = ________________

16) 17 % = ________________

17) 95 % = ________________

18) 0.44 = ________________

19) 0.33 = ________________

20) 18 % = ________________

21) 35 % = ________________

22) 62 % = ________________

23) 29 % = ________________

24) 0.2 = ________________

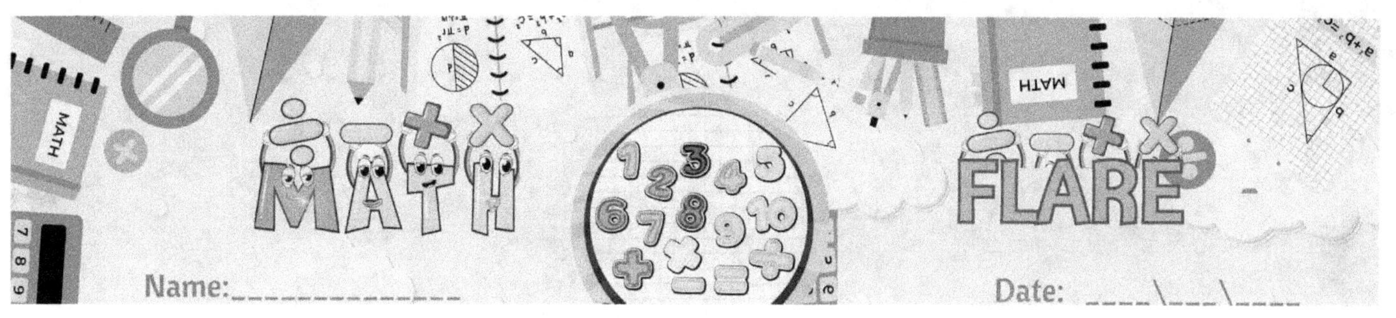

25) 0.75 = ______________

26) 0.68 = ______________

27) 0.26 = ______________

28) 69 % = ______________

29) 36 % = ______________

30) 0.05 = ______________

31) 0.09 = ______________

32) 0.19 = ______________

33) 0.14 = ______________

34) 27 % = ______________

35) 0.1 = ______________

36) 0.71 = ______________

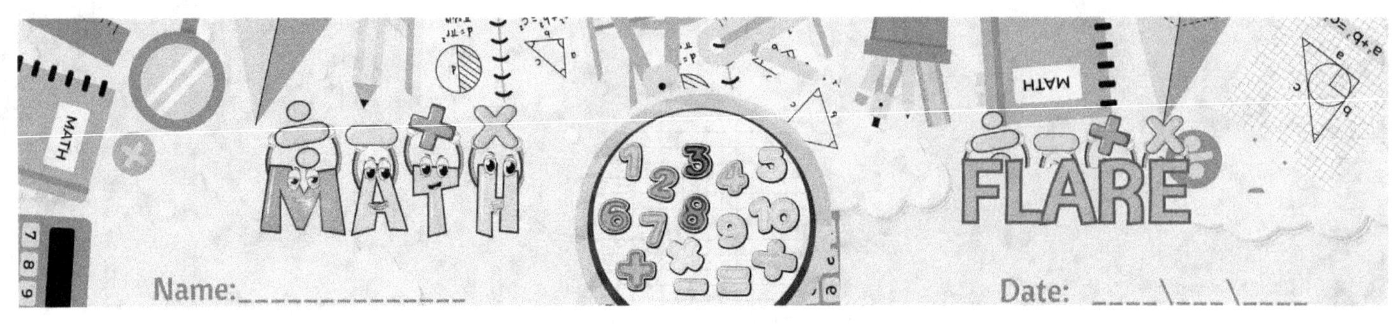

37) 0.97 = _____________

38) 0.04 = _____________

39) 0.07 = _____________

40) 87 % = _____________

41) 0.02 = _____________

42) 0.65 = _____________

43) 0.88 = _____________

44) 0.85 = _____________

45) 53 % = _____________

46) 0.84 = _____________

47) 58 % = _____________

48) 0.74 = _____________

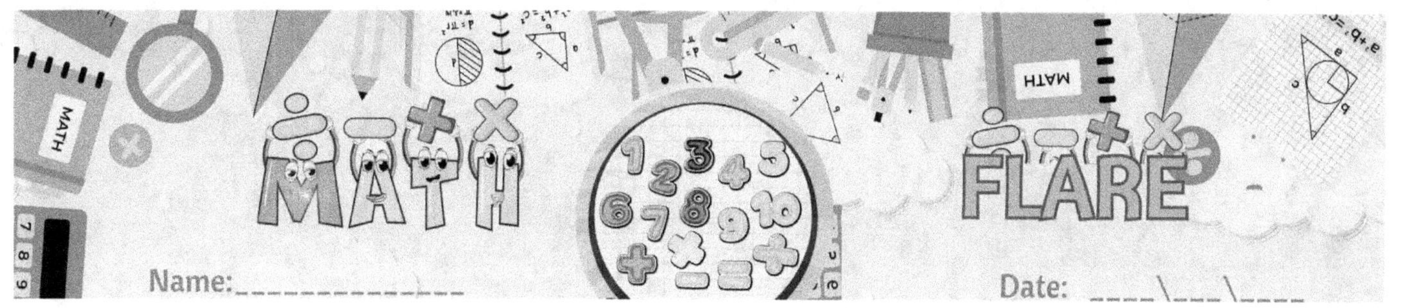

49) 42 % = _______________

50) 0.77 = _______________

51) 31 % = _______________

52) 6 % = _______________

53) 0.08 = _______________

54) 28 % = _______________

55) 66 % = _______________

56) 22 % = _______________

57) 0.45 = _______________

58) 0.57 = _______________

59) 61 % = _______________

60) 41 % = _______________

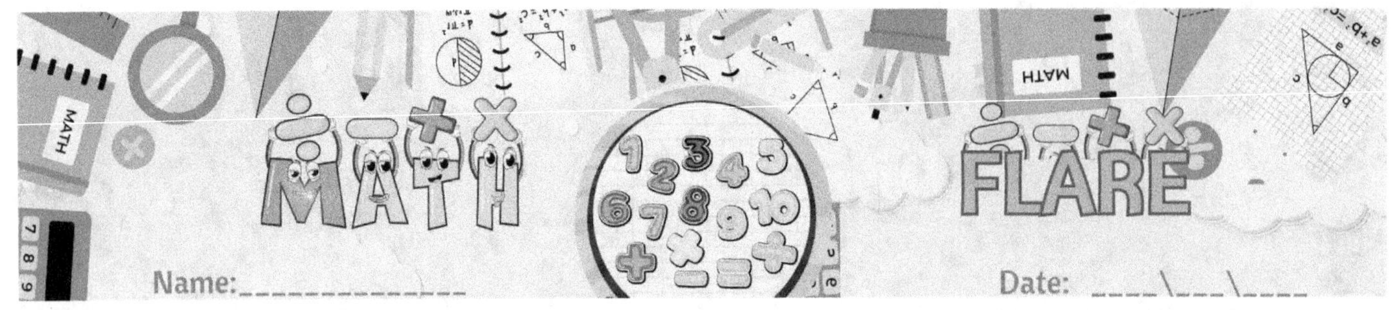

Convert: Ratio, Fraction, Percent, and Decimals

1)

	Ratio	Fraction	Percent	Decimal
a.		18/18		
b.		10/14		
c.				0.833
d.			90.9%	
e.	1:6			
f.				0.632
g.	9:19			
h.		1/19		
i.				0.5
j.	5:19			
k.		9/16		
l.			9.1%	
m.				0.333
n.				0.25
o.				0.875

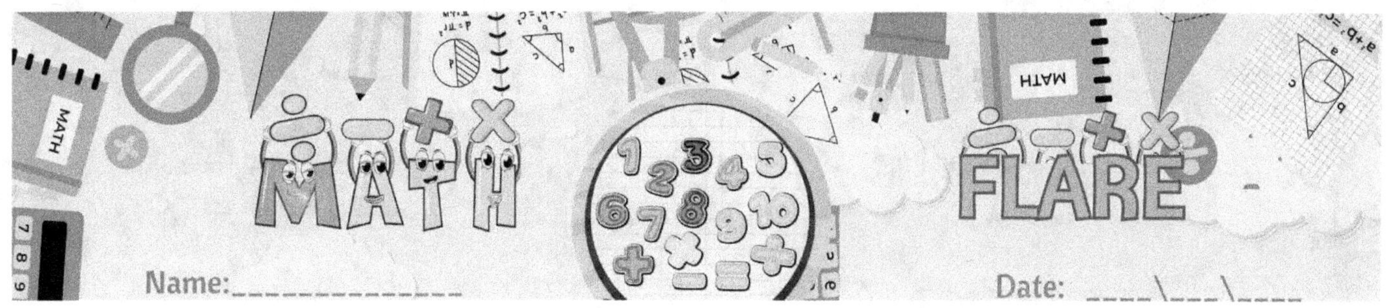

2)

	Ratio	Fraction	Percent	Decimal
a.				0.632
b.	8:20			
c.				0.211
d.	3:4			
e.	1:2			
f.		9/17		
g.		5/19		
h.				0.125
i.		13/19		
j.				0.8
k.				1
l.		4/6		
m.			84.2%	
n.	1:6			
o.				0.455

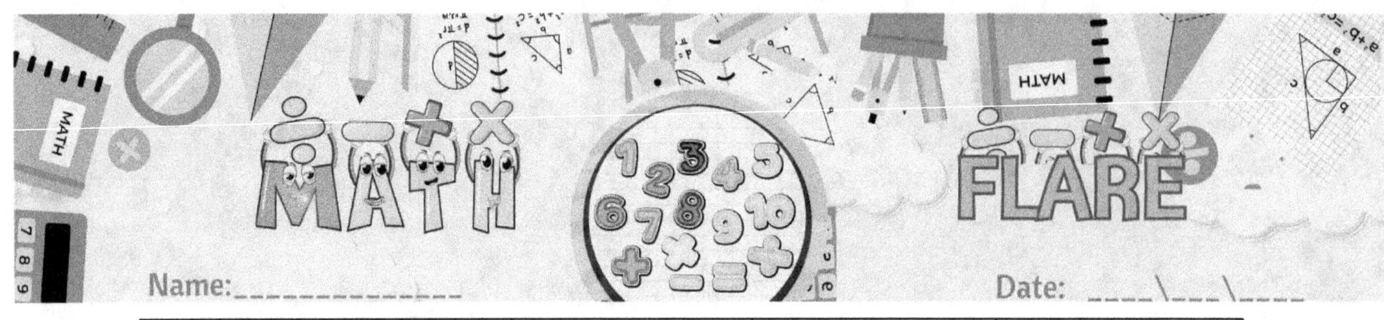

3)

	Ratio	Fraction	Percent	Decimal
a.		1/1		
b.	6:14			
c.		1/2		
d.	3:4			
e.		1/14		
f.	1:3			
g.	4:5			
h.			37.5%	
i.	5:19			
j.				0.278
k.				0.25
l.	13:19			
m.			28.6%	
n.	14:19			
o.	11:20			

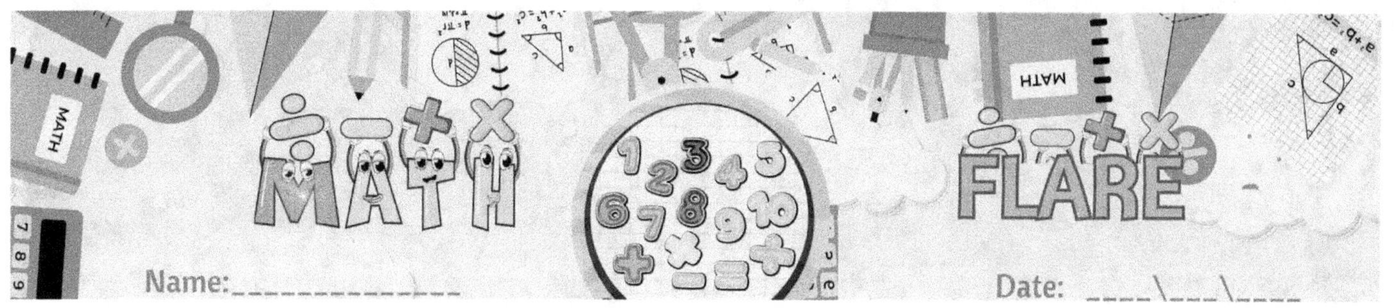

Name:________________   Date: ____________

4)

	Ratio	Fraction	Percent	Decimal
a.			40%	
b.	3:5			
c.				0.625
d.			41.7%	
e.		6/12		
f.		1/2		
g.	2:8			
h.	3:16			
i.	1:1			
j.				0.818
k.	1:3			
l.			92.3%	
m.		1/14		
n.		3/11		
o.		7/20		

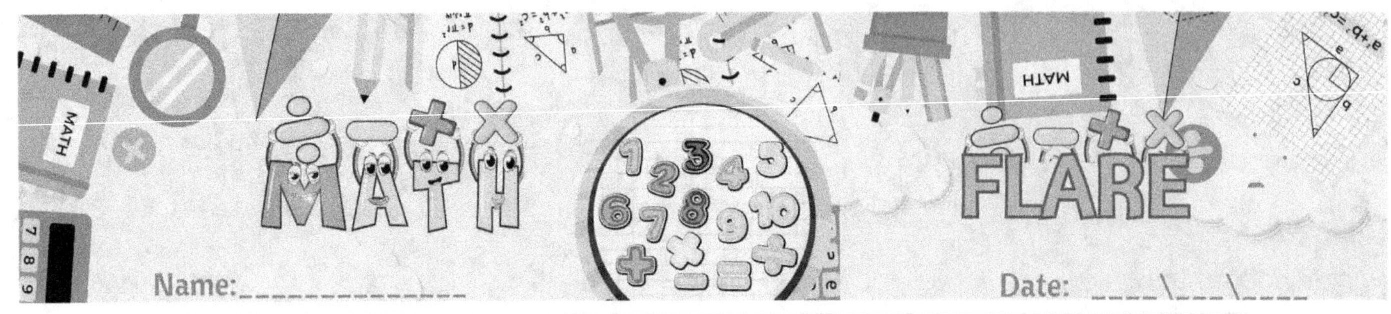

5)

	Ratio	Fraction	Percent	Decimal
a.		6/13		
b.		12/13		
c.		2/3		
d.			16.7%	
e.			75%	
f.		5/5		
g.		7/10		
h.				0.429
i.		5/9		
j.		12/16		
k.		1/16		
l.		11/13		
m.		18/20		
n.		2/14		
o.				0.5

Chapter. 05

Geometry

Area and Perimeter

The area of a shape represents the amount of space it occupies. The perimeter of a shape is the total distance around its outer edge.

Area of Rectangle

For a square, since all four sides are equal, we only need to know the length of one side to find its area. We can calculate the area of a square by multiplying the length of one side by itself (squared). So, if the length of one side of the square is 's', then the area (A) is given by:

$A = s \times s$

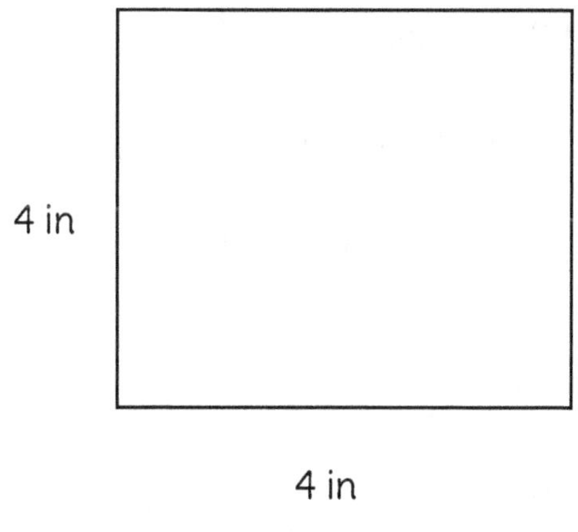

$A = 4 \times 4$

$A = 16$

Perimeter of Rectangle

For a square, since all four sides are equal, we can find the perimeter by adding up the lengths of all four sides. If 's' represents the length of one side, then the perimeter (P) is given by:

$$P = 4 \times s$$

$$P = 4 \times 4$$

$$P = 16$$

Area of Triangle:

The area of a triangle represents the amount of space enclosed within its three sides. The formula for calculating the area of a triangle depends on the type of triangle. For a general triangle, we use the formula:

$$A = \frac{1}{2} \times base \times height$$

Where:

- *A* represents the area of the triangle.

- The base is the length of any one side of the triangle.

- The height is the perpendicular distance from the base to the opposite vertex.

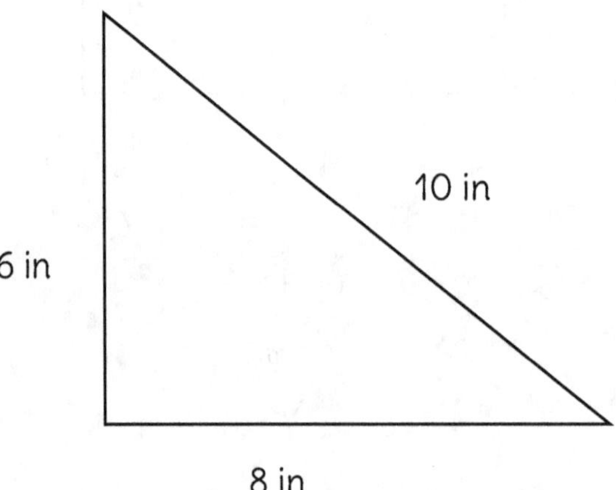

MathFlare - Math Workbook 6th and 7th Grade

$$A = \frac{1}{2} \times \text{base} \times \text{height}$$

$$A = \frac{1}{2} \times 6 \times 8$$

$$A = \frac{1}{2} \times 48$$

$$A = 24$$

Perimeter of Triangle:

The perimeter of a triangle is the total length of its three sides. To find the perimeter, we simply add the lengths of all three sides together:

$$P = \text{side1} + \text{side2} + \text{side3}$$

$$P = 6 + 8 + 10$$

$$P = 24$$

Equilateral Triangle

An equilateral triangle is a triangle in which all three sides are equal in length. To find the area and perimeter of an equilateral triangle, we can use the following formulas:

- Area (A): $\frac{\sqrt{3}}{4} \times a^2$ where a is the length of one side of the equilateral triangle.

- Perimeter (P): $P = 3a$ where a is the length of one side of the equilateral triangle.

Let's solve a problem:

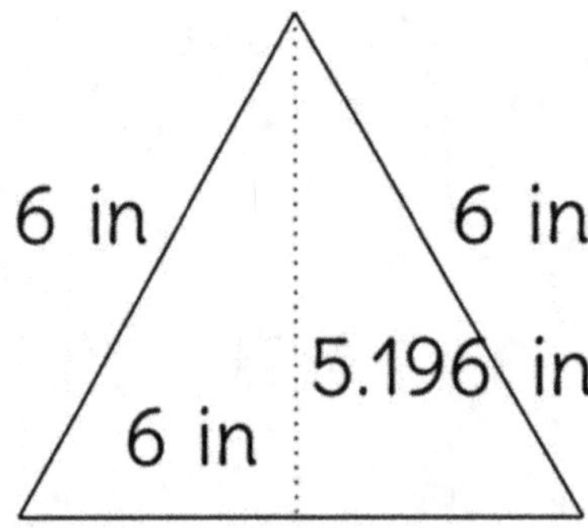

Area of Equilateral Triangle:

$$\text{Area (A): } \frac{\sqrt{3}}{4} \times (6)^2$$

$$\text{Area (A): } \frac{\sqrt{3}}{4} \times 36$$

$$\text{Area (A): } \frac{36\sqrt{3}}{4}$$

$$\text{Area (A): } \frac{36(1.73)}{4}$$

$$\text{Area (A): } \frac{62.35}{4}$$

$$\text{Area (A): } 15.59 \text{ in}^2$$

Perimeter of Equilateral Triangle:

$$P = 3a$$

$$P = 3(6) = 18$$

Isosceles Triangle

An isosceles triangle is a triangle with at least two sides of equal length. The angles opposite the equal sides are also equal.

Area of Isosceles Triangle

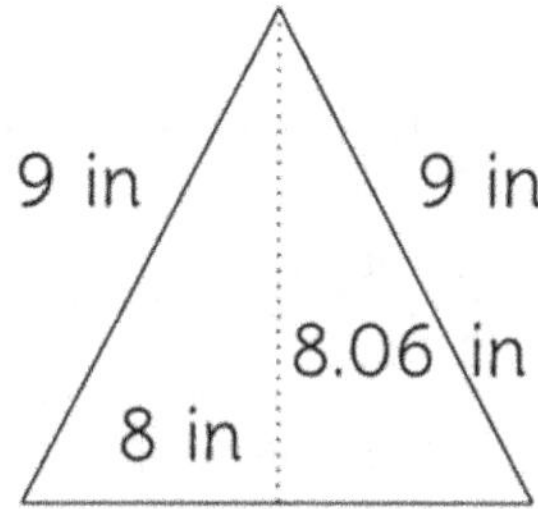

$$A = \frac{1}{2} \times base \times height$$

$$A = \frac{1}{2} \times 8 \times 8$$

$$A = \frac{1}{2} \times 64$$

$$A = 32$$

Perimeter of Isosceles Triangle

The perimeter of a triangle is the total length of its three sides. To find the perimeter, we simply add the lengths of all three sides together:

$$P = side1 + side2 + side3$$

$$P = 9 + 9 + 8$$

$$P = 26$$

Scalene Triangle

A scalene triangle is a triangle with no equal sides and no equal angles. The formula for finding various properties of a scalene triangle is as follows:

Area (A): The area of a scalene triangle can be calculated using Heron's formula, which is given by:

$$A = \sqrt{s(s-a)(s-b)(s-c)}$$

where s is the semi-perimeter of the triangle,

and a, b, and c are the lengths of its three sides.

Perimeter (P): The perimeter of a scalene triangle is the sum of the lengths of its three sides.

$$P = side1 + side2 + side3$$

Let's find the Area and Perimeter of a Scalene Triangle:

15.6 cm   16.6 cm

15.52 cm

7.7 cm

Area (A): First, we calculate the semi-perimeter (s):

$$S = \frac{a+b+c}{2} = \frac{15.6 + 16.6 + 7.7}{2} = \frac{39.8}{2} = 19.9 \text{ cm}$$

Heron's formula to find the area:

$$A = \sqrt{s(s-a)(s-b)(s-c)}$$

$$A = \sqrt{19.9\,(19.9-15.6)(19.9-16.6)(19.9-7.7)}$$

$$A = \sqrt{19.9 \times 4.3 \times 3.3 \times 12.2}$$

$$A = \sqrt{3445} \approx 59$$

Perimeter (P):

$$P = side1 + side2 + side3$$

$$P = 15.6 + 16.6 + 7.7$$

$$P = 39.8$$

Area and Perimeter of an L-shape

The L-shaped figure typically consists of two rectangles joined together to form an L-shape. To find the area and perimeter of an L-shaped figure, we will need to calculate the areas and perimeters of each rectangle and then combine them.

Area=Area of Rectangle 1 + Area of Rectangle 2

Perimeter=Perimeter of Rectangle 1 + Perimeter of Rectangle 2

Let's find the Area and Perimeter of an L-shape:

Area of L-Shape

$$Area\ 1 = 4.38 \times 4.5 = 19.7\ cm^2$$

$$Area\ 2 = 11.28 \times 6.54 = 73.7\ cm^2$$

$$Area = 19.7 + 73.7$$

$$Area = 93.481\ cm^2$$

Perimeter of L-Shape

$$P = 11.28 + 6.54 + 6.78 + 4.38 + 4.5 + 10.92$$

$$P = 44.4\ cm$$

Area and Perimeter of U-shape

U-shape is basically composed of three rectangles, we'll need to calculate the area and perimeter of each rectangle separately and then sum them up.

Area of the U-shape:

The total area (A) of the U-shape is the sum of the areas of the three rectangles:

$$A = A1 + A2 + A3$$

Perimeter of the U-shape: The total perimeter (P) of the U-shape is the sum of the perimeters of the three rectangles:

$$P = P1 + P2 + P3$$

Let's find the area and perimeter of the following U-shape:

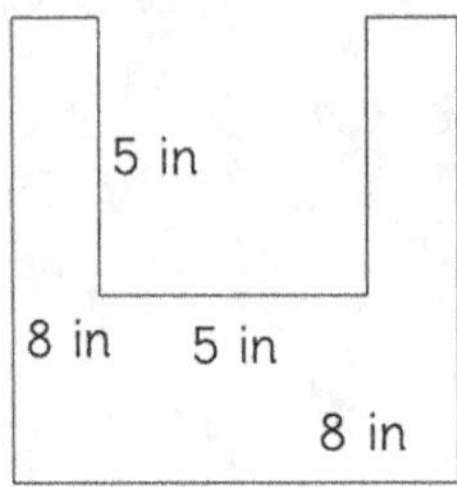

Area:

$$A1 = 8 \times 1.5 = 12 + A2 = 3 \times 5 = 15 + A3 = 8 \times 1.5 = 12$$

$$= 12 + 15 + 12$$

$$= 39 \text{ in}^2$$

Perimeter:

$$2 \times 8 + 2 \times 5 + 2 \times 8$$

$$= 16 + 10 + 16$$

$$= 42$$

Area and Circumference of circles

To find the area (A) and circumference (C) of a circle, we use the following formulas:

1. Area of a Circle (A) = $\pi \times (radius)^2$
   - where π (pi) is a constant with value of (3.14). It is a ratio of the circumference of a circle to its diameter,
   - the radius (r) is the distance from the center of the circle.
2. Circumference of a Circle (C) = $2 \times \pi \times radius$

Let's solve an example: suppose a swimming pool has a radius of 11 meters, we are required to calculate its Area and Circumference:

$$\text{Area } (A) = \pi \times (radius)^2$$

$$A = 3.14 \times 11^2$$

$$A = 3.14 \times 121$$

$$A = 379.94 \text{ square meters}$$

$$\text{Circumference } (C) = 2 \times \pi \times radius$$

$$C = 2 \times 3.14 \times 11$$

$$C = 69.08 \text{ square meters}$$

Angles

Types of Angles: Angles can be classified based on their measures:

- **Acute Angle:** An angle less than 90°.

- **Right Angle:** An angle exactly equal to 90°.

- **Obtuse Angle:** An angle greater than 90° and less than 180°.

- **Straight Angle:** An angle exactly equal to 180°.

- **Reflex Angle:** An angle greater than 180° and less than 360°.

- **Full Angle:** An angle equal to 360°.

Measure angles with a protractor. It looks like a semicircle or a half-disc with degree markings from 0° to 180°.To measure an angle using a protractor, we place the center of the protractor at the vertex of the angle, align one side of the angle with the zero mark on the protractor, and read the degree measure where the other side intersects the protractor.

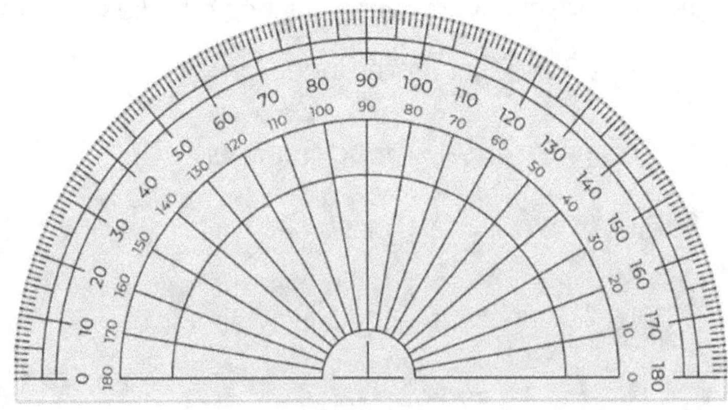

Image: Protector

For example, let's measure the following angle.

The angle is 140°.

We also know that the angle is greater than 90° and less than 180°, so this is an Obtuse angle.

Volume and surface Area

Volume refers to the amount of space occupied by a three-dimensional object. For shapes like cubes or rectangular prisms, we calculate volume by multiplying their length, width, and height.

To find the volume V of a rectangular prism, we use the formula:

$$Volume = length \ x \ width \ x \ height$$

Surface Area represents the total area covering all the faces of a three-dimensional object. For shapes like cubes or rectangular prisms, we find the surface area by summing the areas of all its faces.

The formula for surface area SA of a cube or rectangular prism is:

$$Surface \ Area = 2lw + 2lh + 2wh$$

Where: l is the length, w is the width, and h is the height of the object.

For example: Let's find the Volume and Surface Area of following rectangular prisms:

MathFlare - Math Workbook 6th and 7th Grade

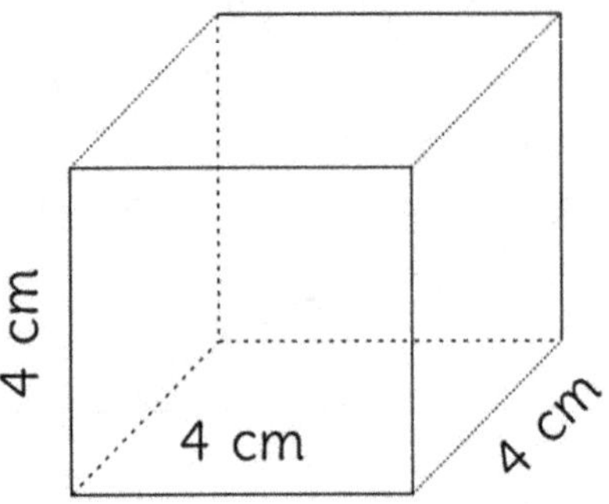

$$Volume = length \times width \times height$$

$$= 4 \times 4 \times 4$$

$$= 64 \text{ cm}^2$$

$$Surface\ Area = 2lw + 2lh + 2wh$$

$$= 2(4 \times 4) + 2(4 \times 4) + 2(4 \times 4)$$

$$= 32 + 32 + 32$$

$$= 96 \text{ cm2}$$

Different 3D objects have unique formulas for finding their volume and surface area. Here are some common ones:

1. Cube:

    - Volume: $V = s^3$ (where s is the length of one side of the cube)

    - Surface area: $SA = 6s^2$

2. Sphere:

    - Volume: $V = \left(\frac{4}{3}\right)\pi r^3$ (where r is the radius of the sphere)

    - Surface area: $SA = 4\pi r^2$

3. Cone:

- Volume: $V = (\frac{1}{3})\pi r^2 h$ (where r is the radius of the base and h is the height of the cone)

- Surface area: $SA = \pi r^2 + \pi r \sqrt{(r^2 + h^2)}$

4. Cylinder:

- Volume: $V = \pi r^2 h$ (where r is the radius of the base and h is the height of the cylinder)

- Surface area: $SA = 2\pi r^2 + 2\pi rh$

5. Pyramid:

- Volume: $V = (\frac{1}{3})Bh$ (where B is the area of the base and h is the height of the pyramid)

- Surface area: $SA = B + \frac{1}{2}Pl$ (where P is the perimeter of the base and l is the slant height of the pyramid)

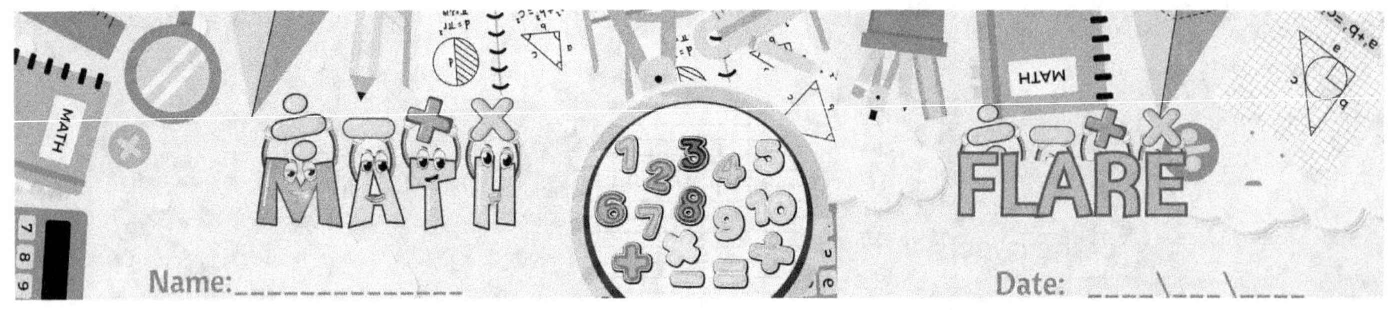

Area and Perimeter

1)

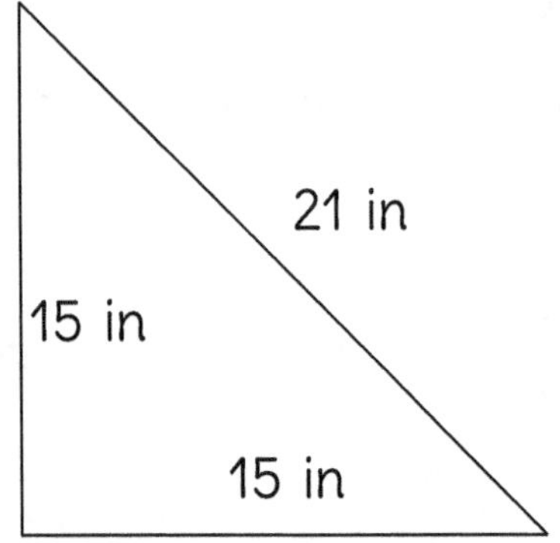

2)

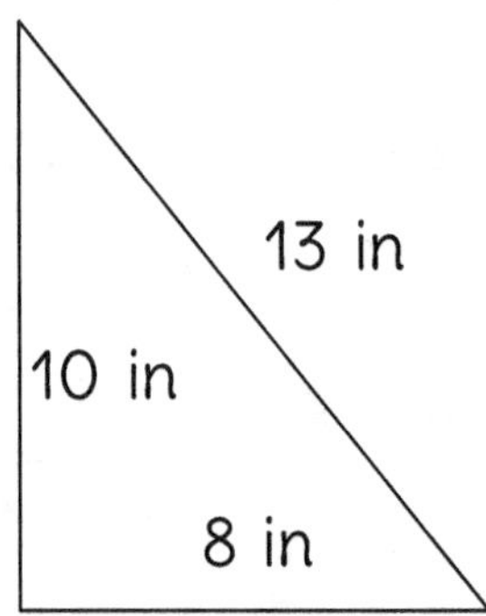

3)

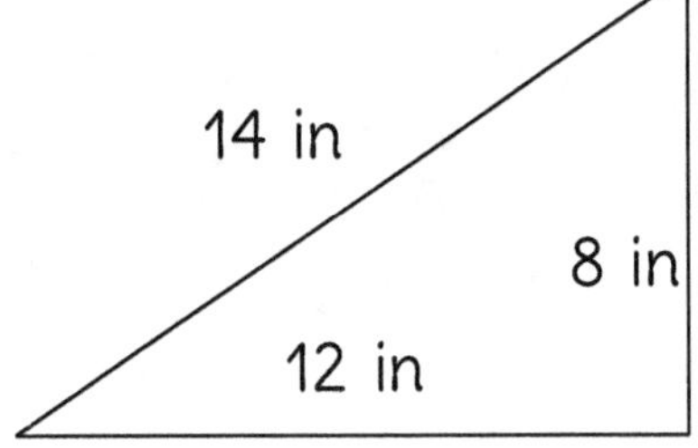

4)

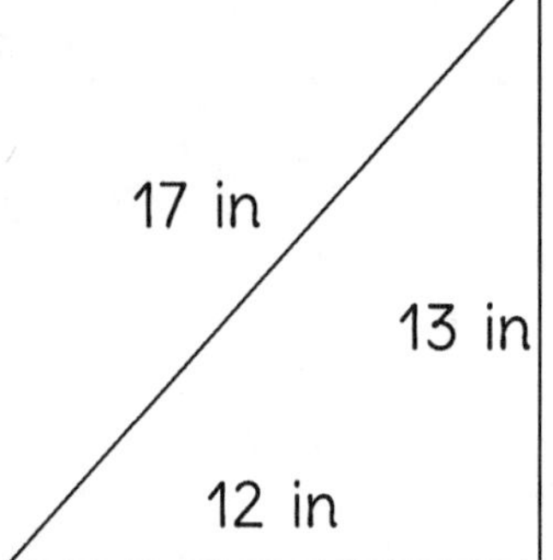

MATH
FLARE
Name:______________
Date: ___________

5)

7 in
10 in
10 in
6 in

6)

16 in
10 in
16 in
7 in

7)

10 in
7 in
7 in

8)

9 in
8 in

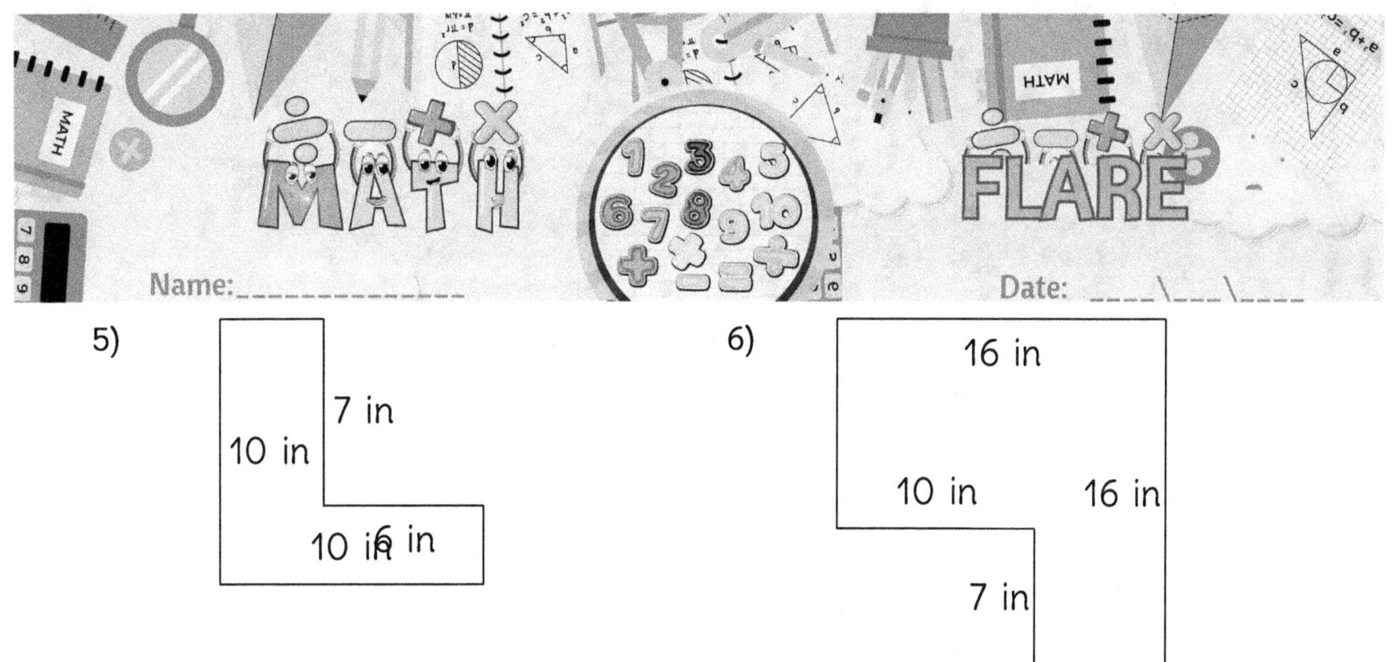

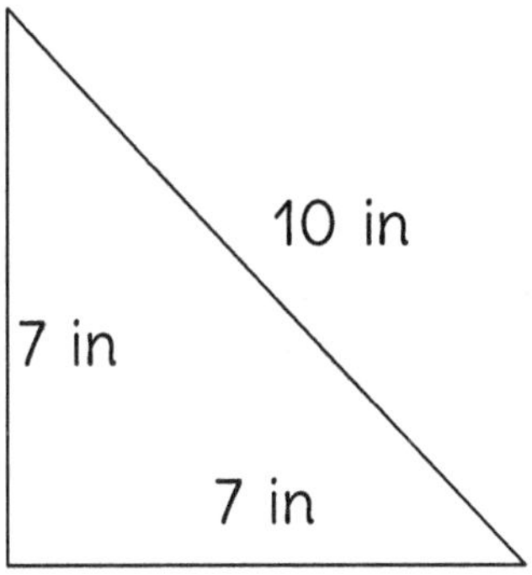

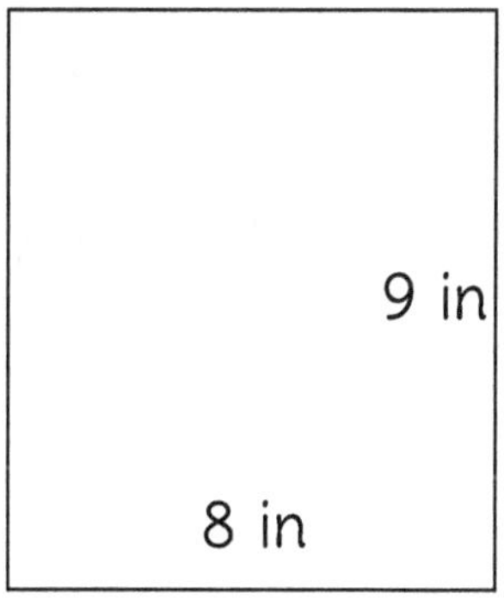

Name:
Date:

9)

6 in
0 in
16 in
16 in

10)

19 in
13 in
14 in

11)

11 in
5 in
4.92 in
12 in

12)

4 in
9 in
5 in
9 in

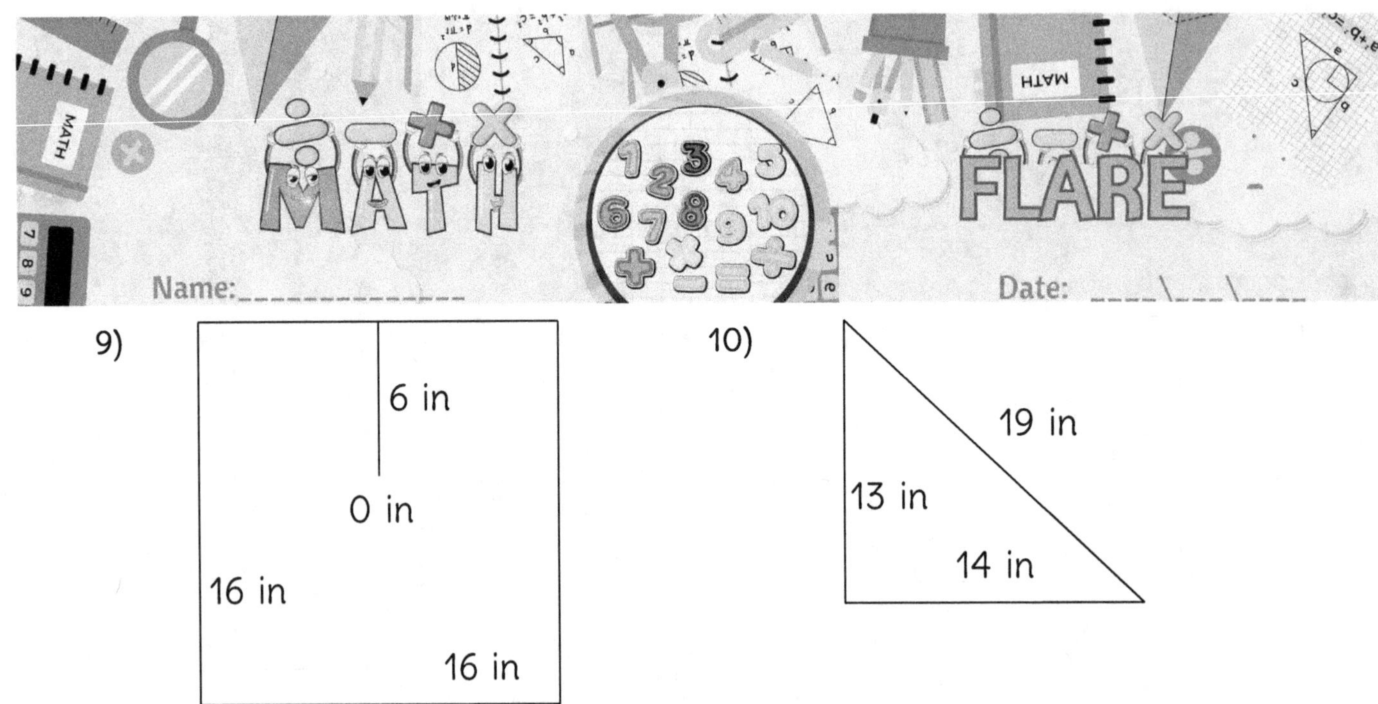

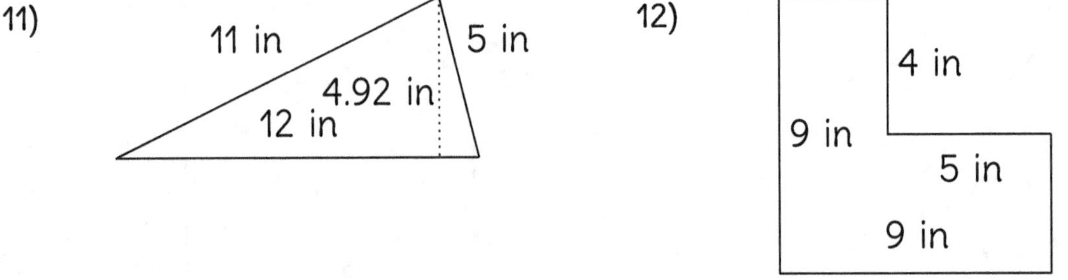

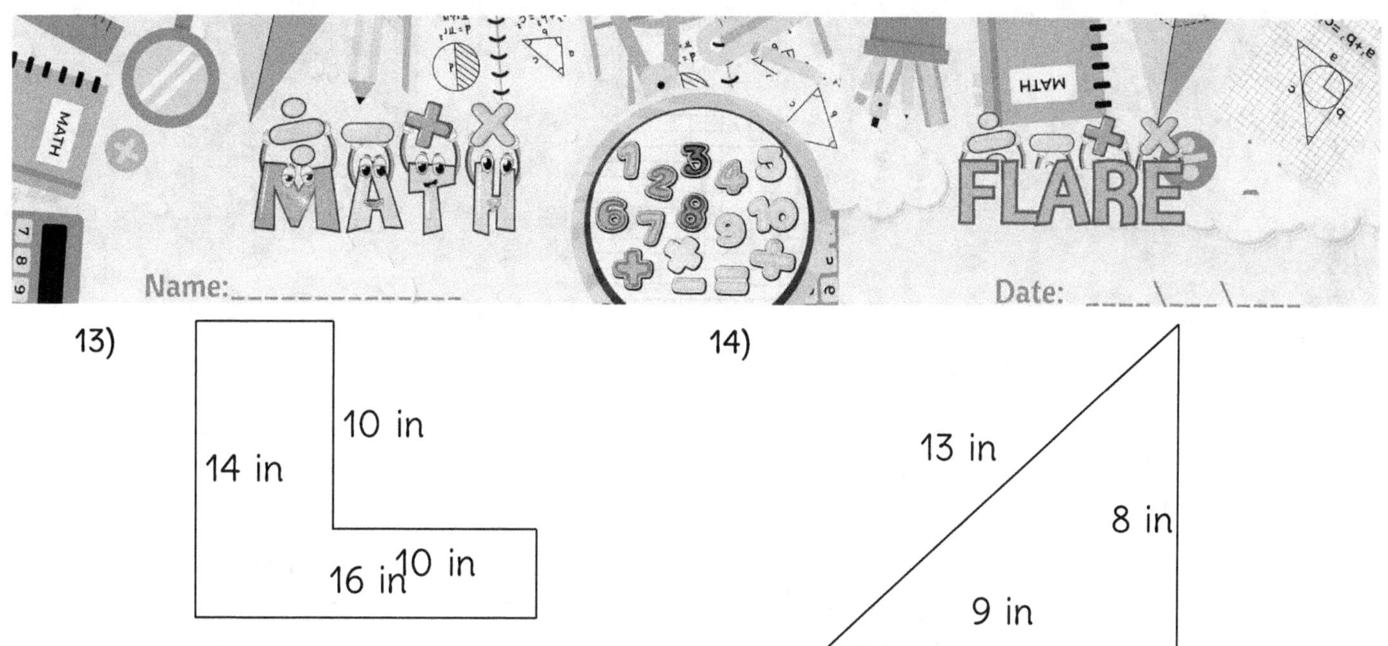

Name: _______________   Date: ____ \ ____ \ ____

13)

14)

10 in
14 in
16 in   10 in

13 in
8 in
9 in

15)

16)

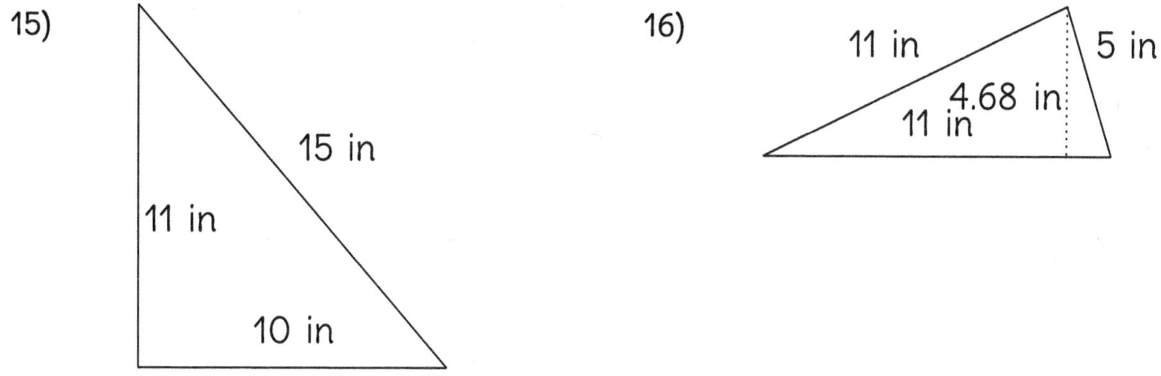

15 in
11 in
10 in

11 in   5 in
4.68 in
11 in

MATH
FLARE
Name:
Date:

17)

2 in
6 in
4 in
7 in

18)
6 in
12 in
0 in
15 in

19)
10 in
10 in
8.660 in
10 in

20)
7 in
12 in
3 in
11 in

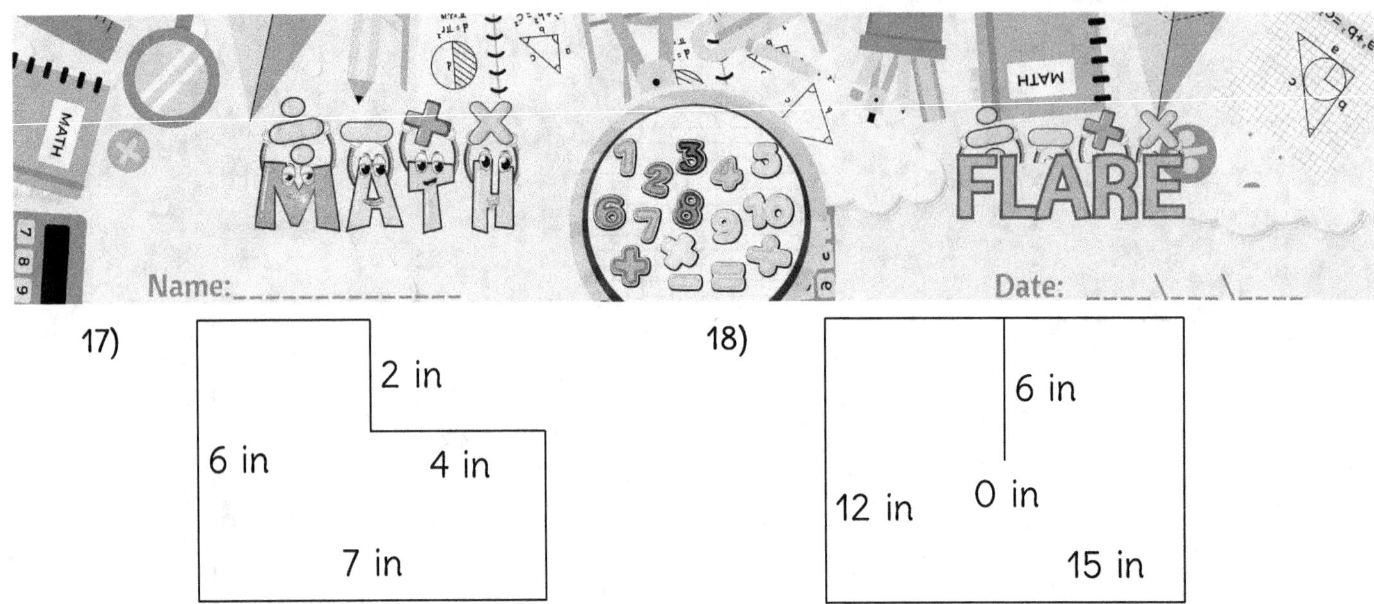

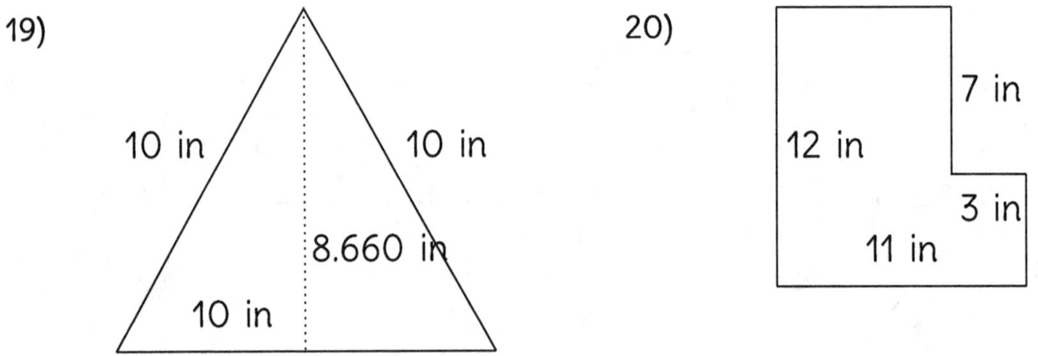

MATH
FLARE
Name:
Date:

21)

11 in
8 in
8 in

22)

8 in
8 in
7.19 in
7 in

23)

11 in
13 in

24)

10 in
16 in
0 in
15 in

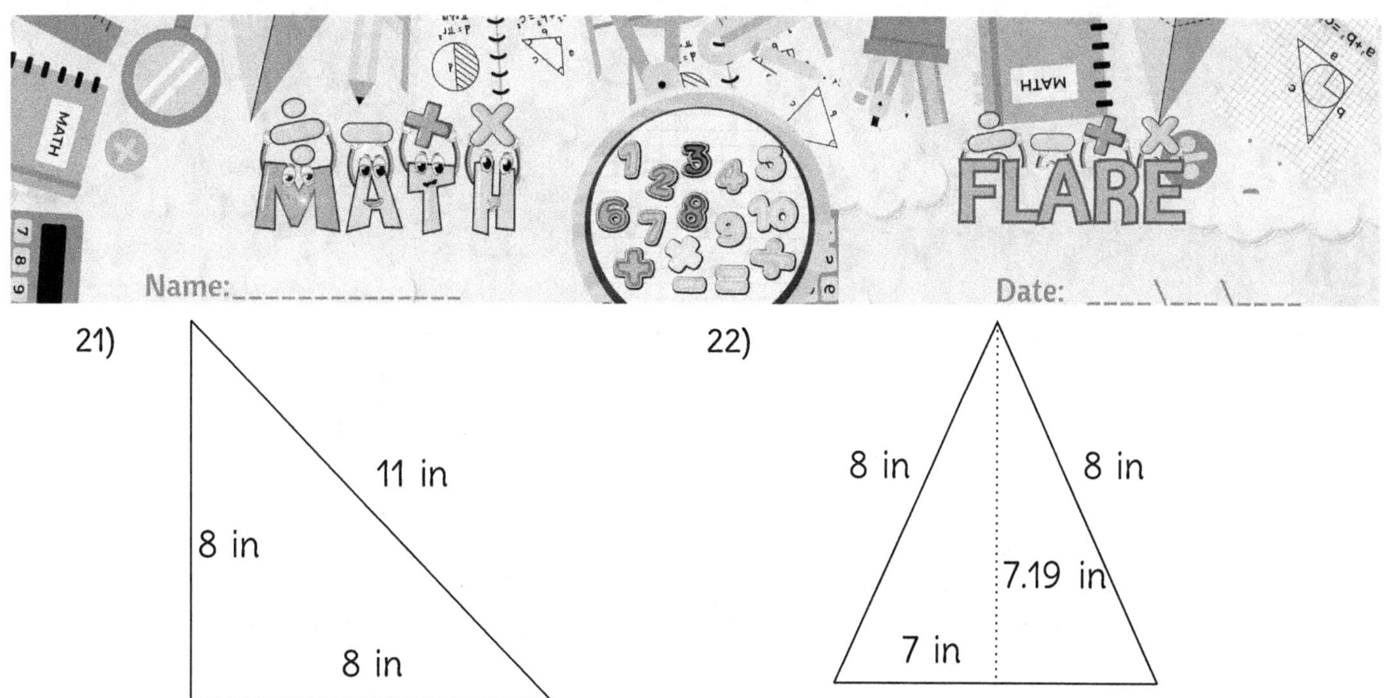

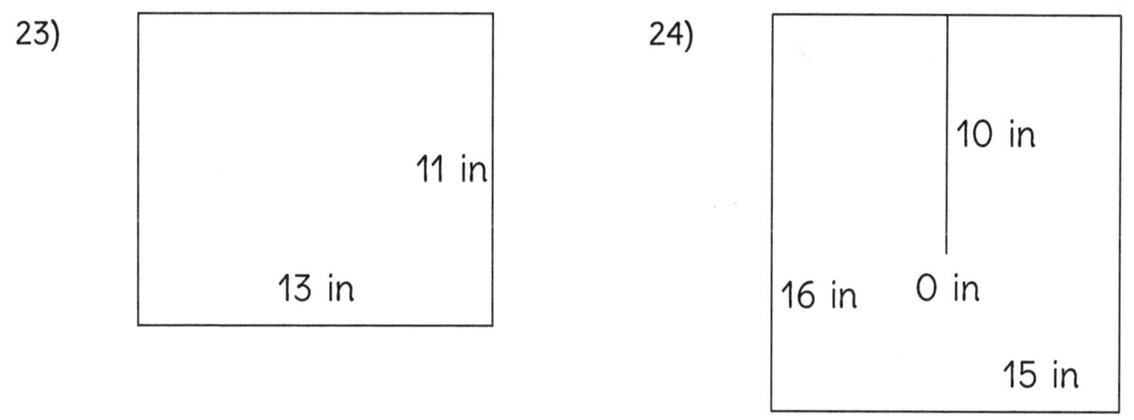

Name:
Date:

25)

6 in
9 in
5 in
8 in

26)

7 in
13 in
0 in
14 in

27)

10 in
7 in

28)

24 in
16 in
18 in

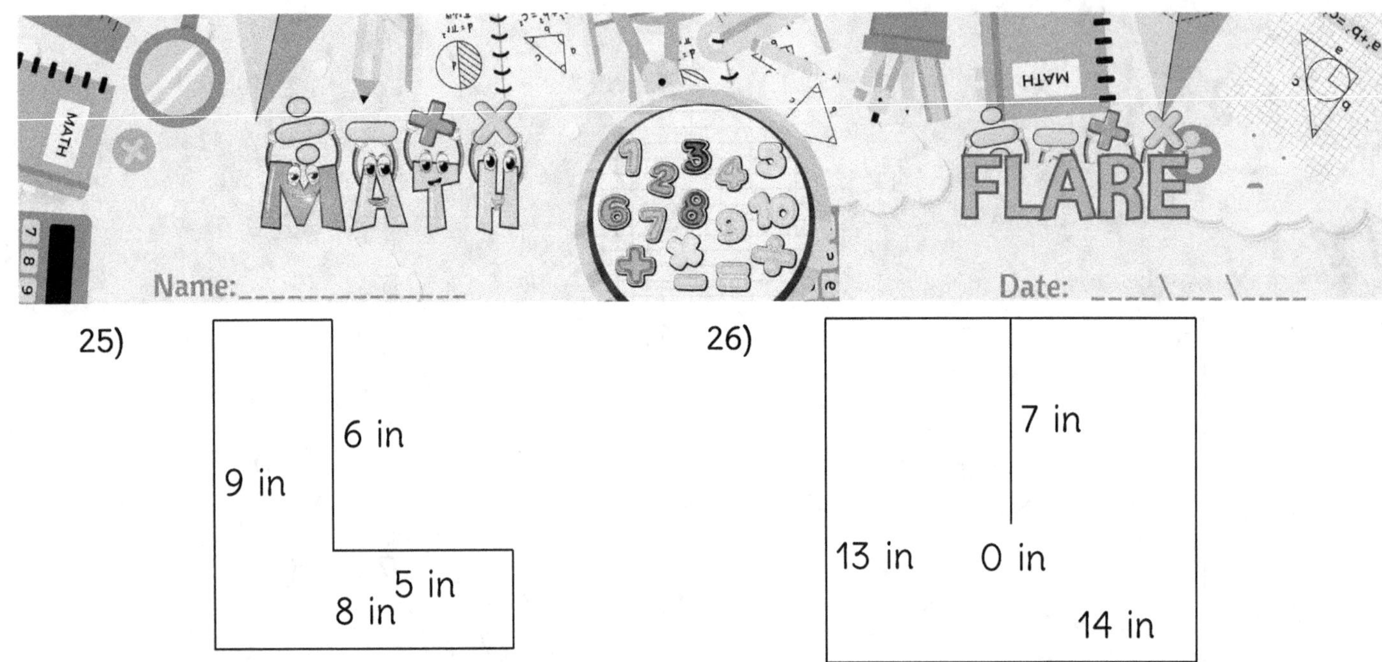

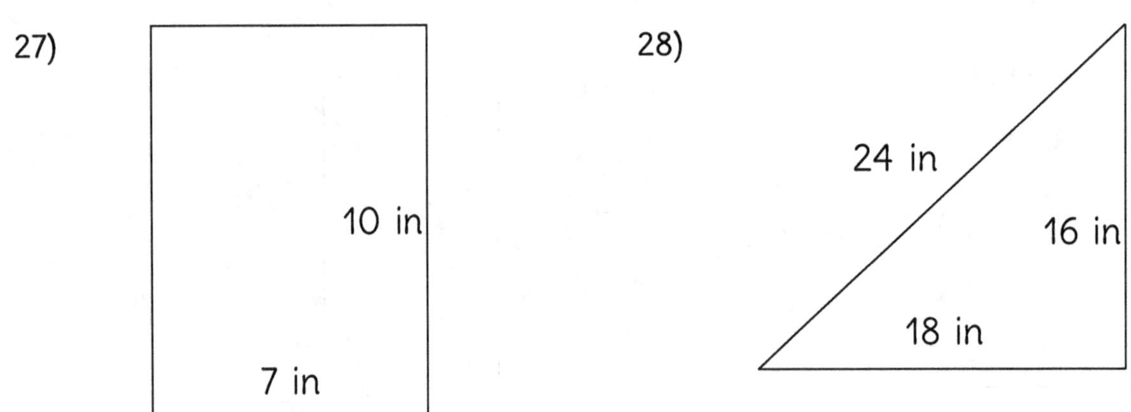

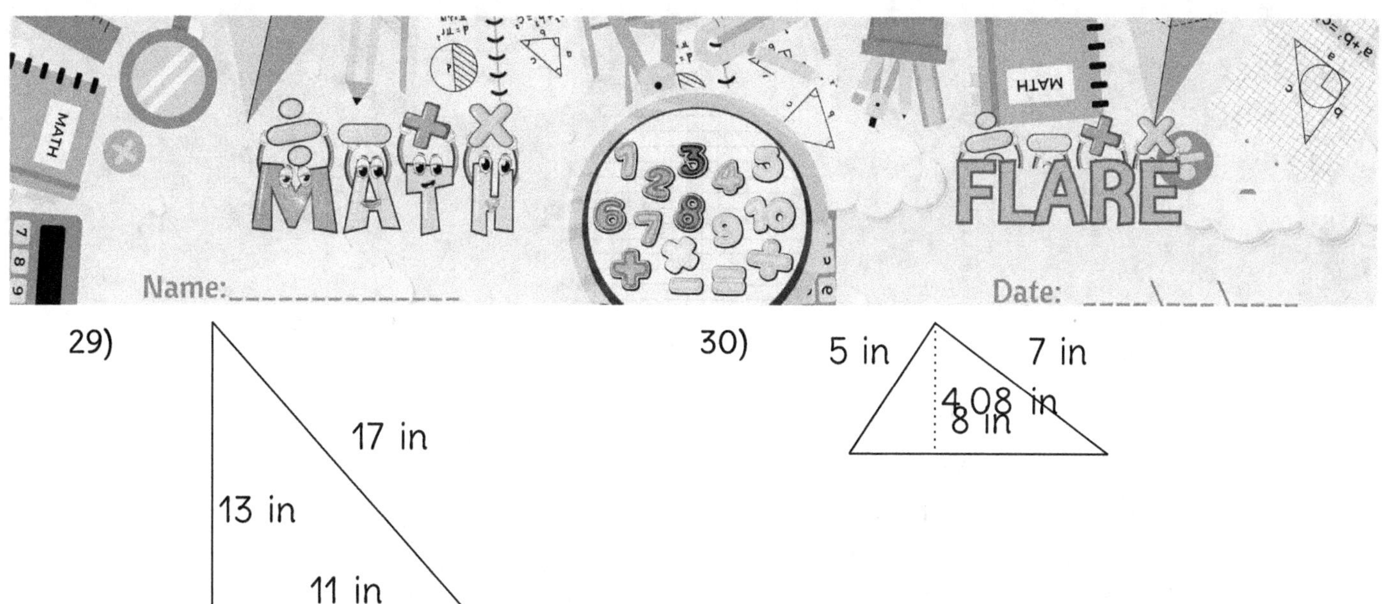

29)

17 in
13 in
11 in

30)

5 in
7 in
4.08 in
8 in

31)

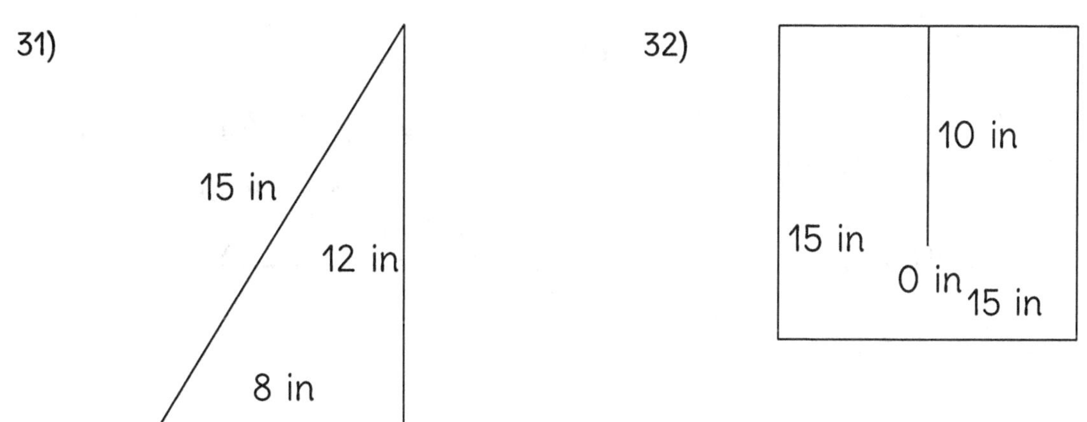

15 in
12 in
8 in

32)

10 in
15 in
0 in
15 in

33)

13 in
13 in
11.53 in
12 in

34)

9 in
8 in
8.25 in
3 in

35)

12 in
12 in
10.392 in
12 in

36)

13 in
13 in
11.258 in
13 in

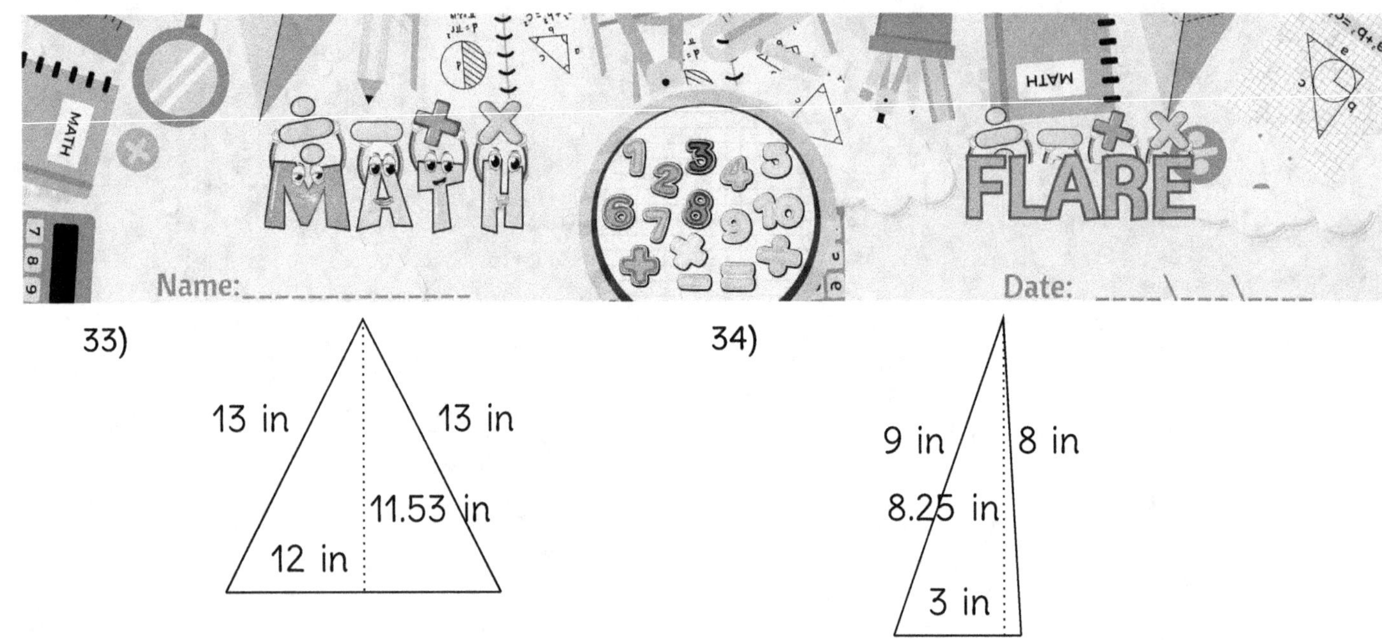

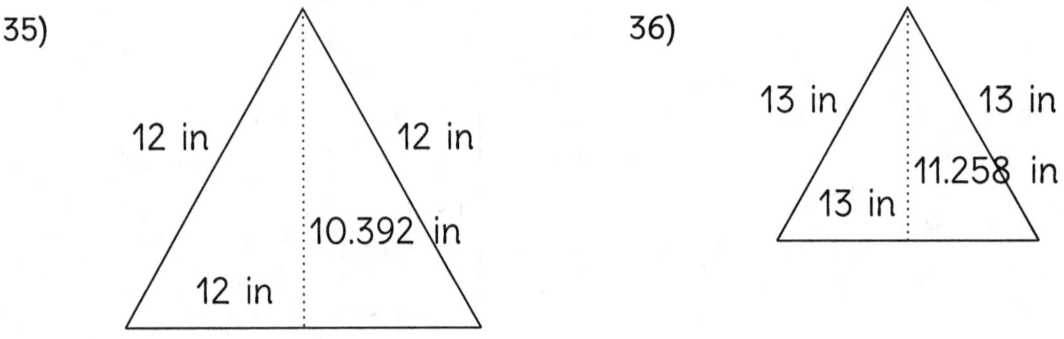

Name:
Date:
MATH
FLARE

37)

2 in
6 in
2 in
8 in

38)

18 in
18 in
16.97 in
12 in

39)

11 in
8 in
7 in

40)

8 in
4 in
3.96 in
9 in

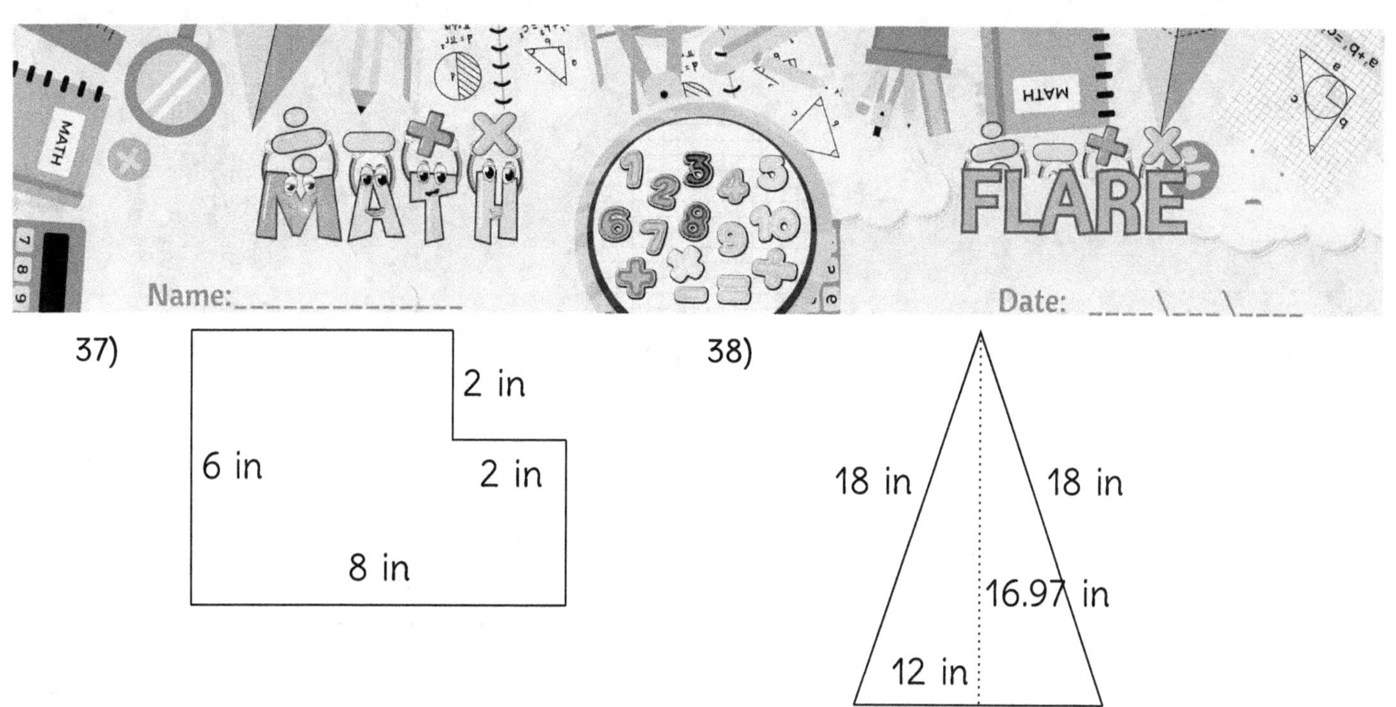

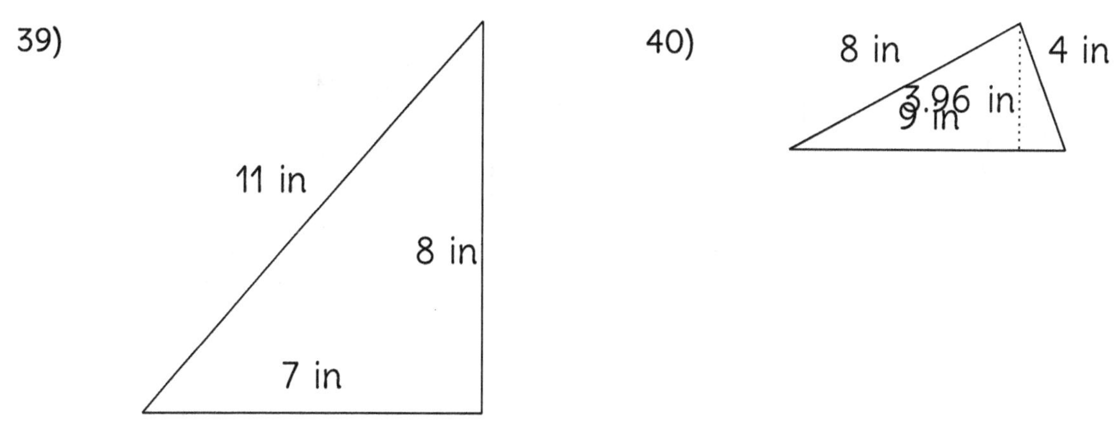

MATH
FLARE
Name:
Date:

41)

9 in
9 in
8.29 in
7 in

42)

5 in
12 in
4 in
13 in

43)

16 in
12 in
11 in

44)

11 in
8 in
8 in

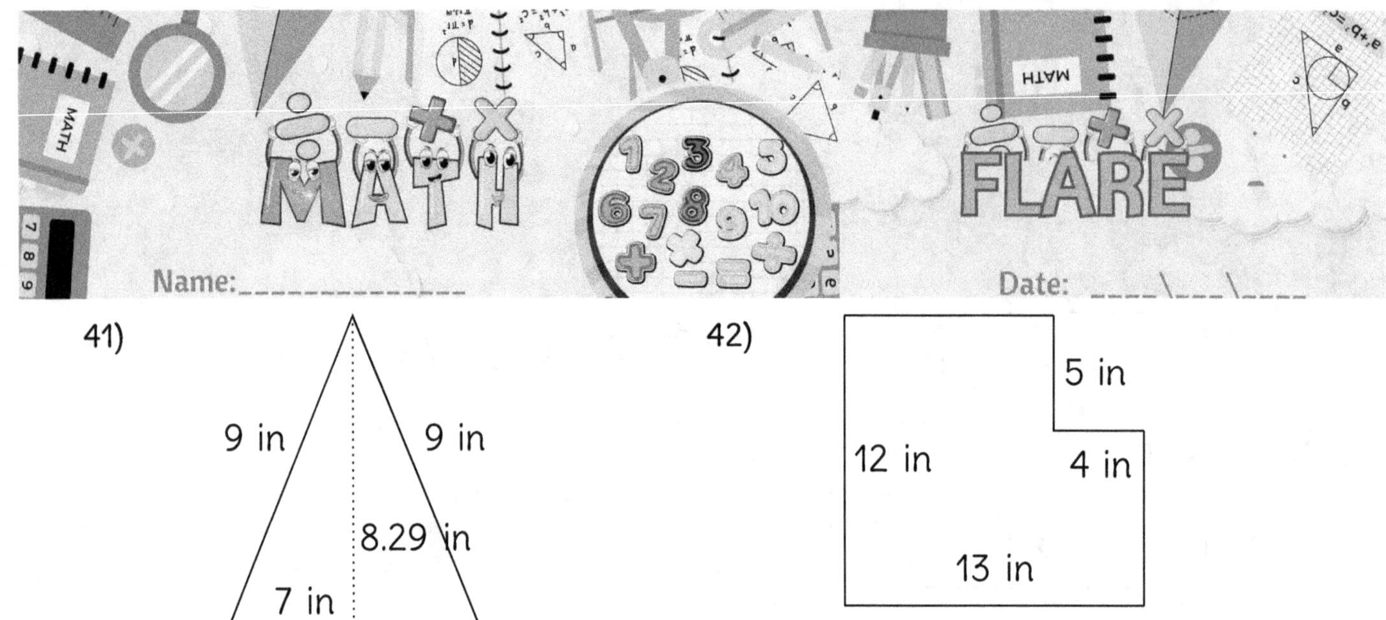

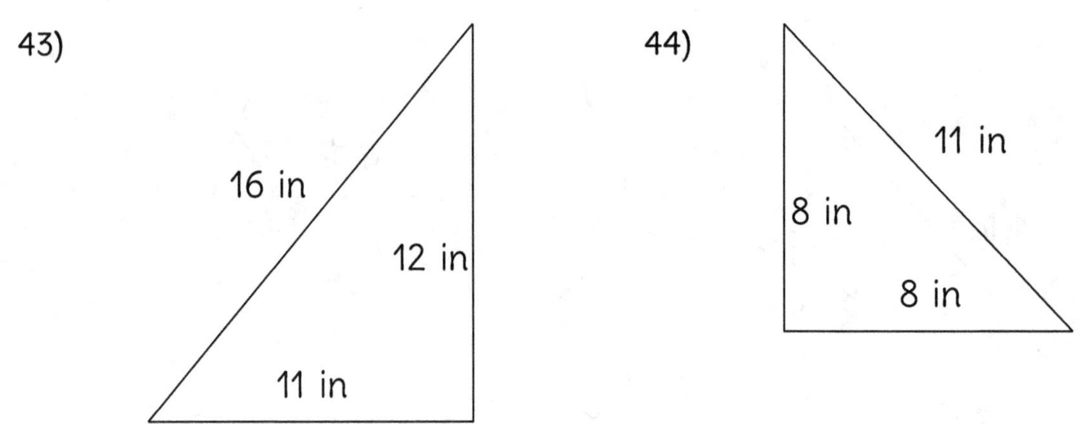

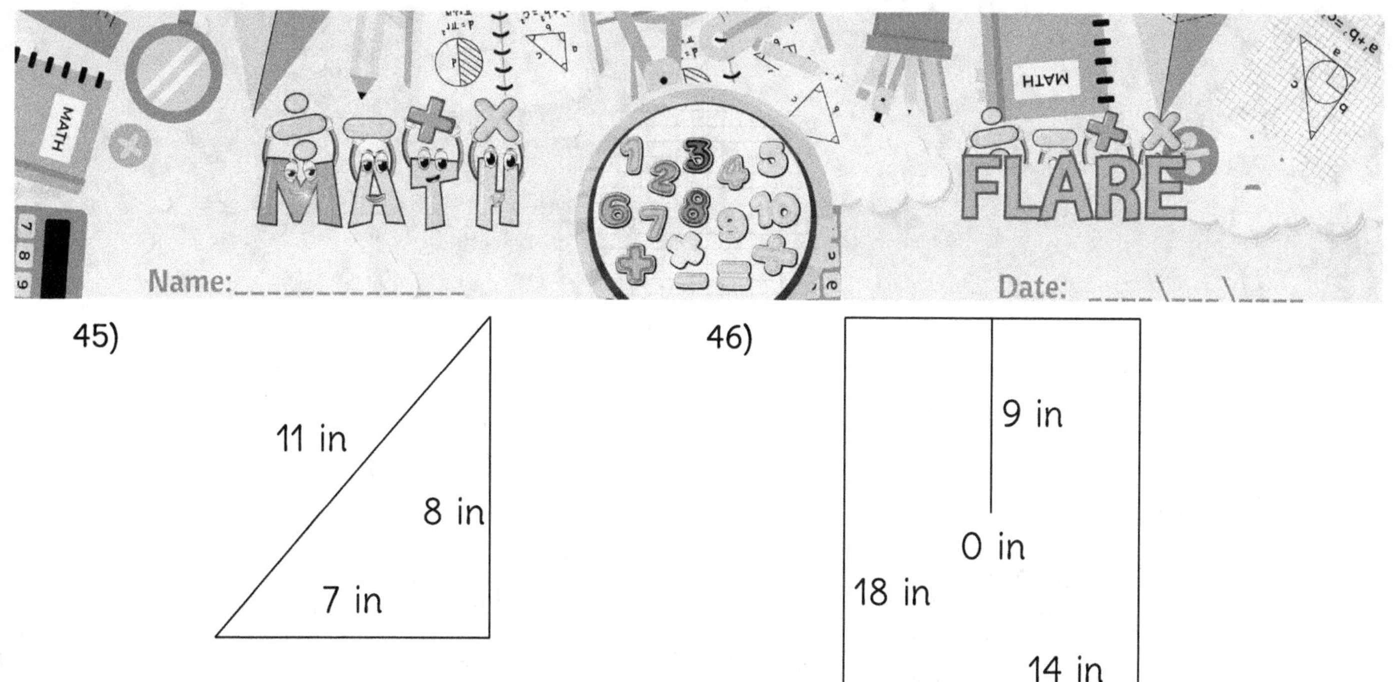

45)

11 in
8 in
7 in

46)

9 in
0 in
18 in
14 in

47)

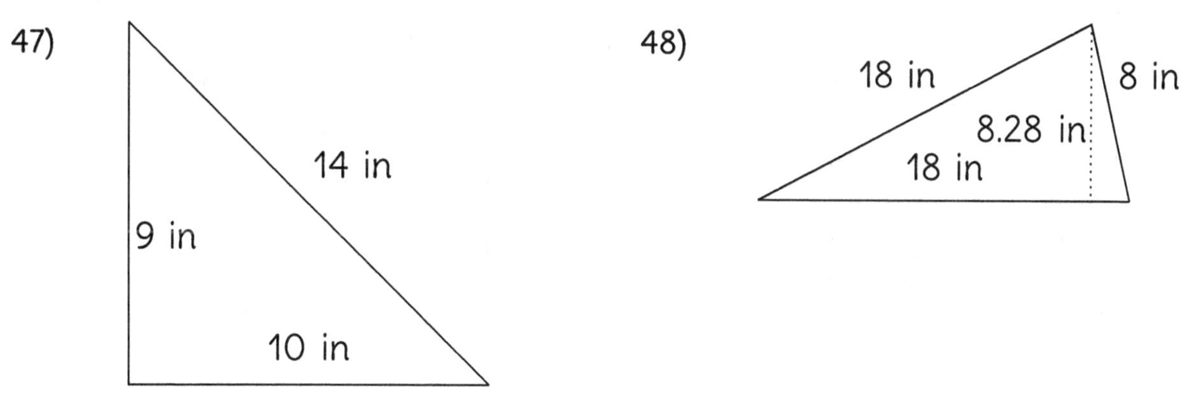

14 in
9 in
10 in

48)

18 in
8 in
8.28 in
18 in

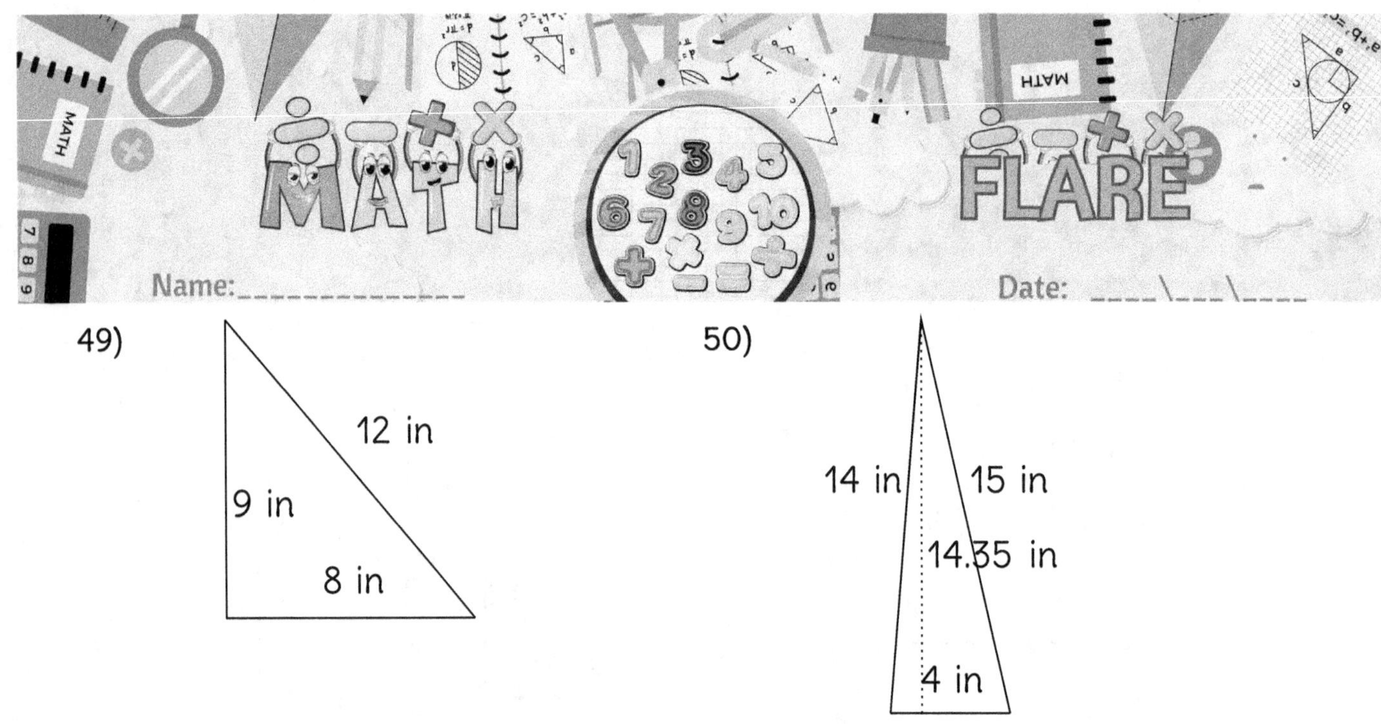

Name:
Date:
49)
12 in
9 in
8 in
50)
14 in
15 in
14.35 in
4 in

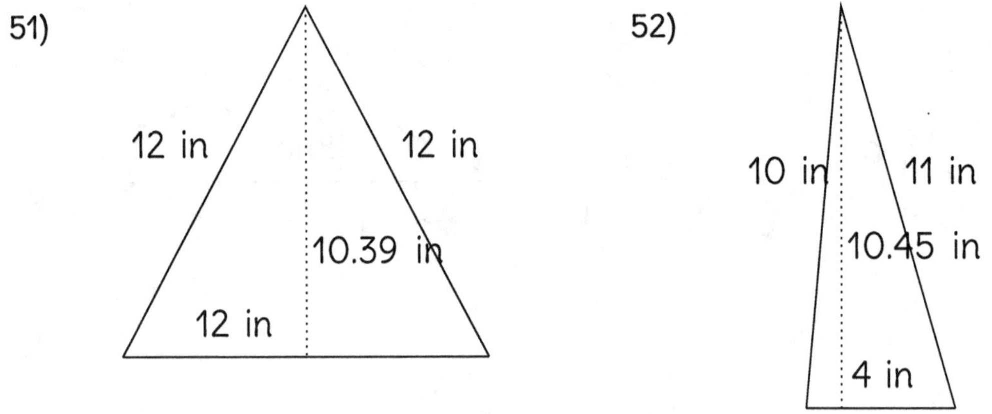

51)
12 in
12 in
10.39 in
12 in
52)
10 in
11 in
10.45 in
4 in

Name:
Date:
MATH
FLARE

53)

11 in
11 in
9.526 in
11 in

54)

16 in
12 in
11 in

55)

6 in
6 in

56)

8 in
8 in
8.16 in
3 in

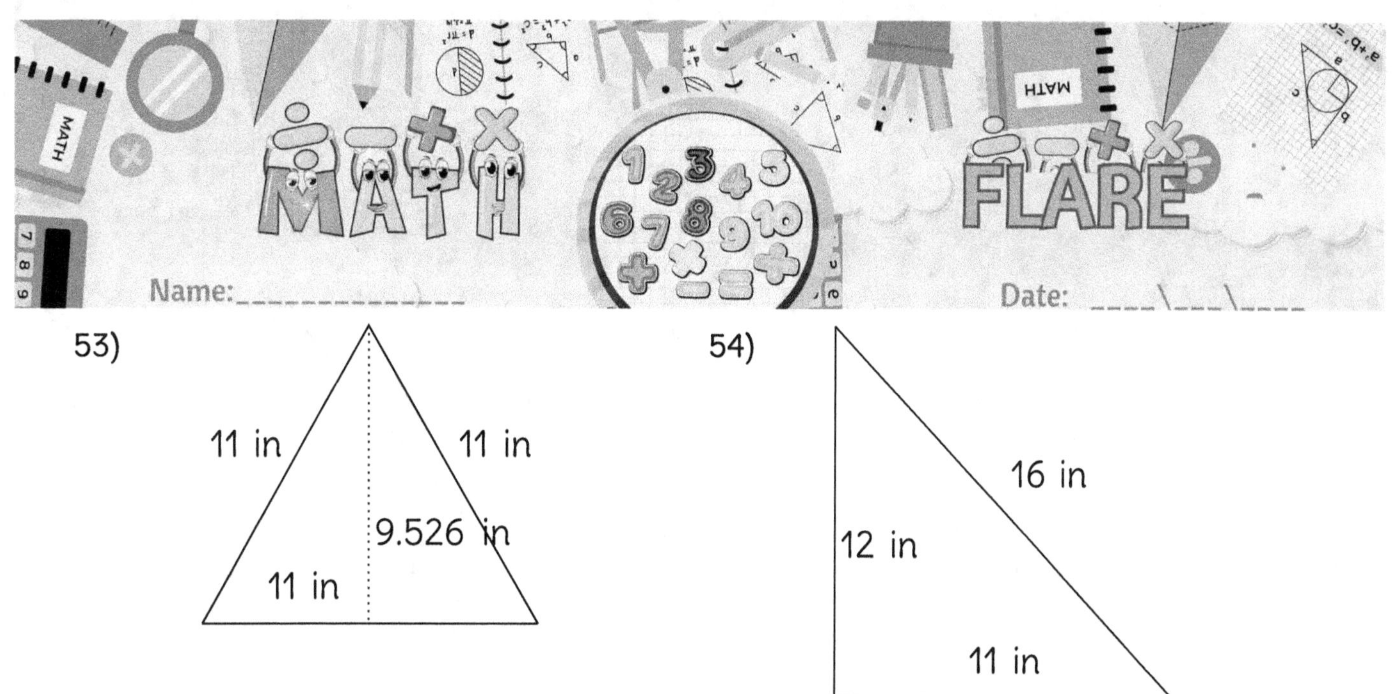

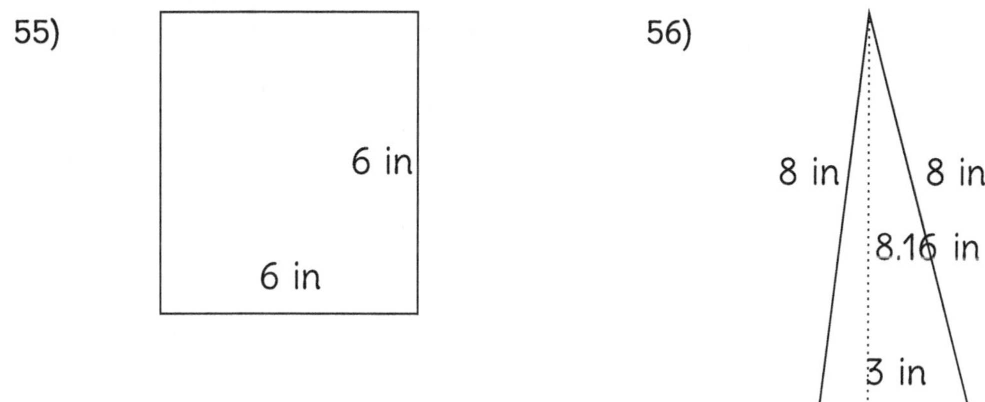

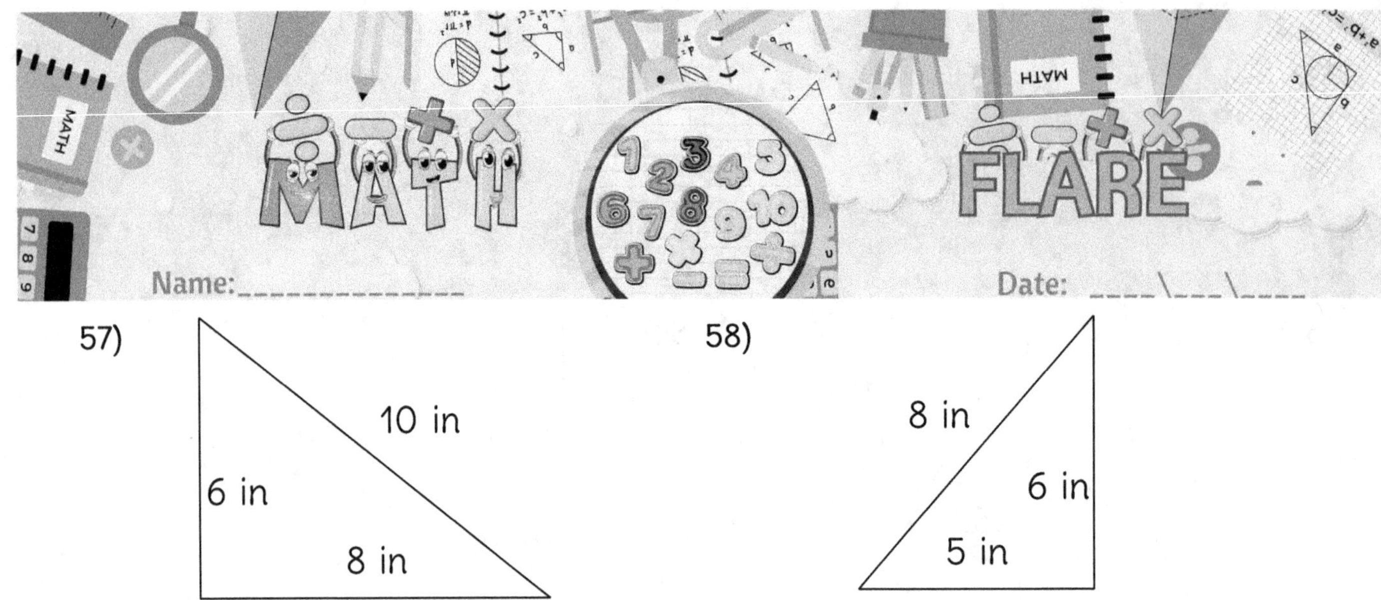

57)

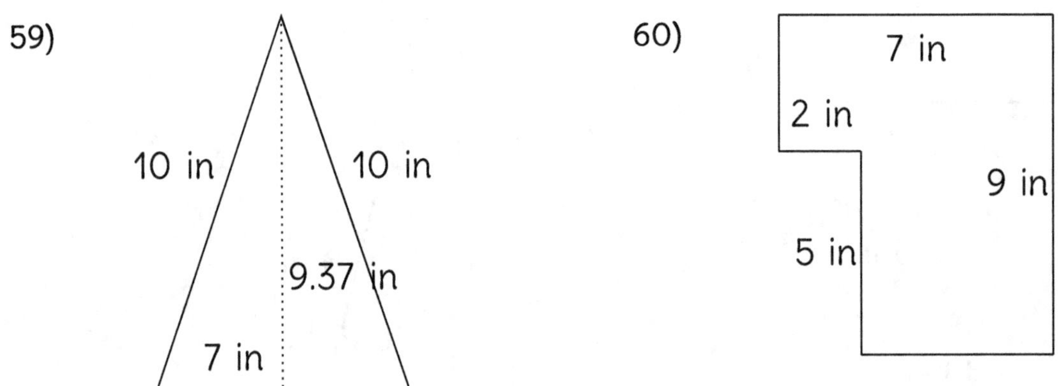

58)

59)

60)

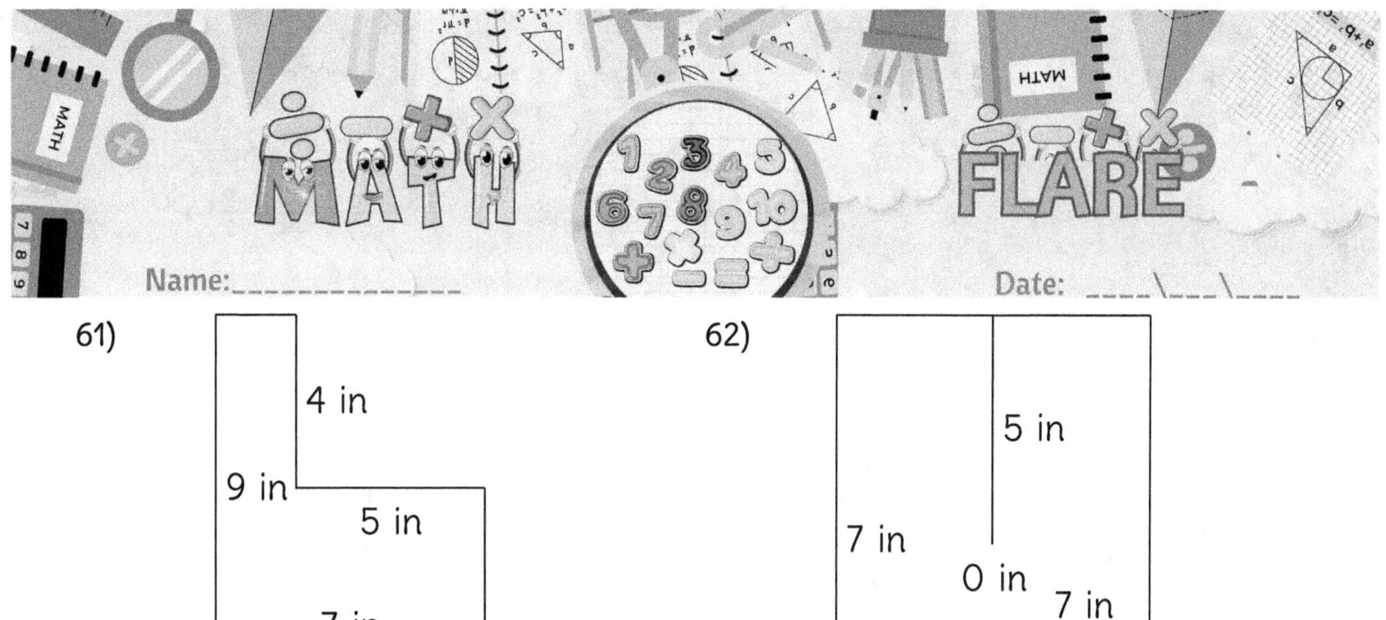

61)

4 in

9 in

5 in

7 in

62)

5 in

7 in

0 in

7 in

63)

5 in

9 in   0 in

8 in

64)

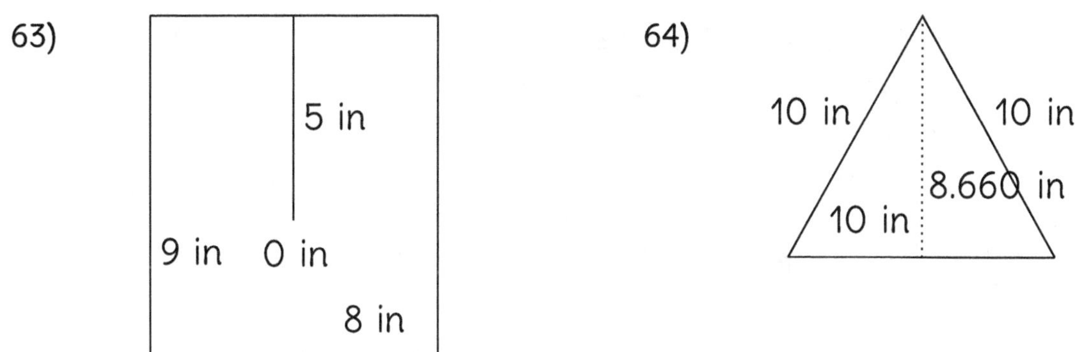

Name:
Date:

65)

8 in
3 in
8 in
5 in

66)

12 in
11 in
11.04 in
5 in

67)

21 in
12 in
17 in

68)

17 in
14 in
10 in

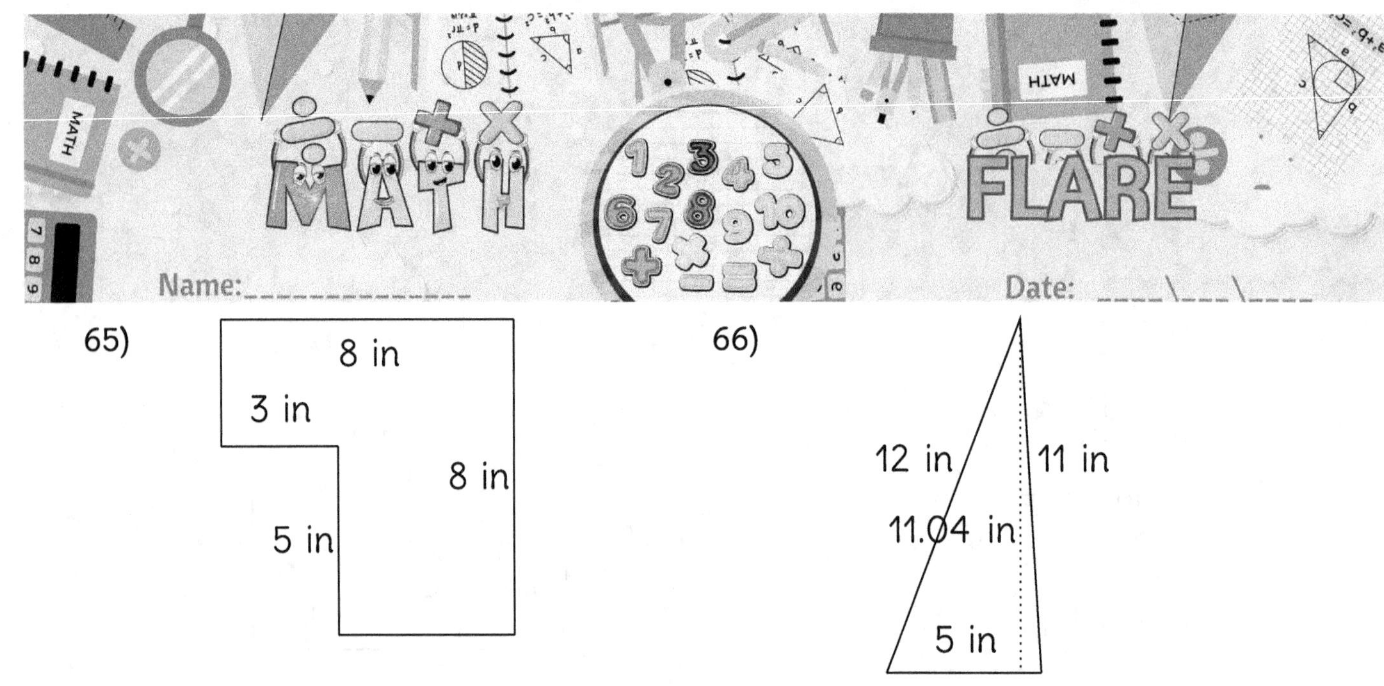

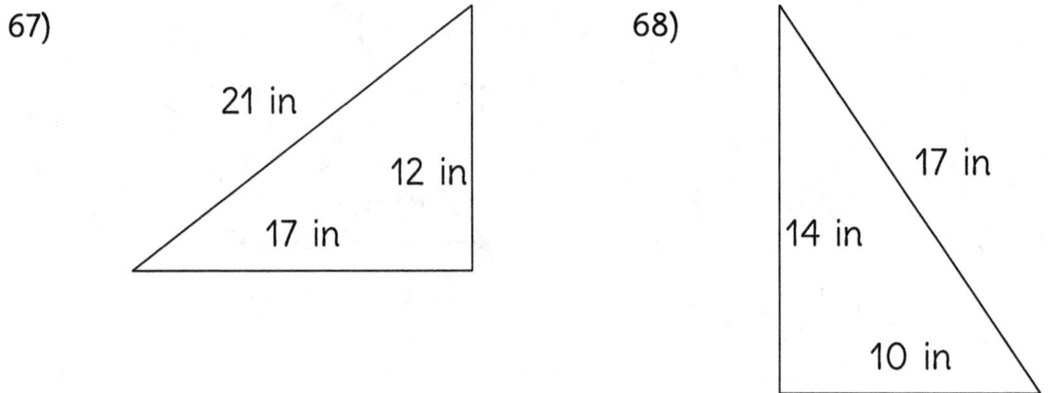

MATH
FLARE
Name:________________
Date: ___________

69)

6 in
0 in
13 in
10 in

70)

4 in 6 in
5 in
4 in

71)

6 in
10 in 0 in
12 in

72)

12 in
9 in
8 in

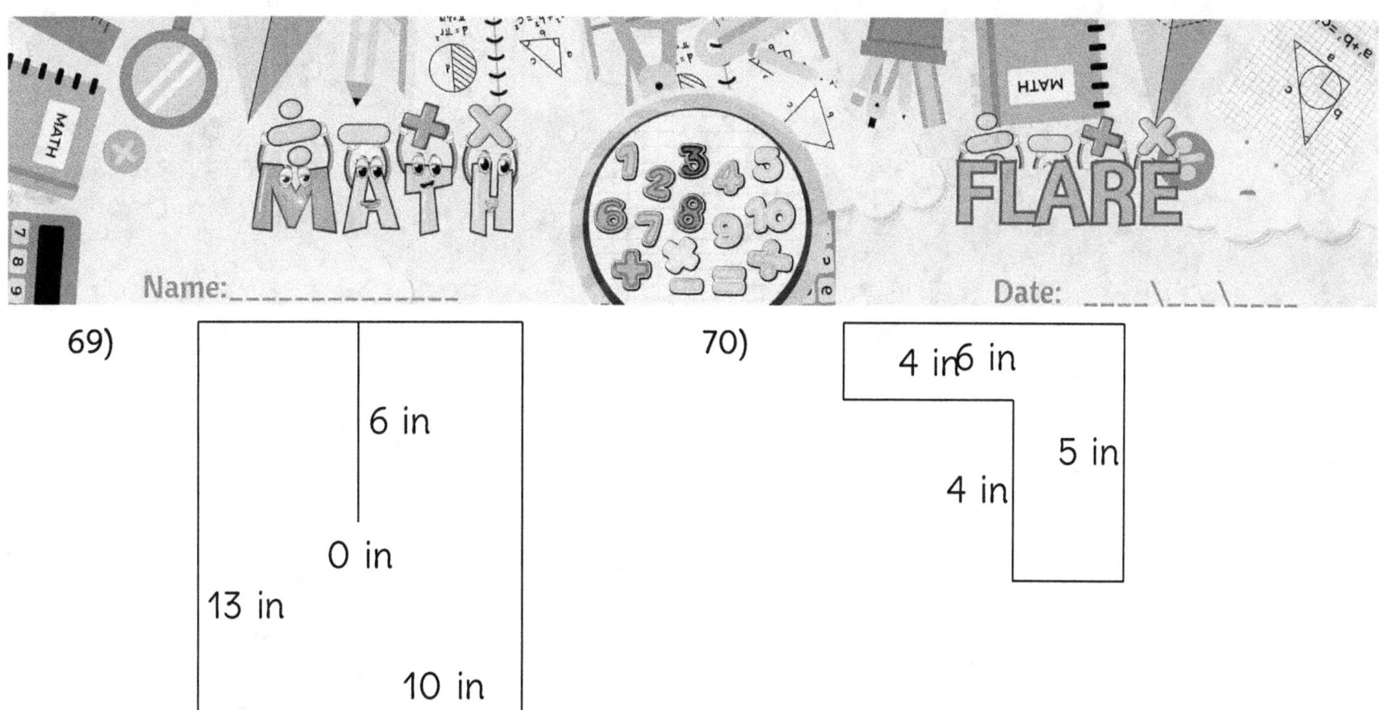

Name:________________   Date: ___________
73)   8 in   10 in
      6.08 in
      14 in
74)   13 in
      18 in
      5 in
      18 in

73)

74)

75)

19 in
11 in
16 in

76)

8 in   8 in
7.42 in
6 in

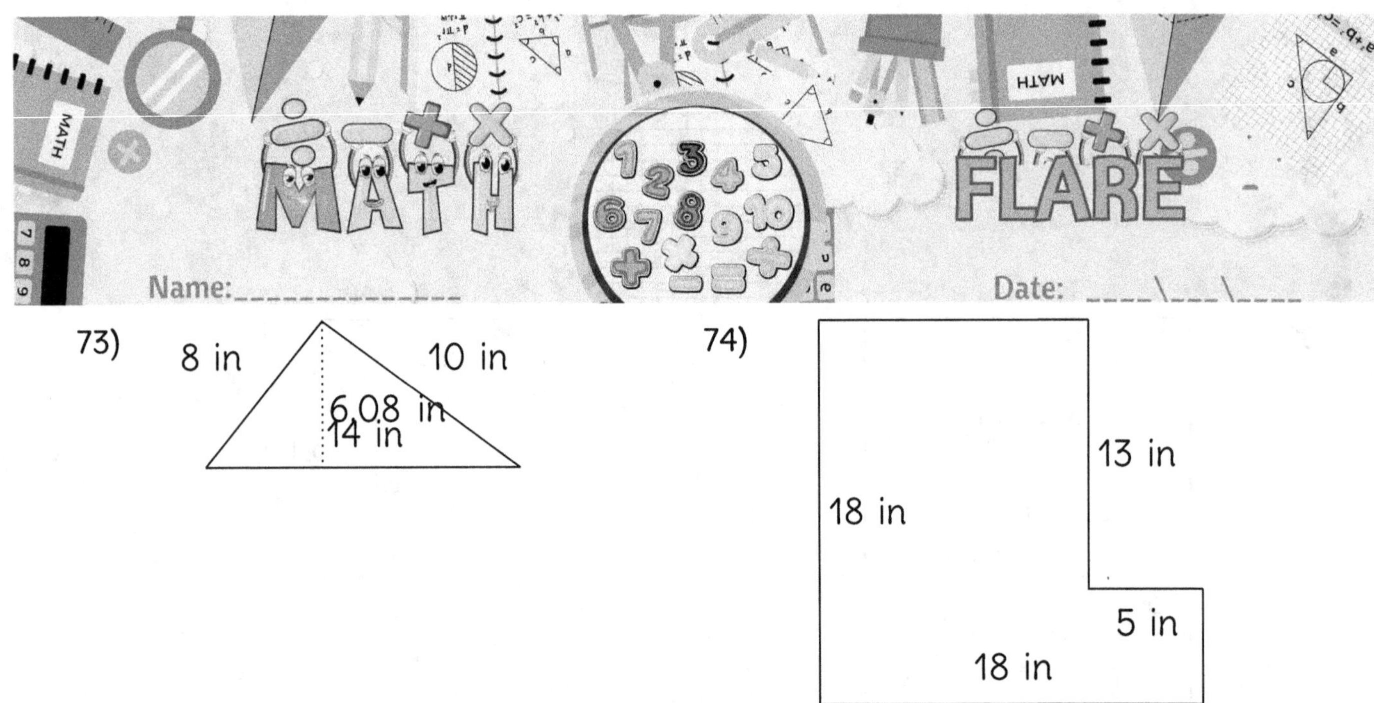

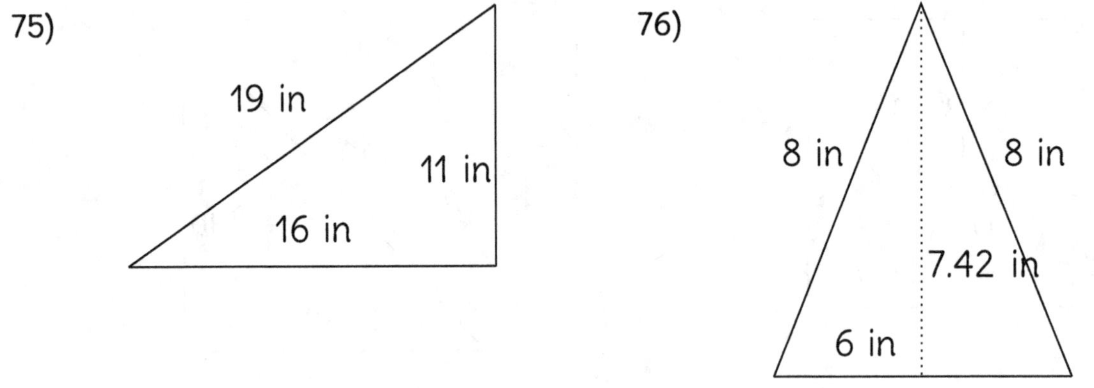

MATH FLARE
Name:_______________
Date: ____________

77)

9 in
7 in
6 in

78)

5 in
11 in
0 in
14 in

79)

4 in
11 in
5 in
12 in

80)

12 in
7 in
13 in
8 in

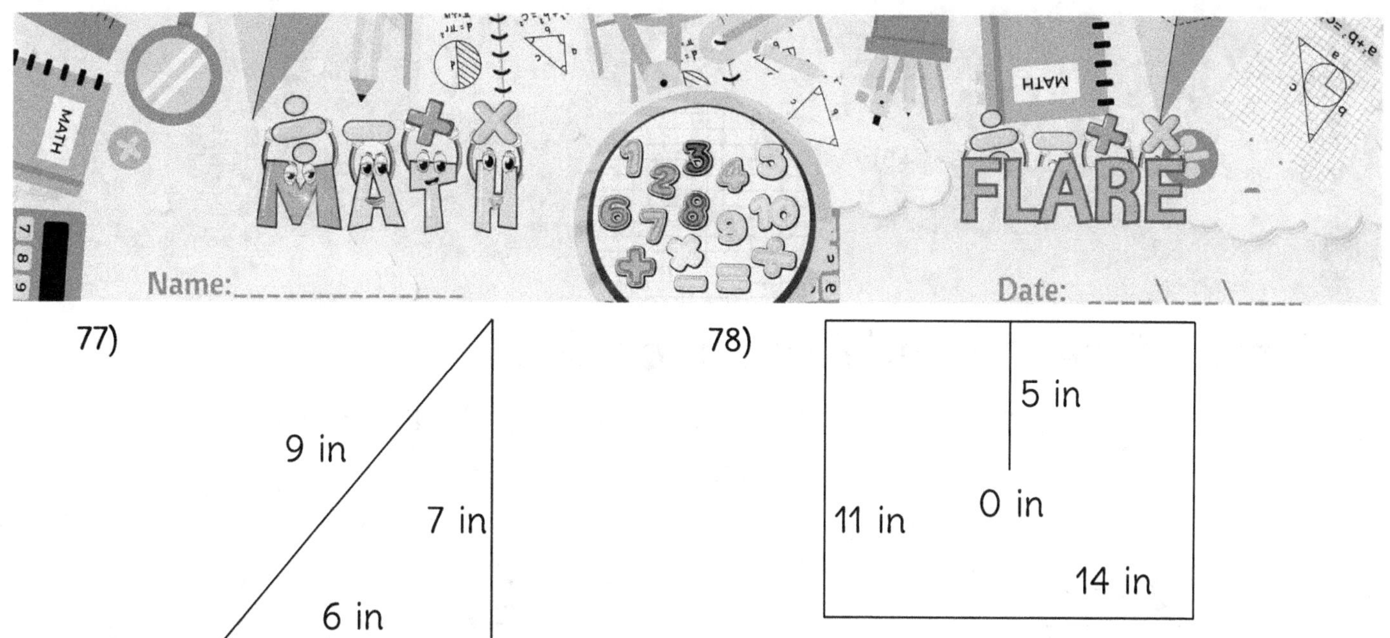

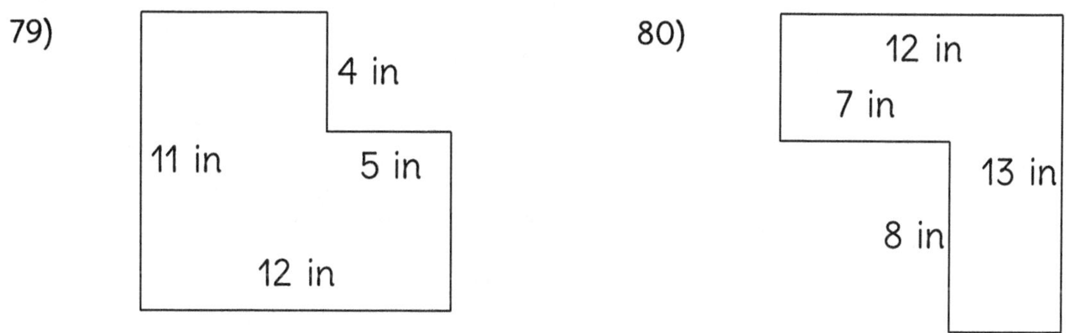

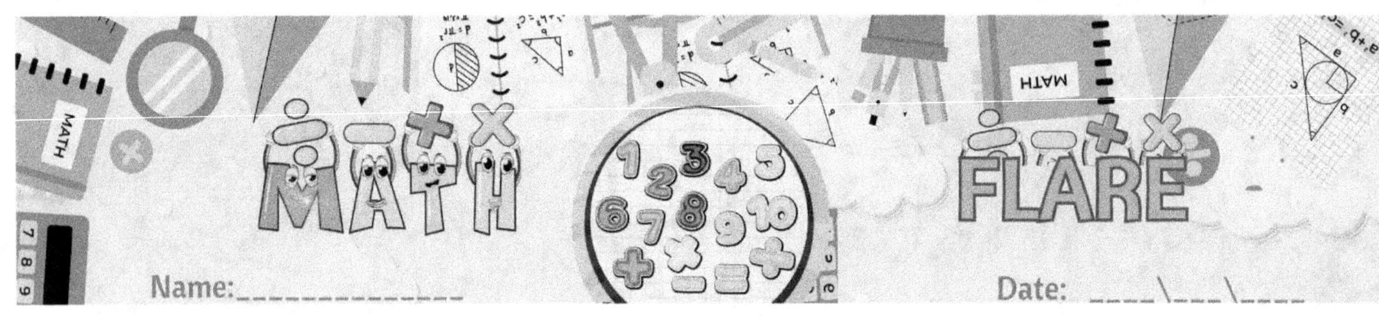

Circumference and Area of circles

Calculate the circumference of each circle. Pi Value = 3.14

1)
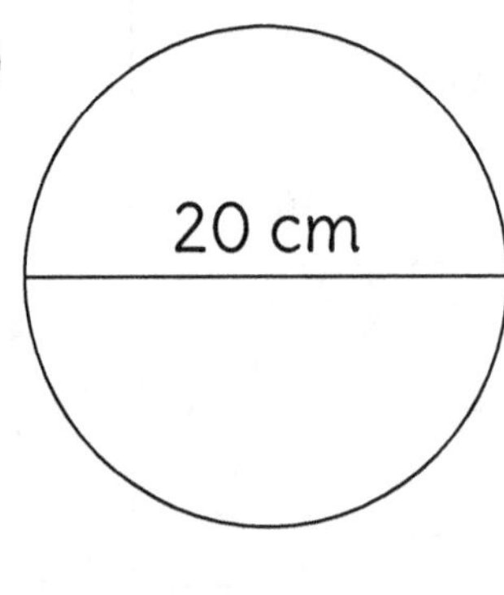

____
____

2)
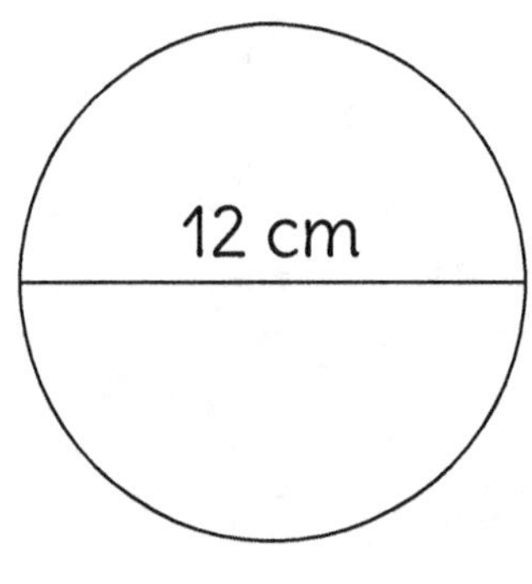

____
____

3)
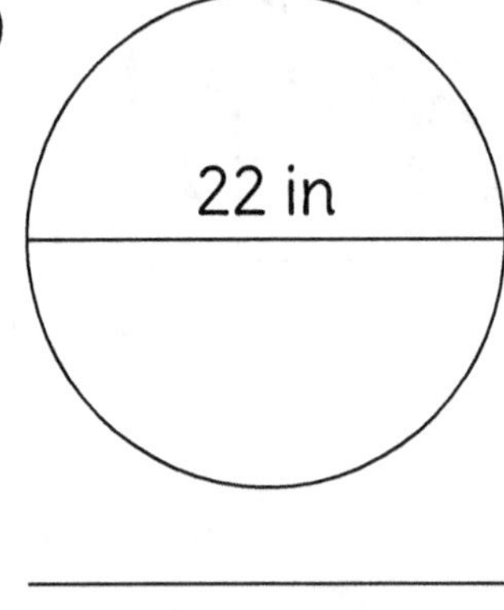

____
____

4)
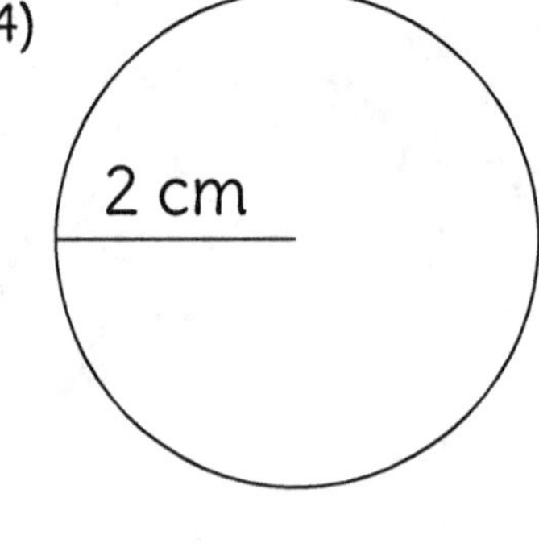

____
____

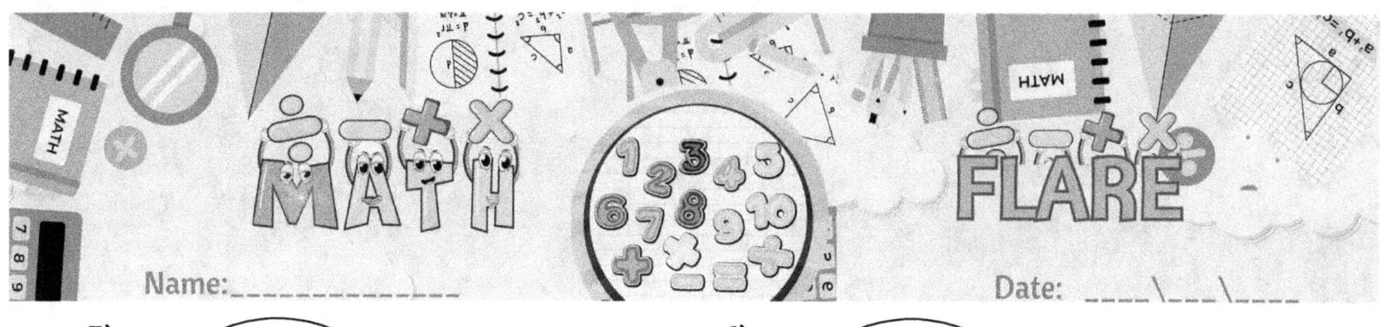

5)

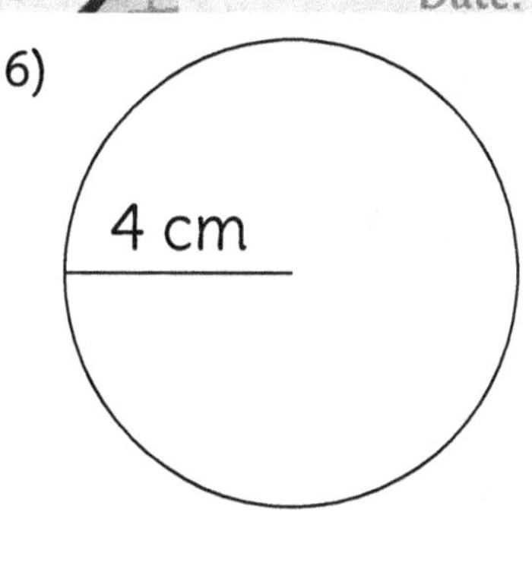

____
____

6)

____
____

7)

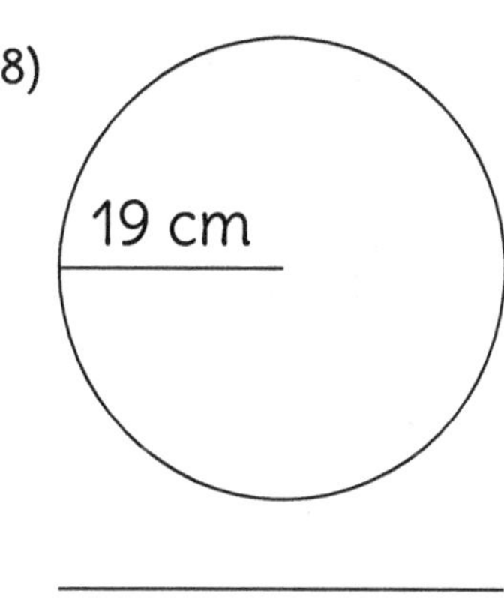

____
____

8)

____
____

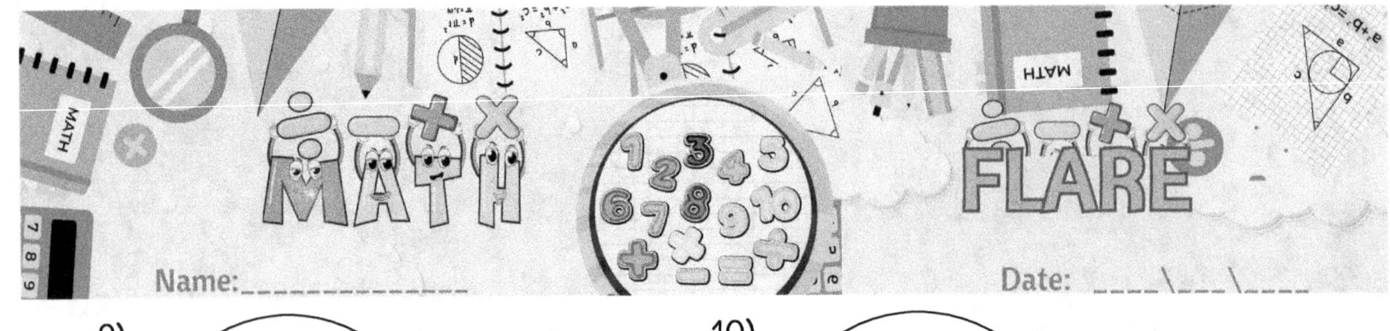

9)

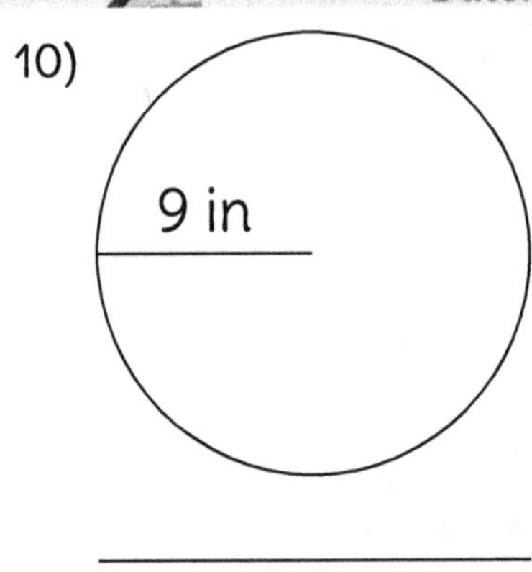

____
____

10)

9 in

____
____

11)

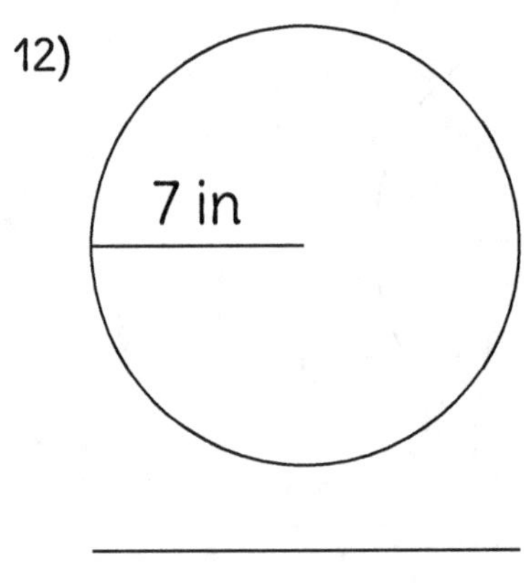

____
____

12)

7 in

____
____

13)

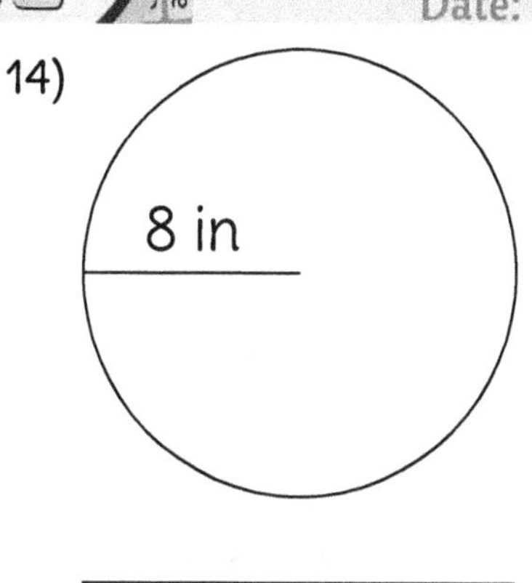

____
____

14)

____
____

15)

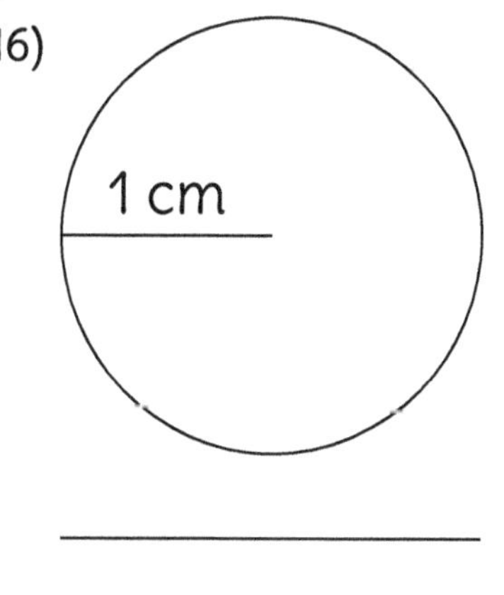

____
____

16)

____
____

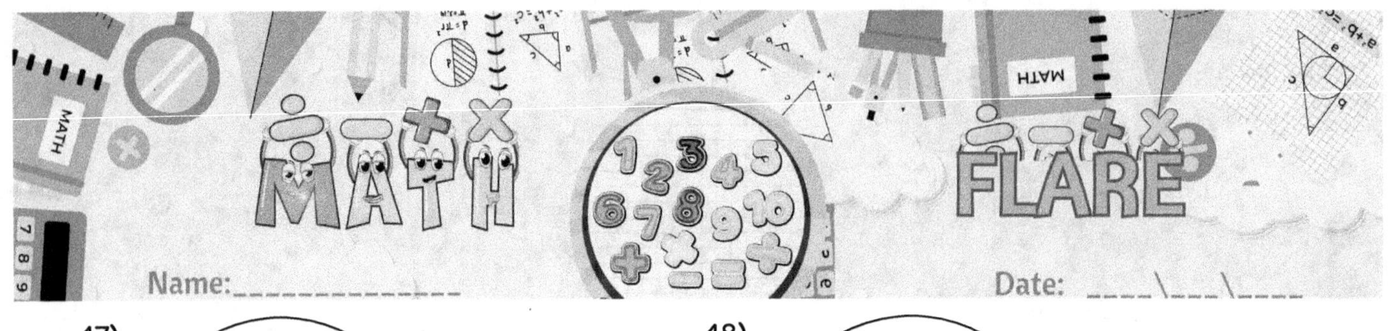

17)

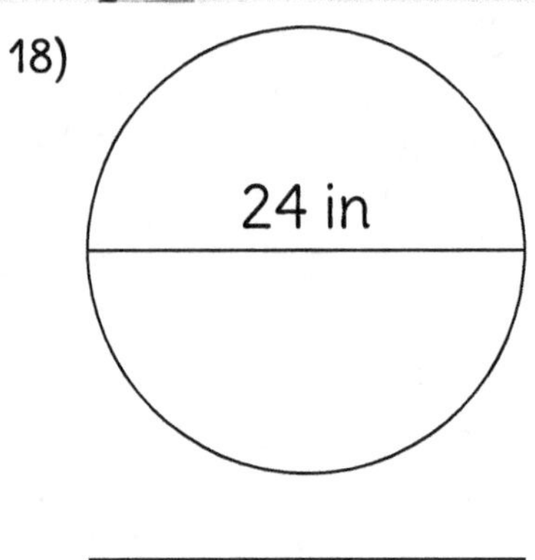

____

____

18)

____

____

19)

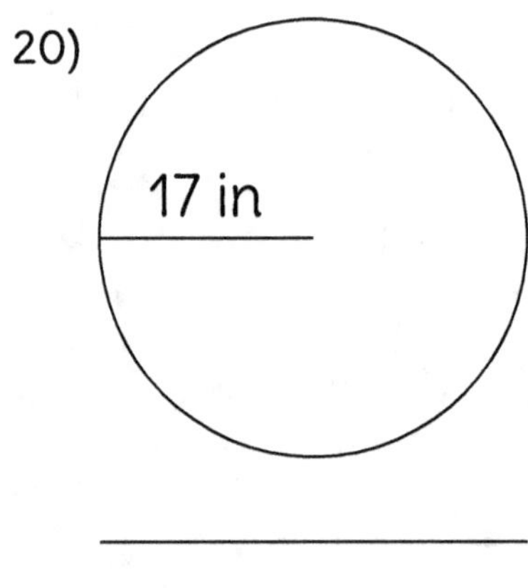

____

____

20)

____

____

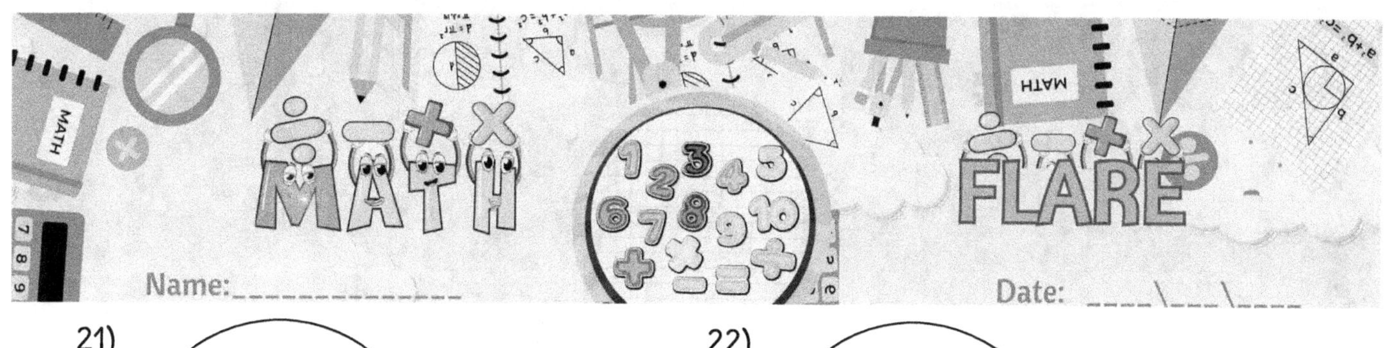

21)

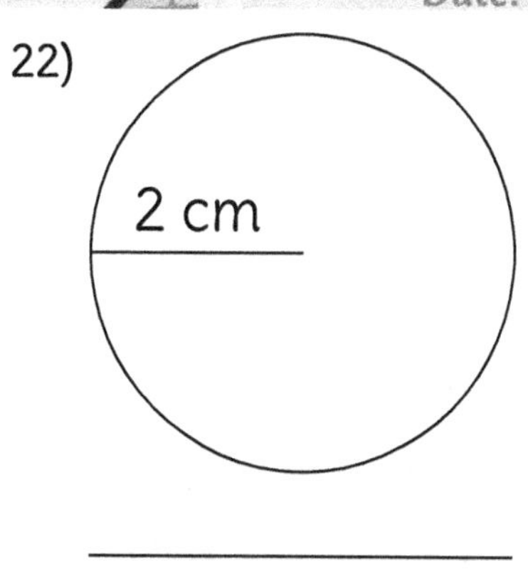

____
____

22)

____
____

23)

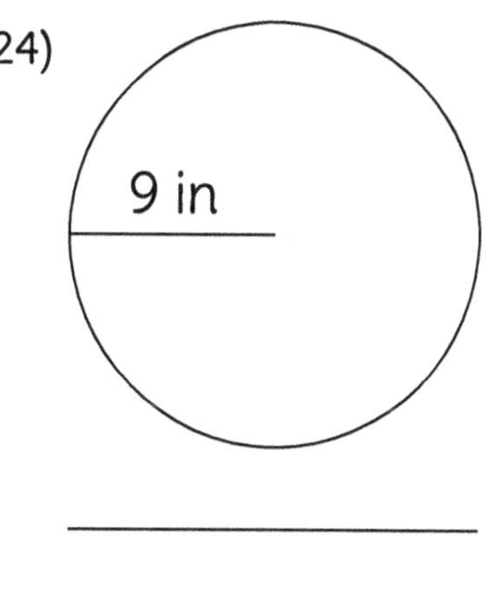

____
____

24)

____
____

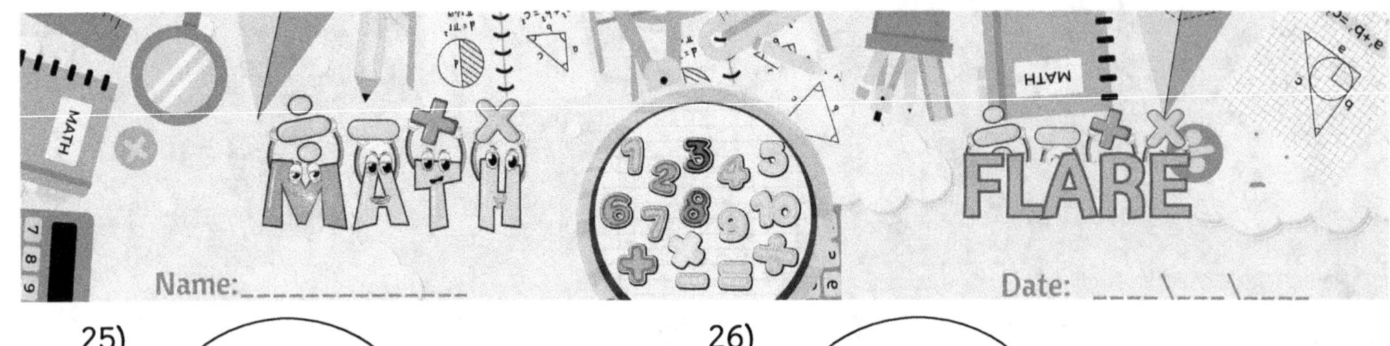

25)

32 cm

____
____

26)

12 in

____
____

27)

6 in

____
____

28)

14 cm

____
____

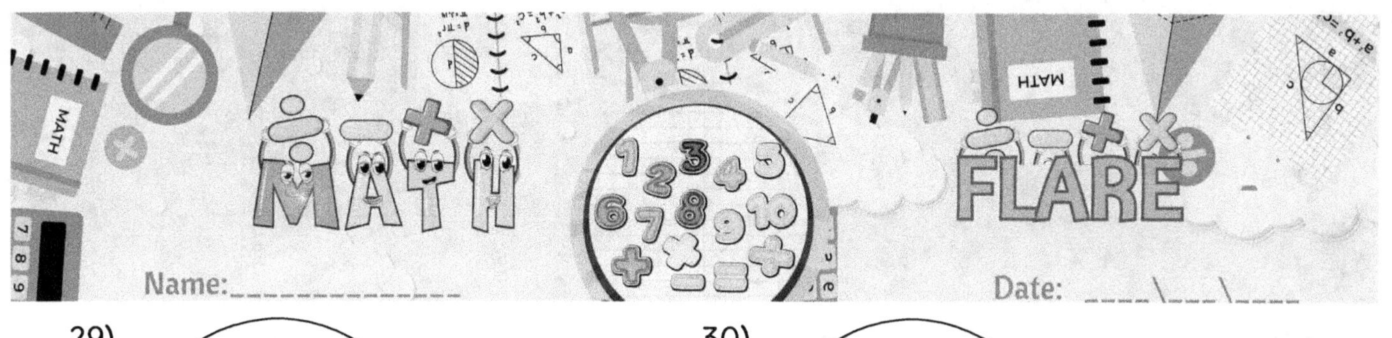

29)

4 cm

____
____

30)

6 cm

____
____

31)

18 cm

____
____

32)

26 cm

____
____

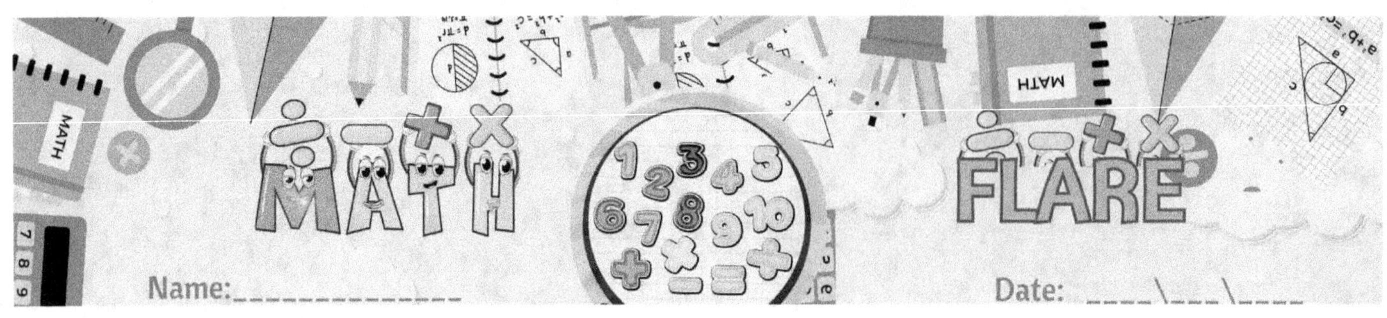

Classify and Measure Angles

1)

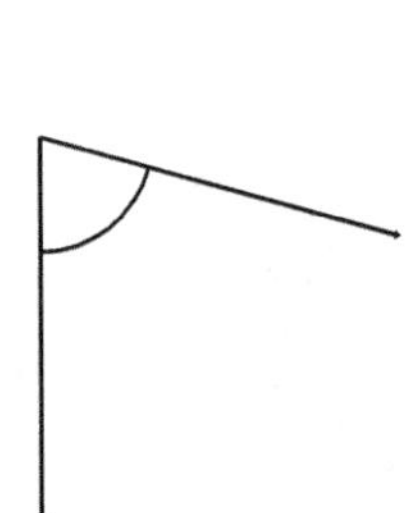

____

2)

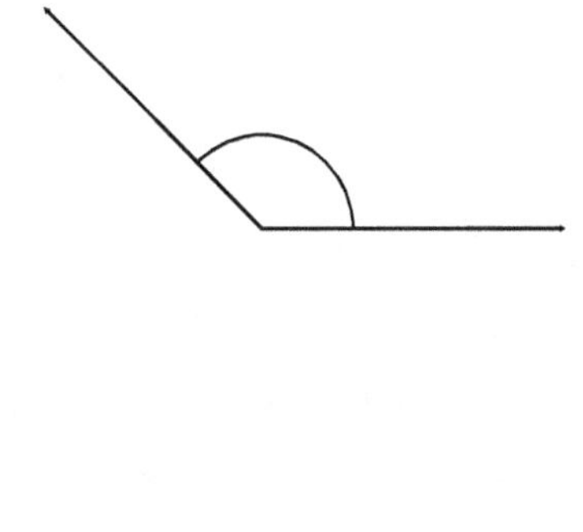

____

3)

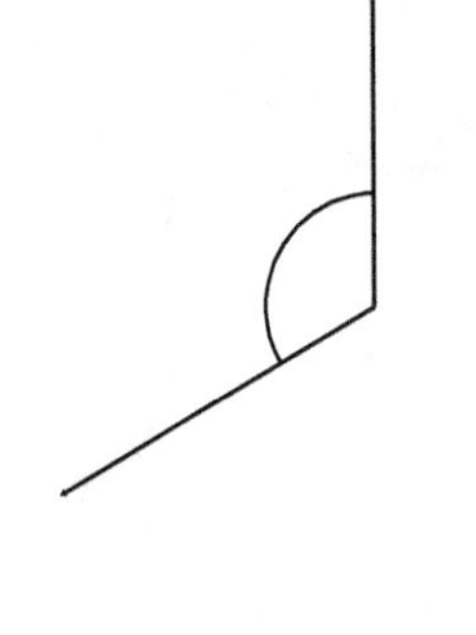

____

4)

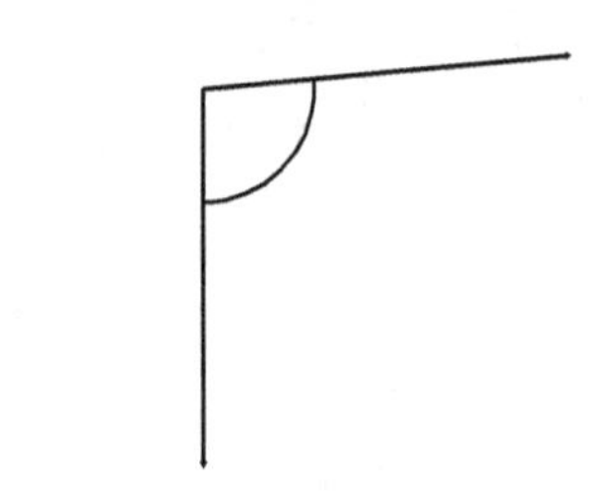

____

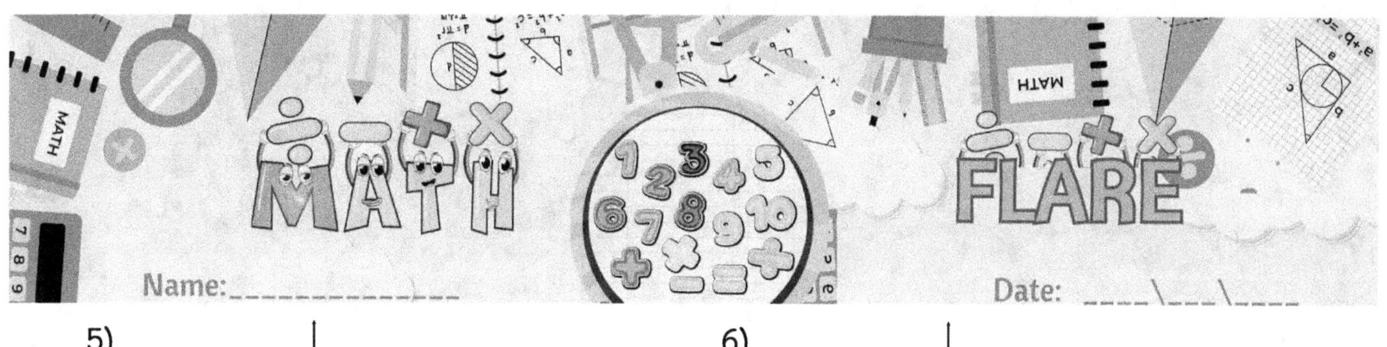

5)

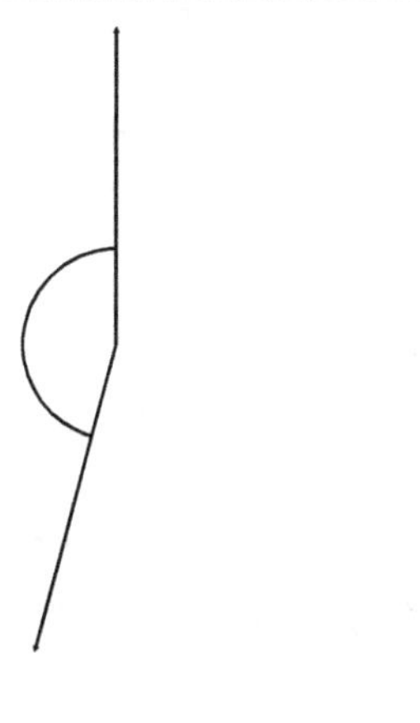

____

6)

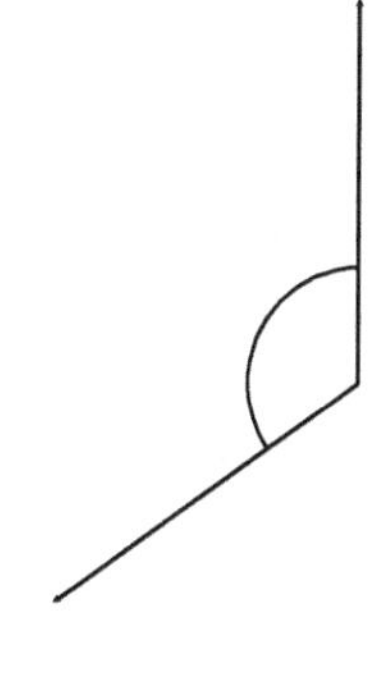

____

7)

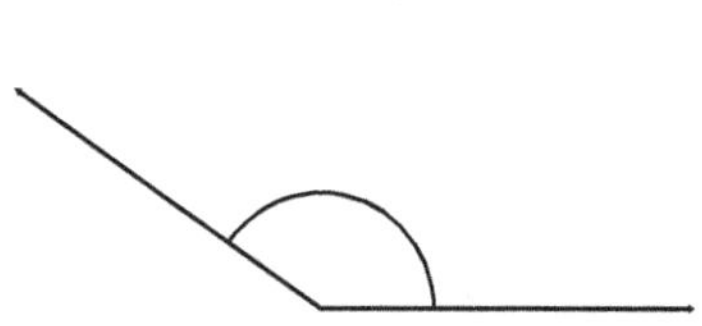

____

8)

____

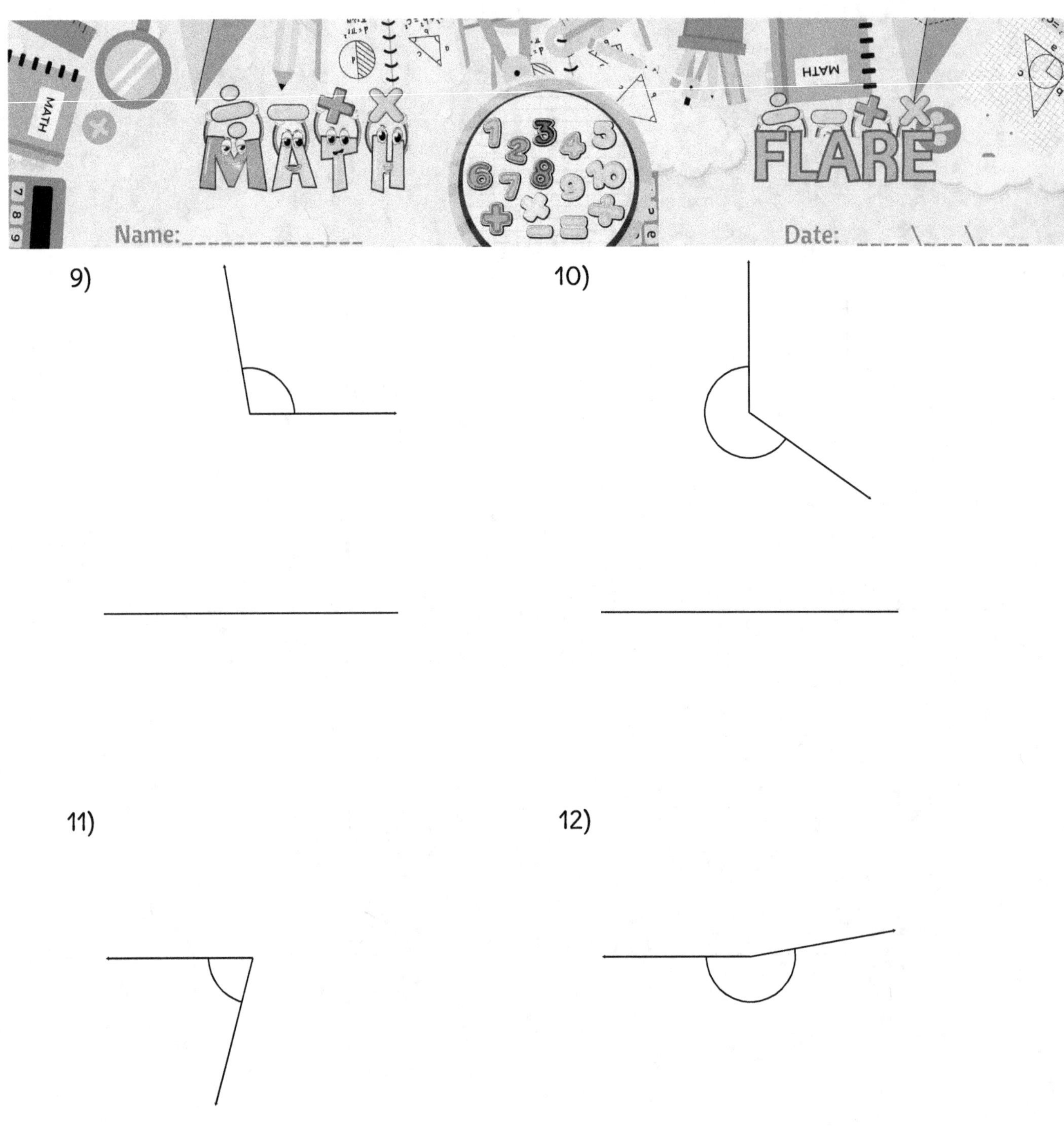

Name:____________________

Date: ____________

9)

____

10)

____

11)

____

12)

____

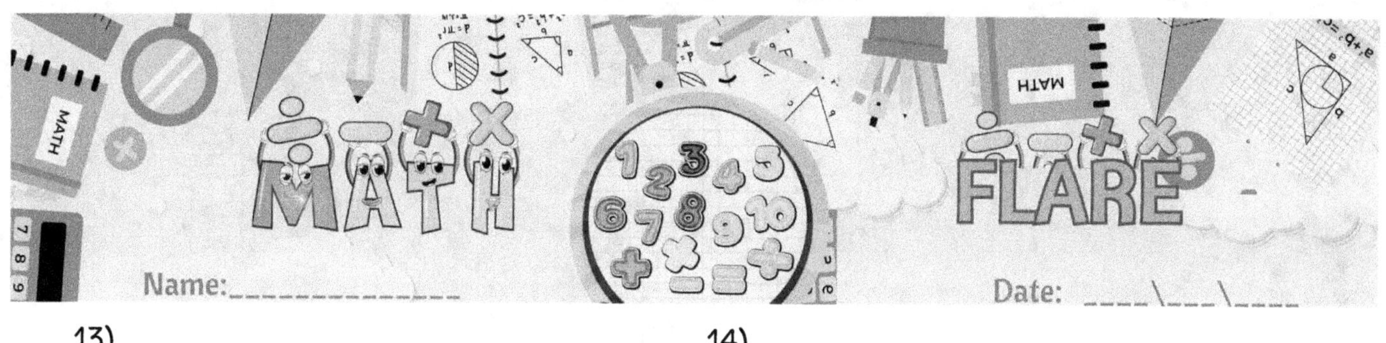

13)

14)

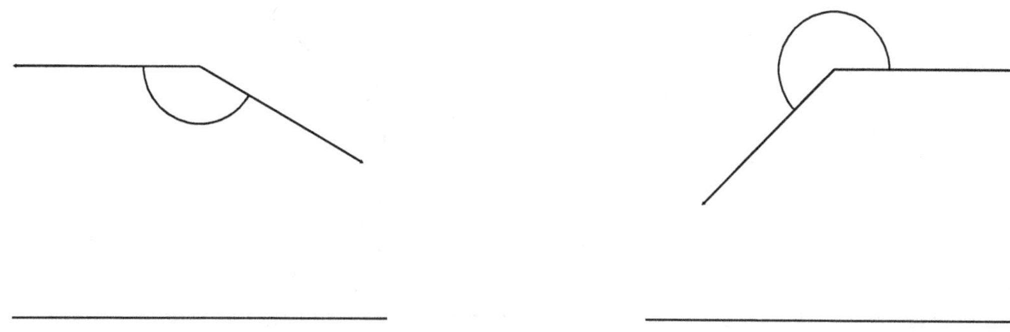

15)

16)

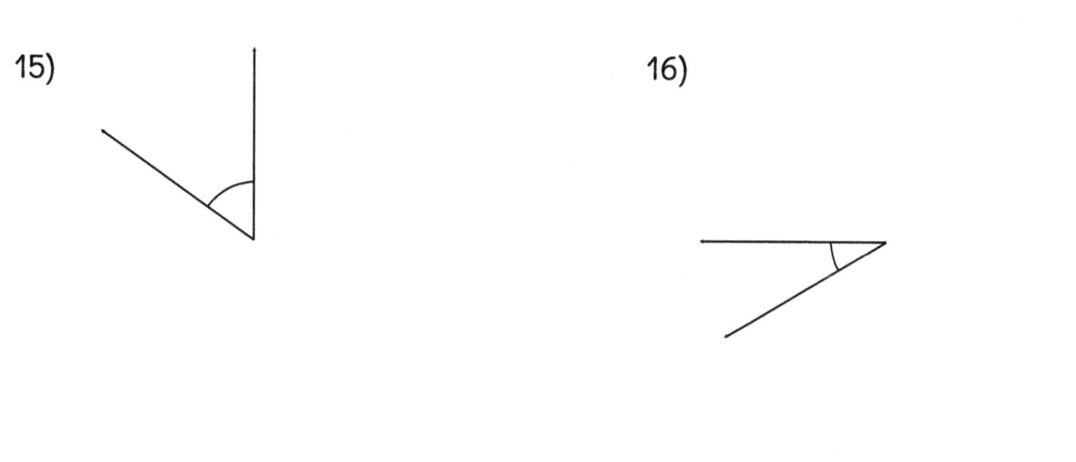

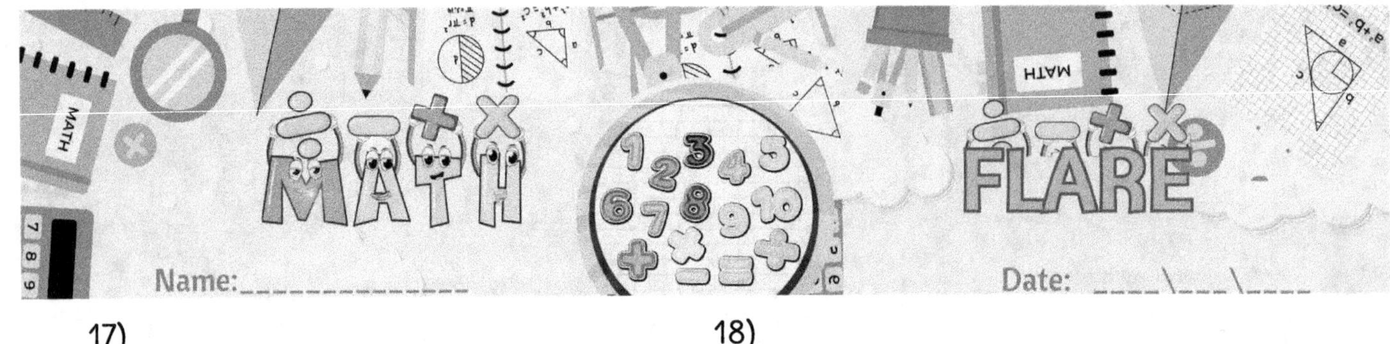

17)

18)

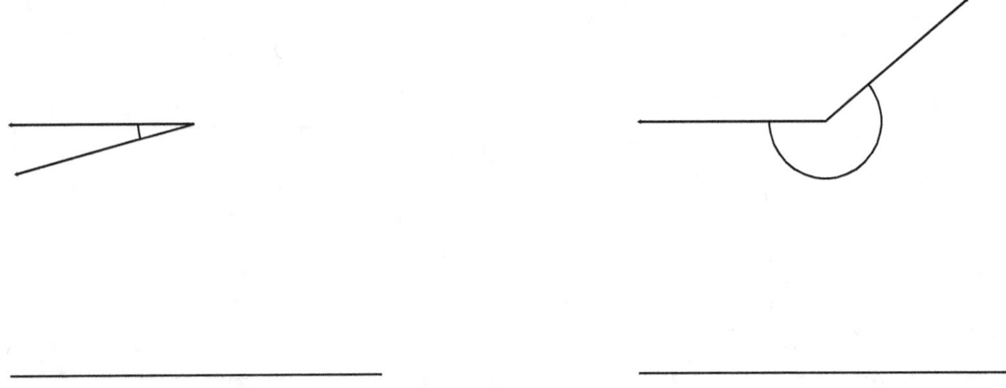

19)

20)

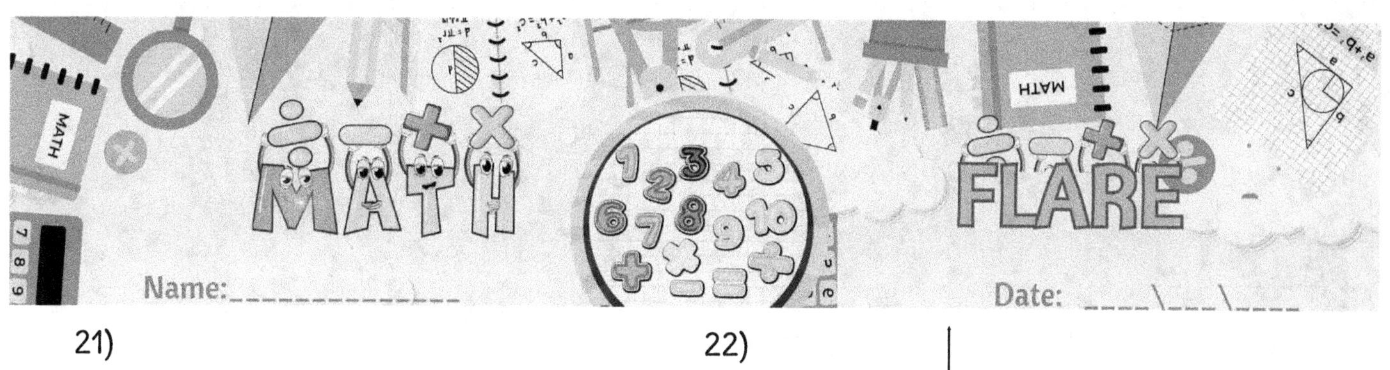

21)

22)

23)

24)

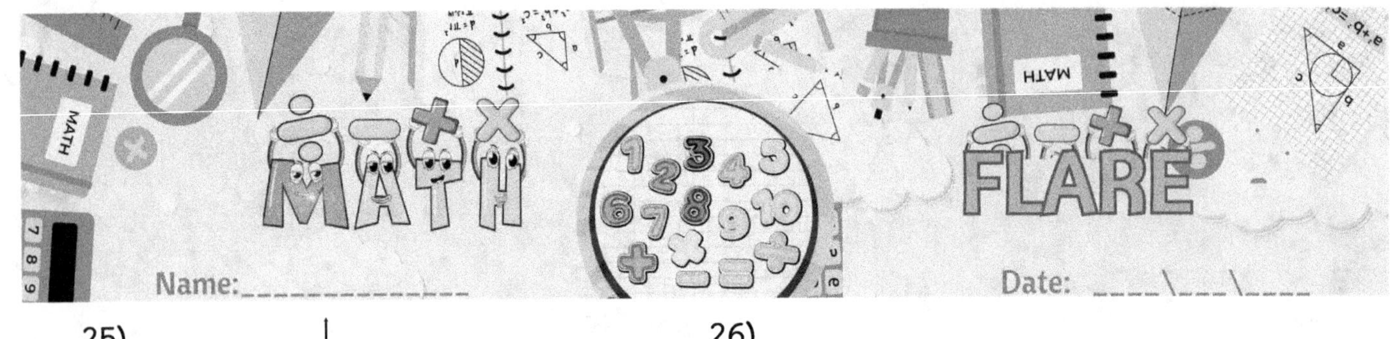

25)

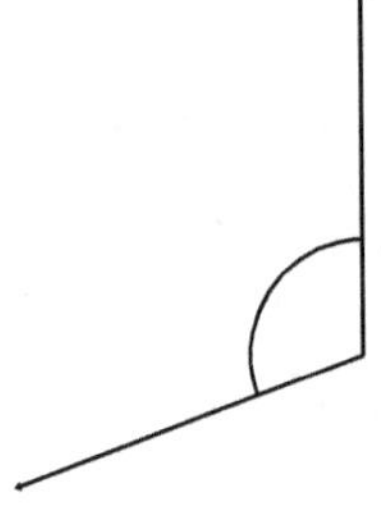

____

26)

____

27)

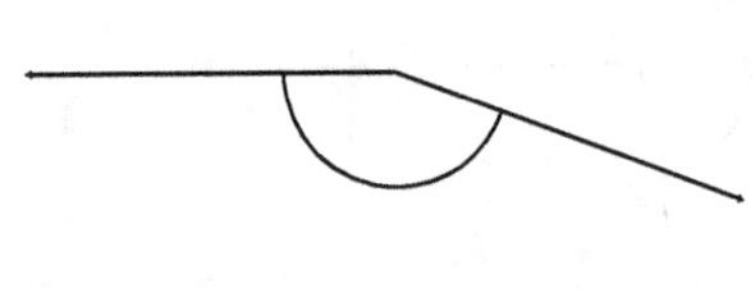

____

28)

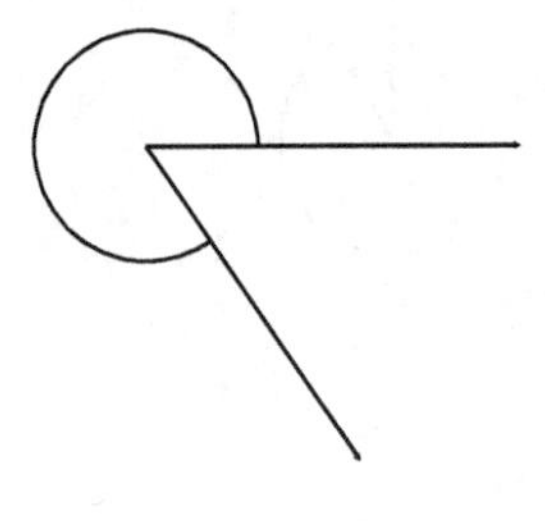

____

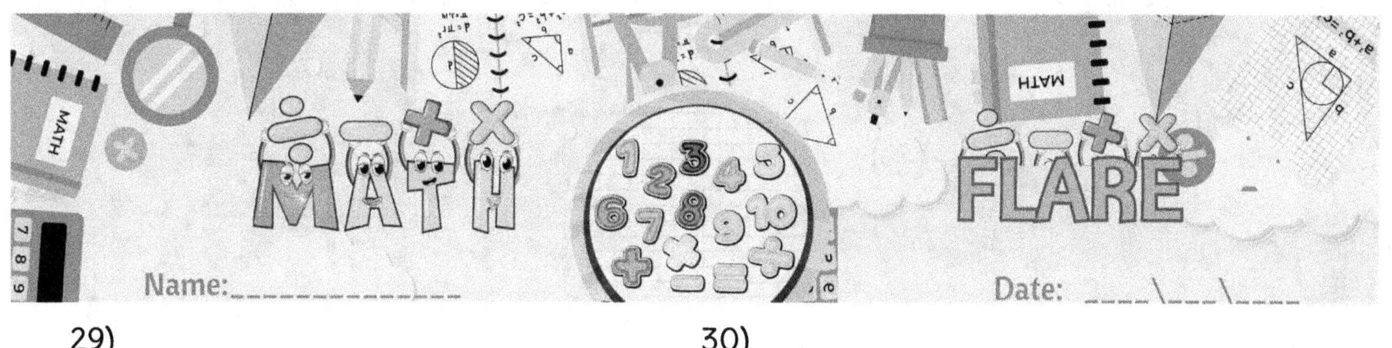

29)

30)

____

31)

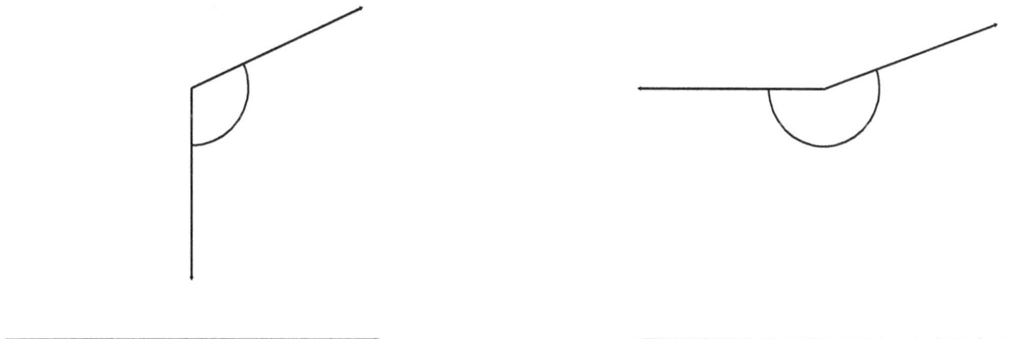

32)

____

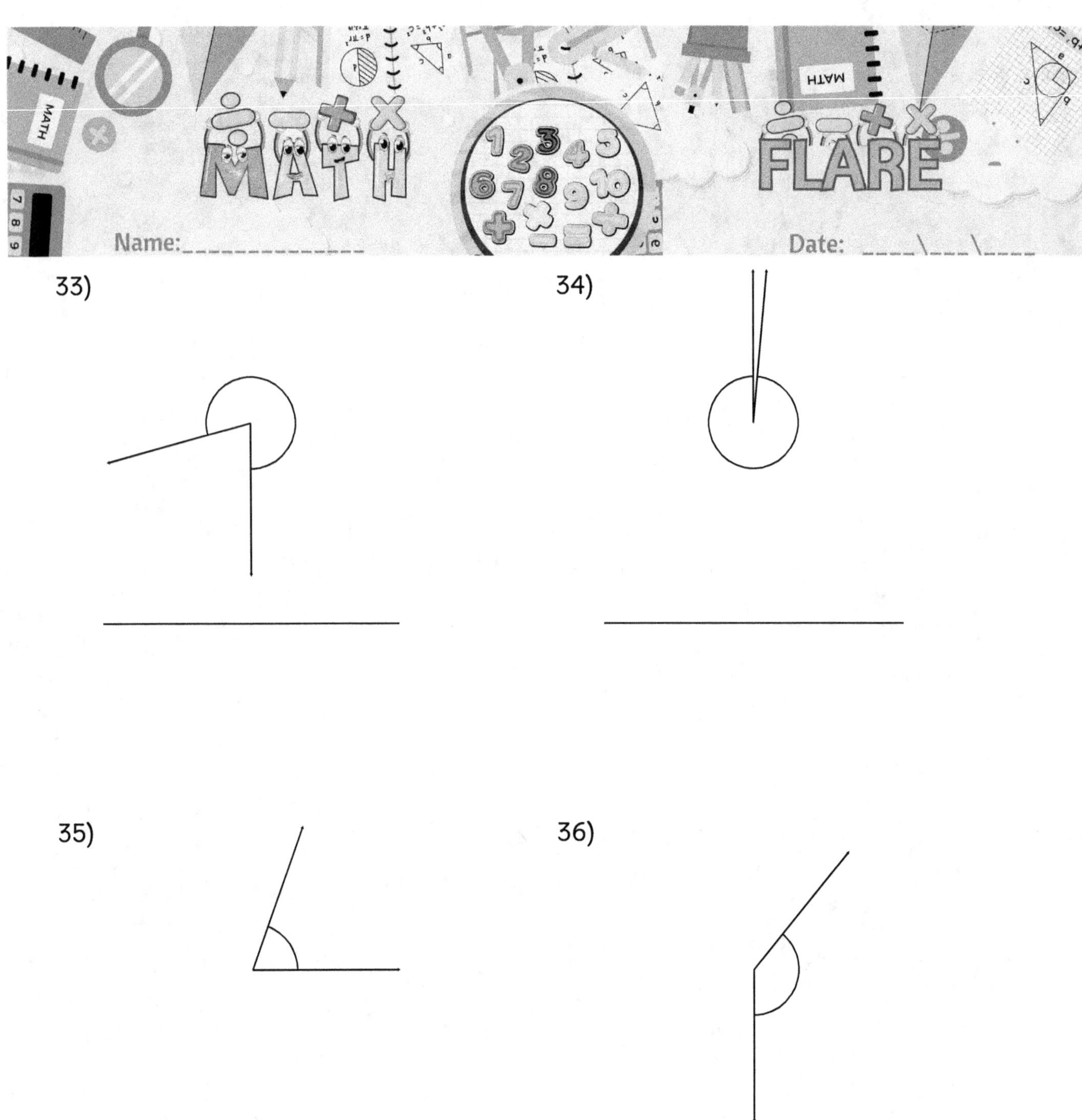

33)

____

34)

____

35)

____

36)

____

37)

38)

39)

40)

41)

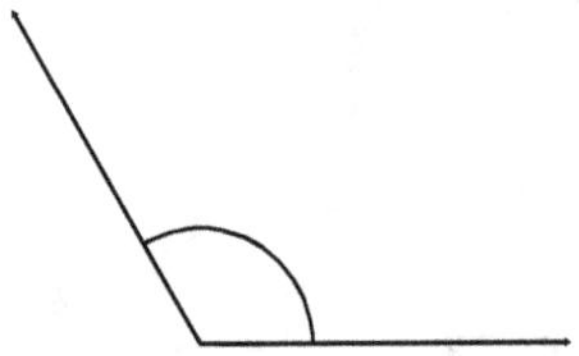

42)

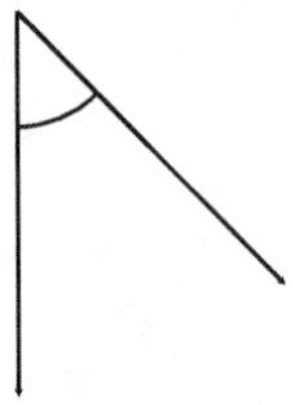

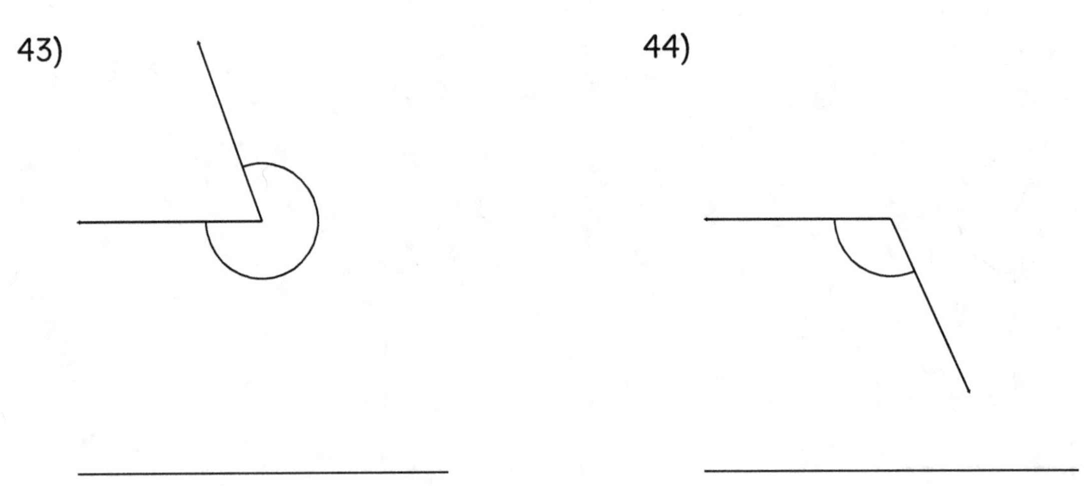

43)

44)

45)

46)

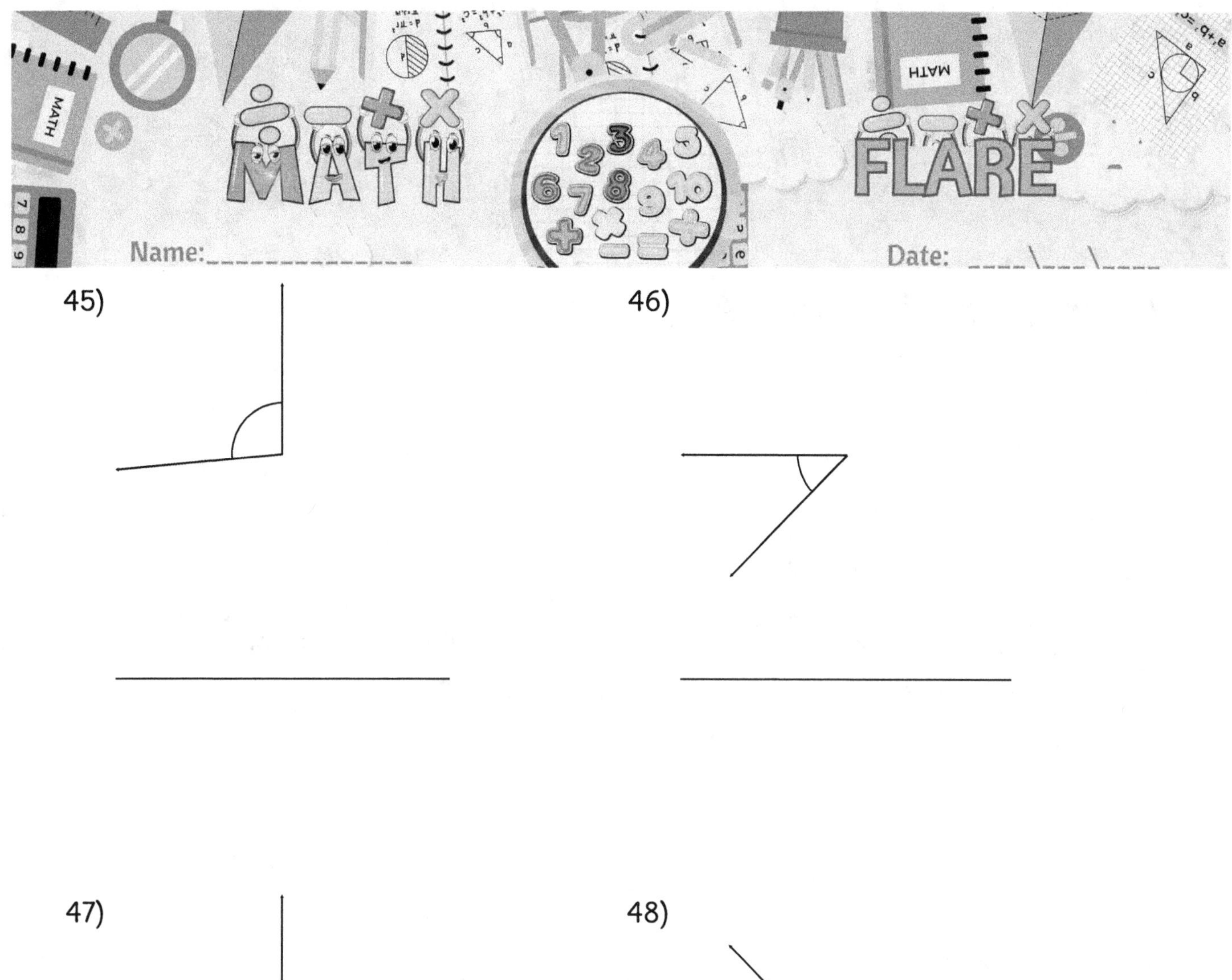

47)

48)

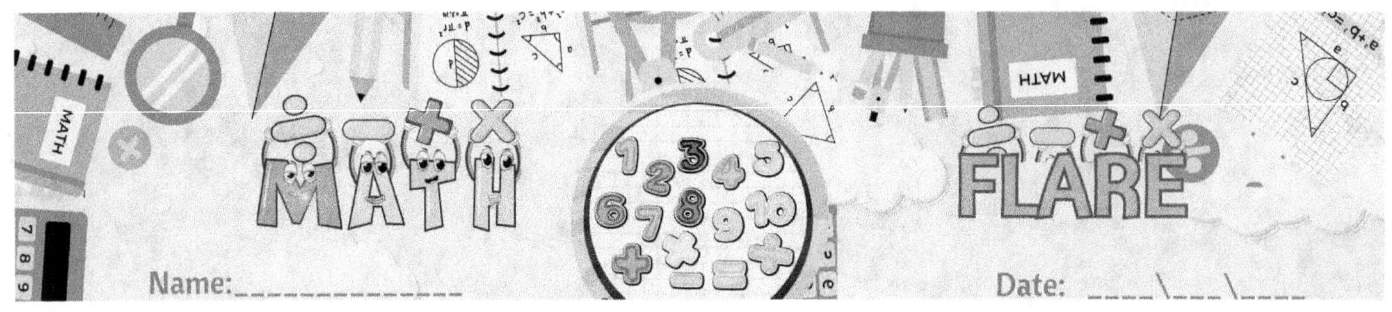

Volume and Surface Area

1)

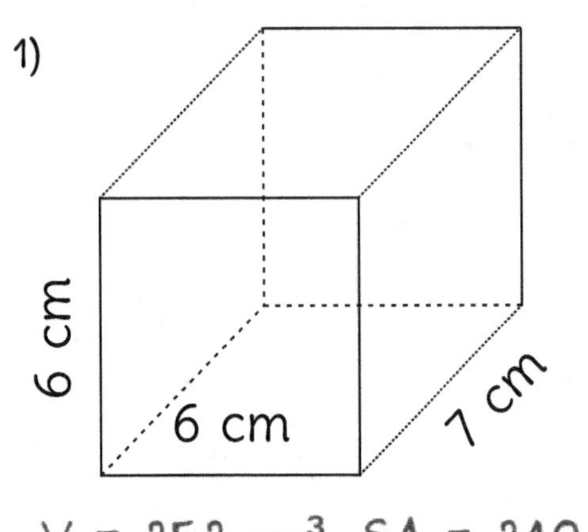

V = 252 cm³ SA = 240 cm²

2)

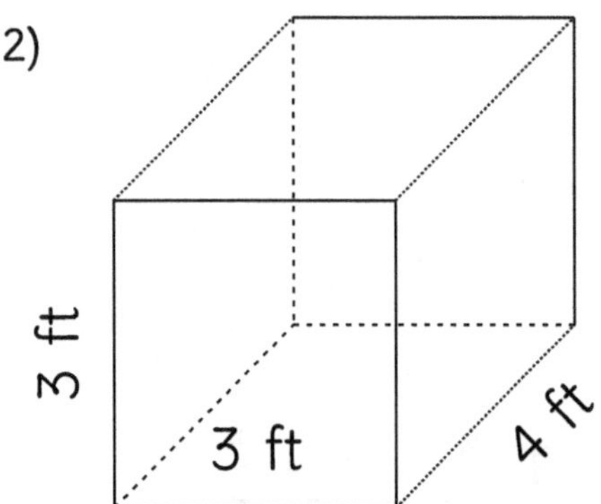

3)

4)

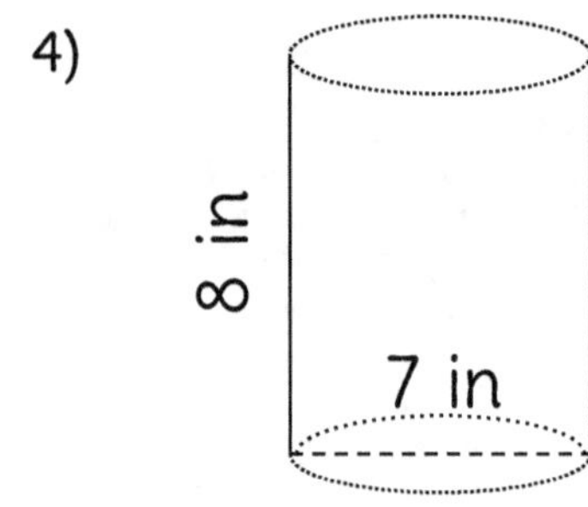

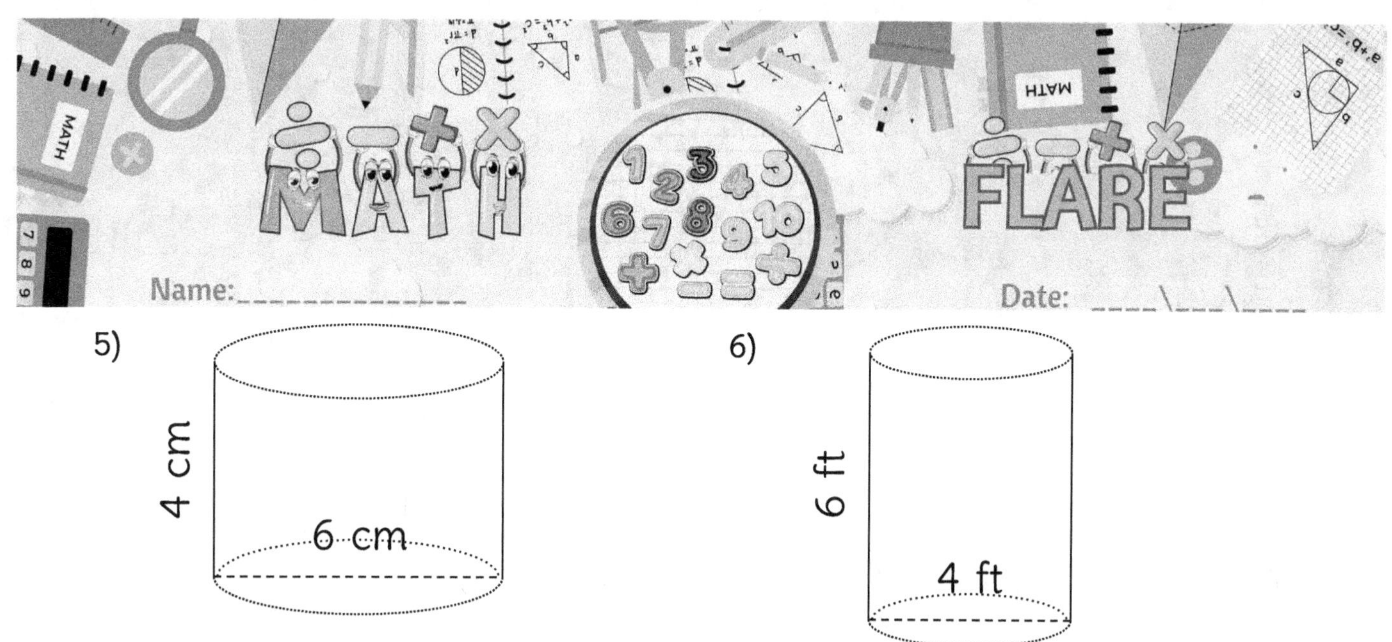

5) 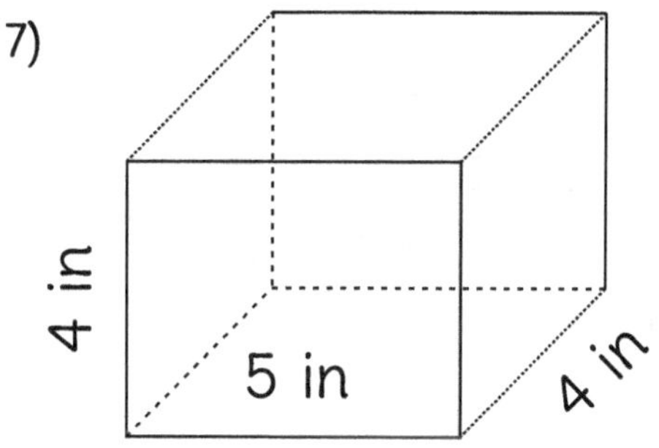

6)

7) 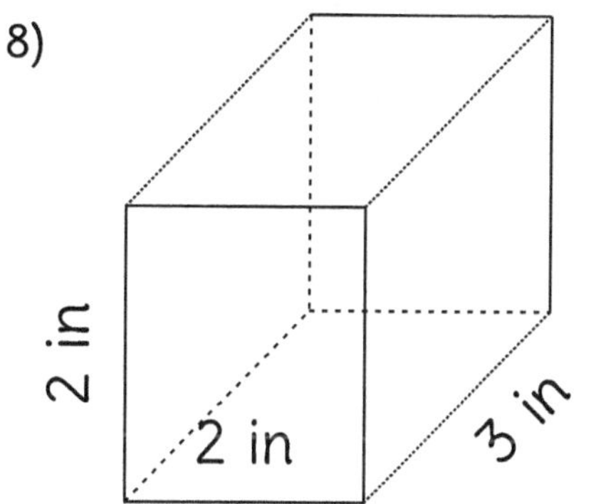

8)

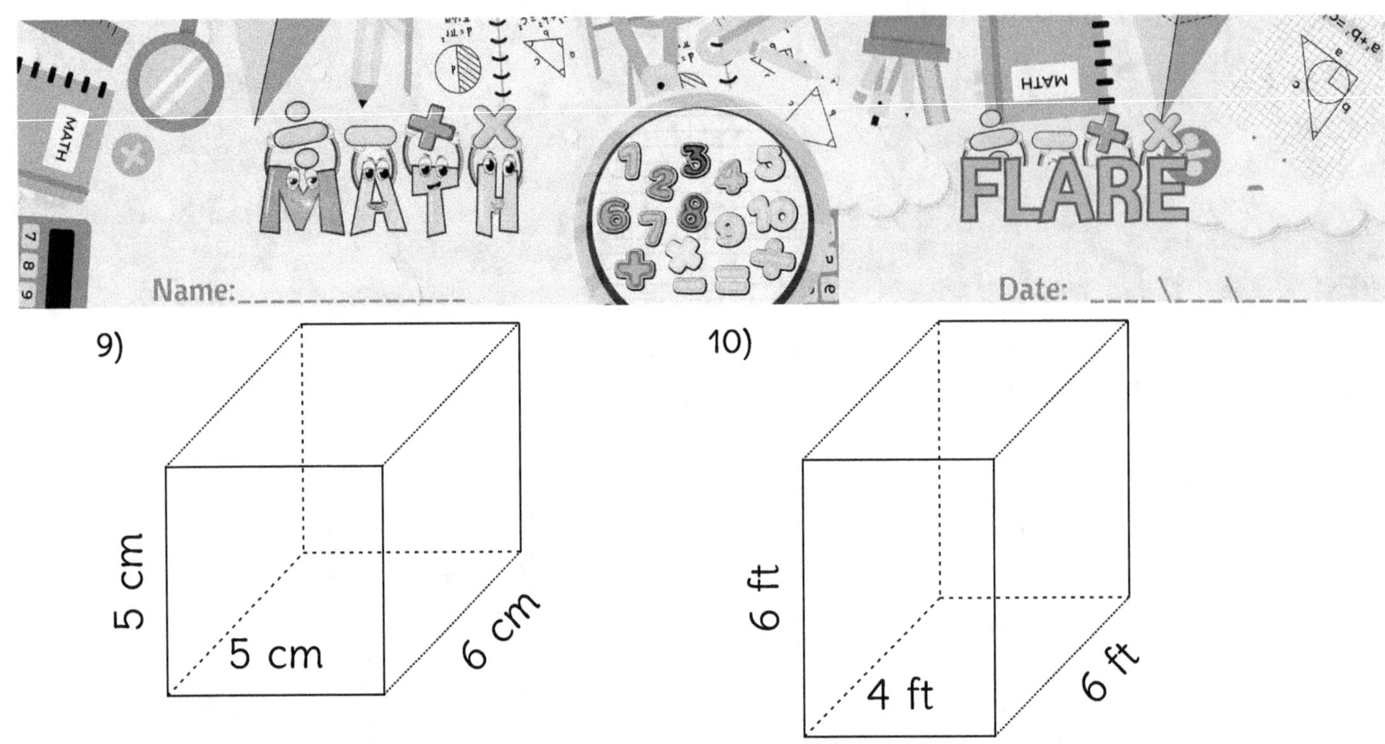

9)

10)

11) 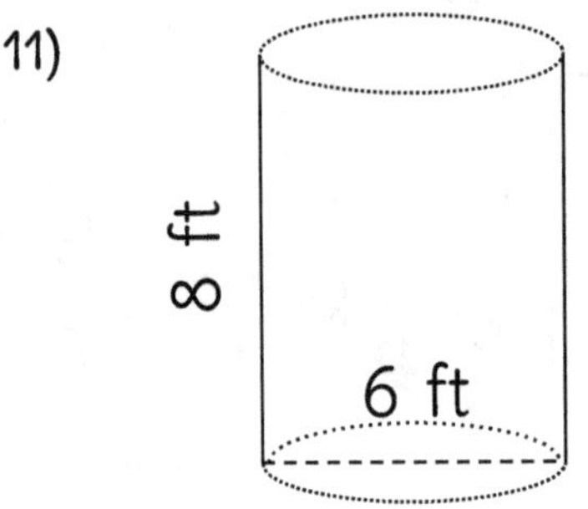

12) 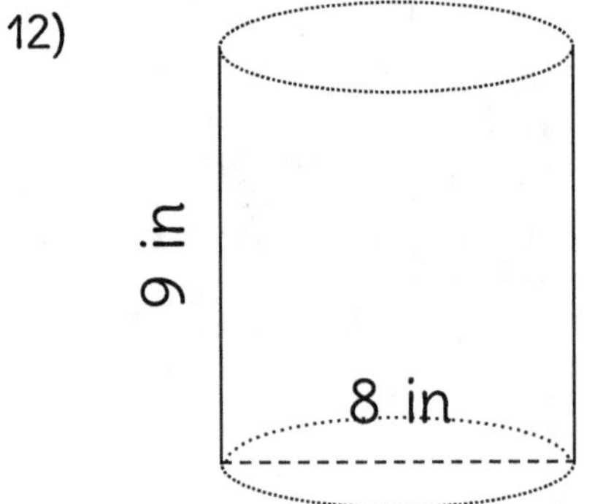

MATH
FLARE
Name:
Date:

13)

7 cm
7 cm
8 cm

14)

4 cm
5 cm
5 cm

15)

7 ft
6 ft

16)

3 in
3 in
3 in

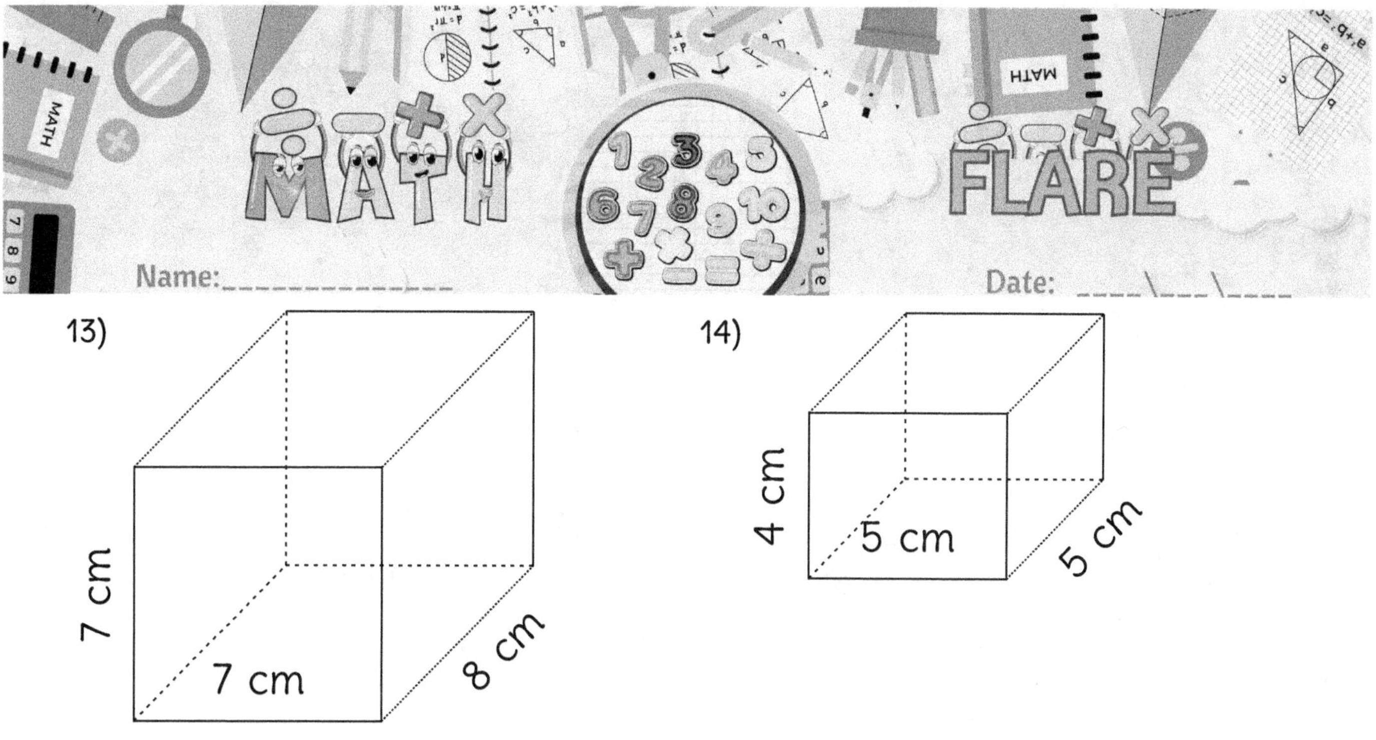

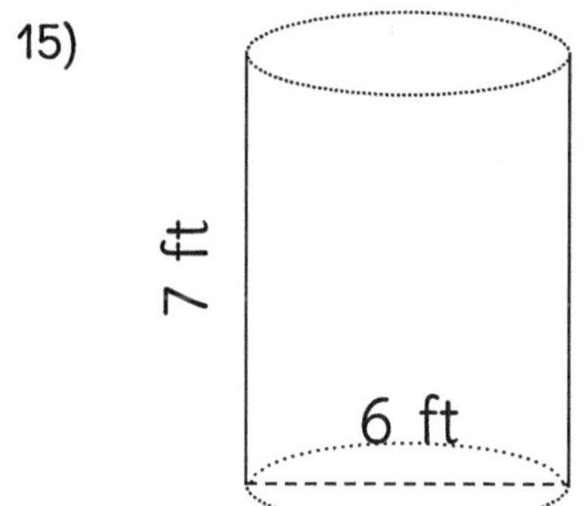

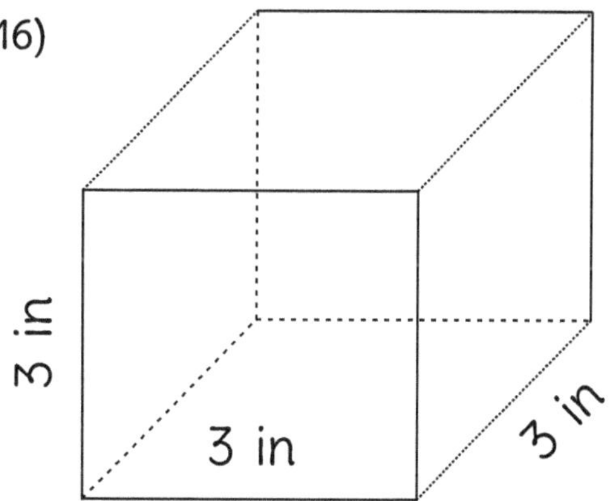

MATH
FLARE
Name:
Date:

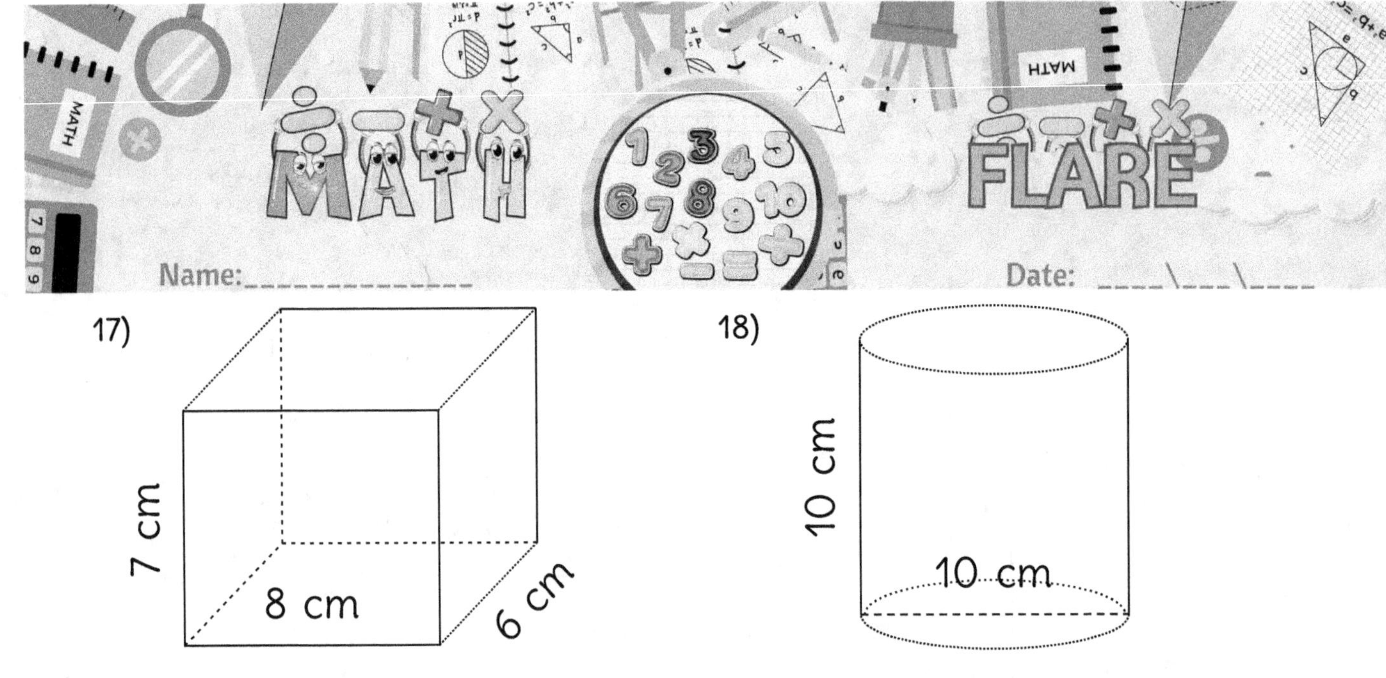

17)

7 cm
8 cm
6 cm

18)

10 cm
10 cm

19)

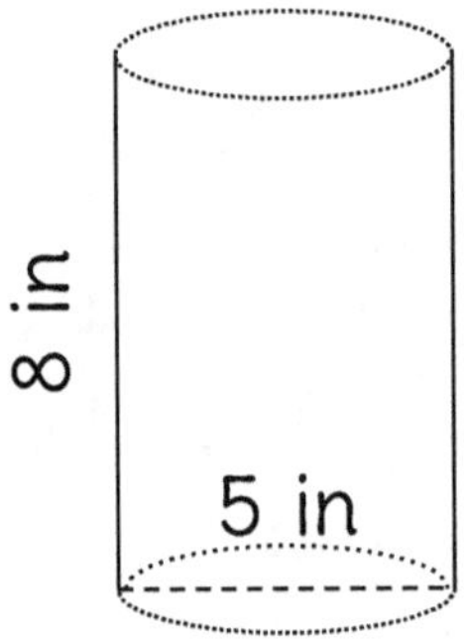

8 in
5 in

20)

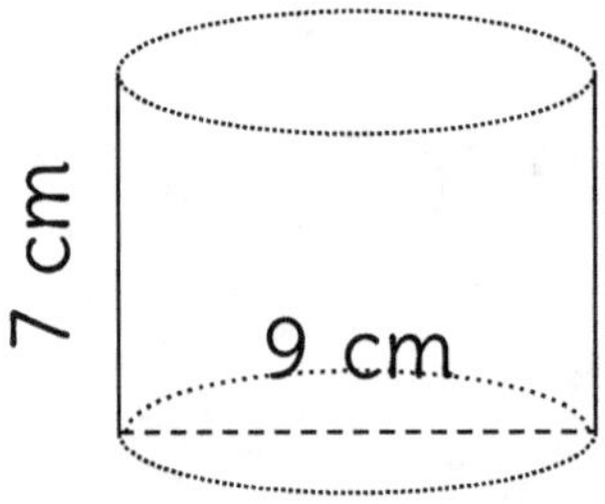

7 cm
9 cm

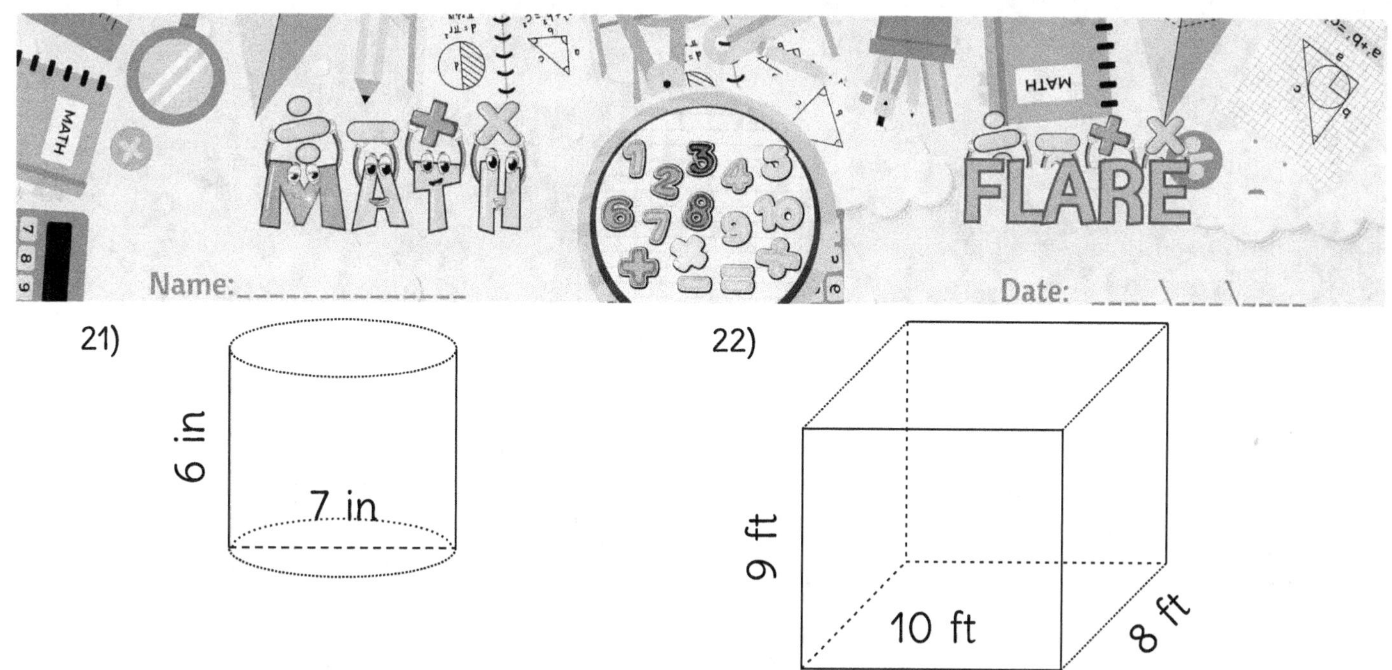

21)

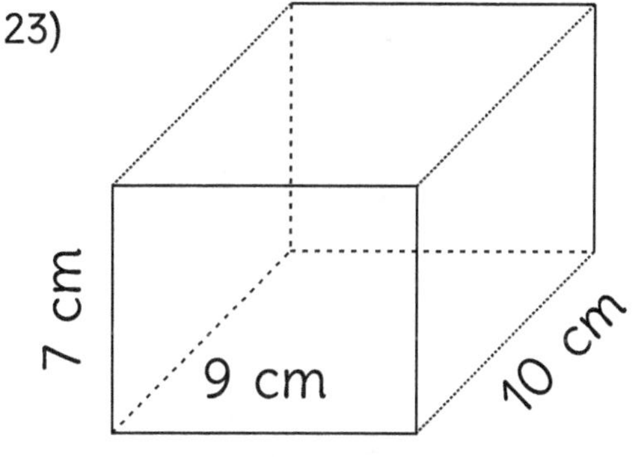

22)

23)

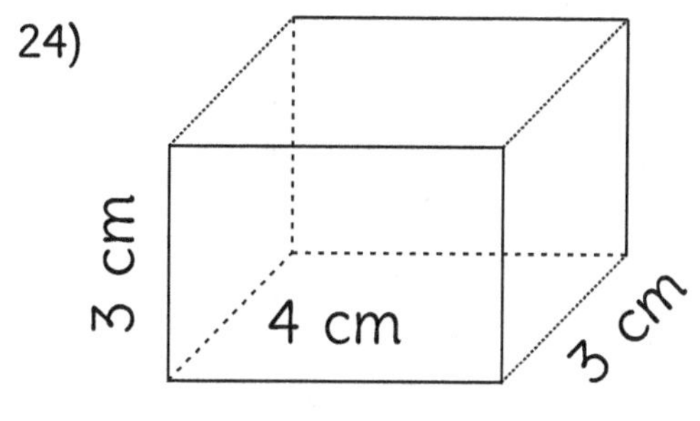

24)

143

MATH
FLARE
Name:____________
Date:____________

25)

4 in
6 in
8 in

26)

3 in
2 in
2 in

27)

3 cm
5 cm
4 cm

28)

7 in
7 in
7 in

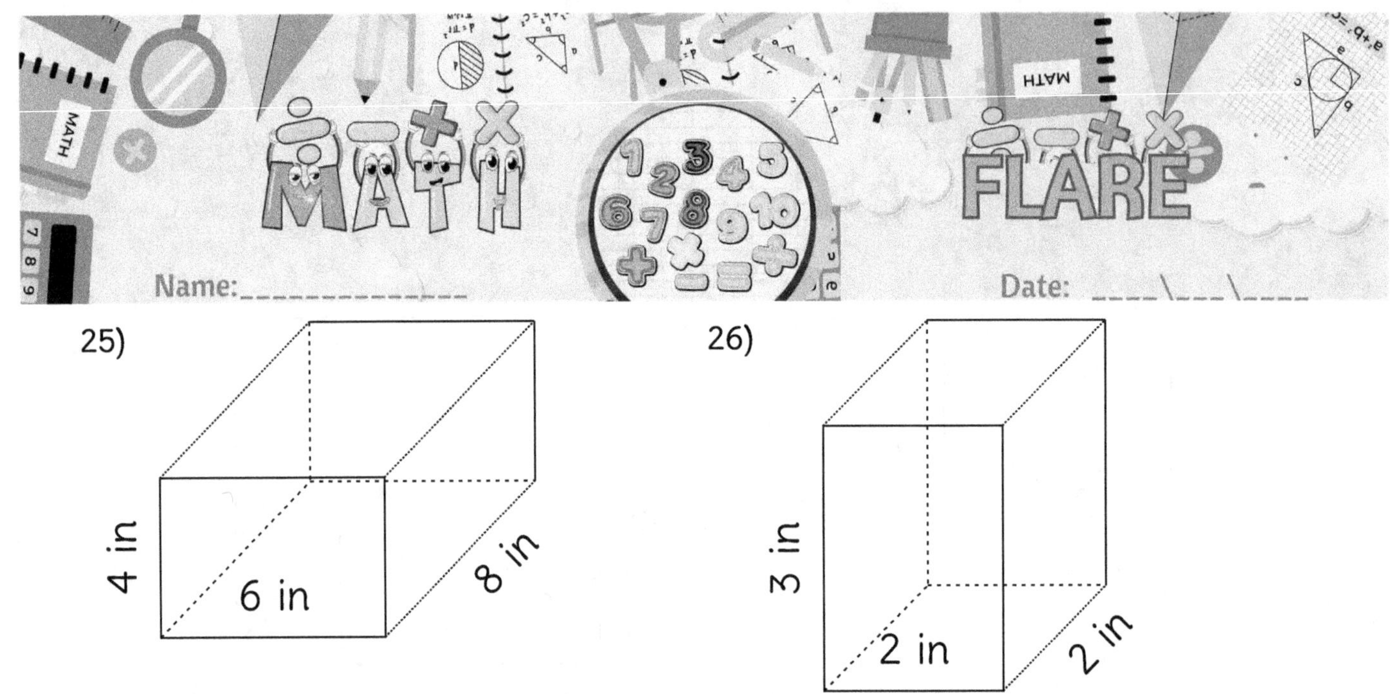

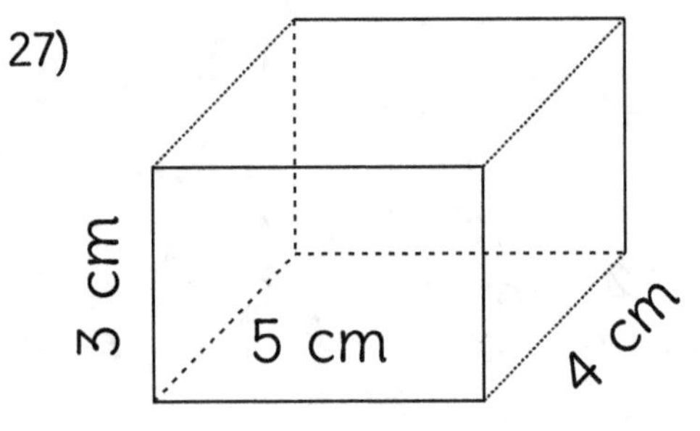

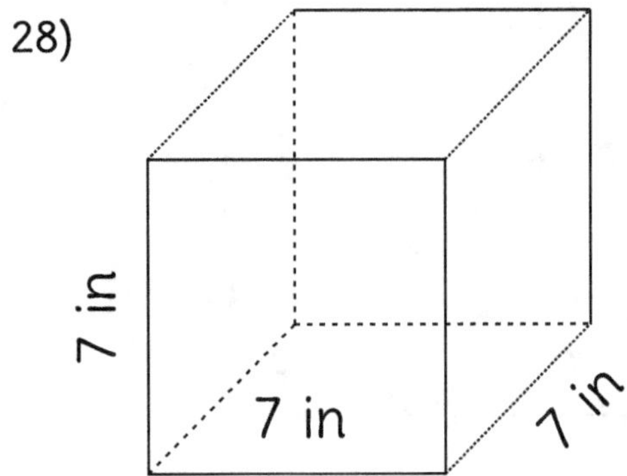

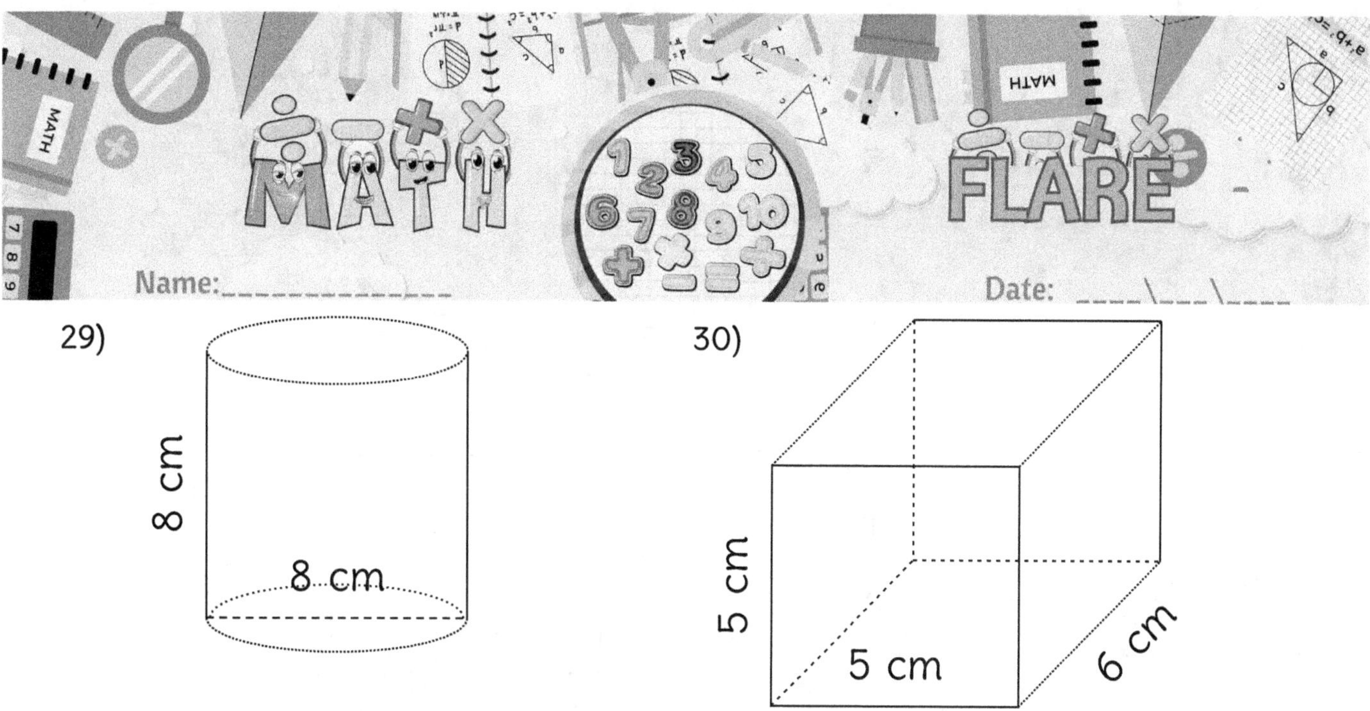

29)

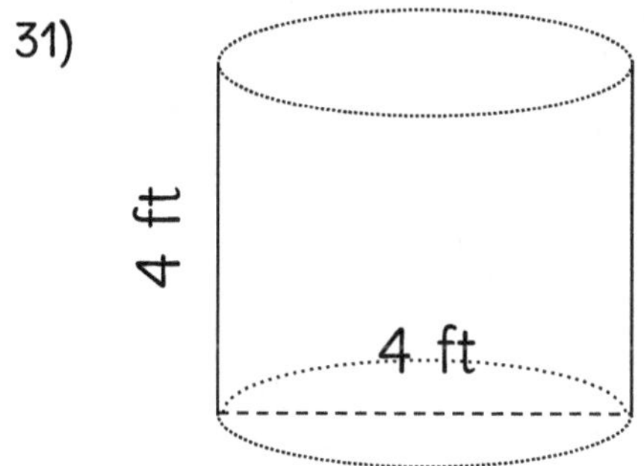

30)

31)

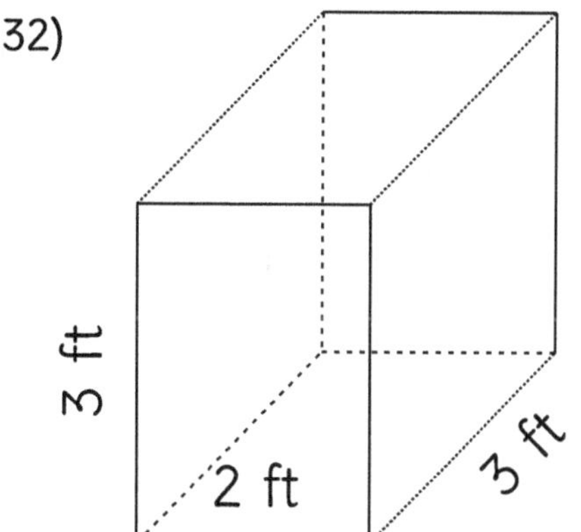

32)

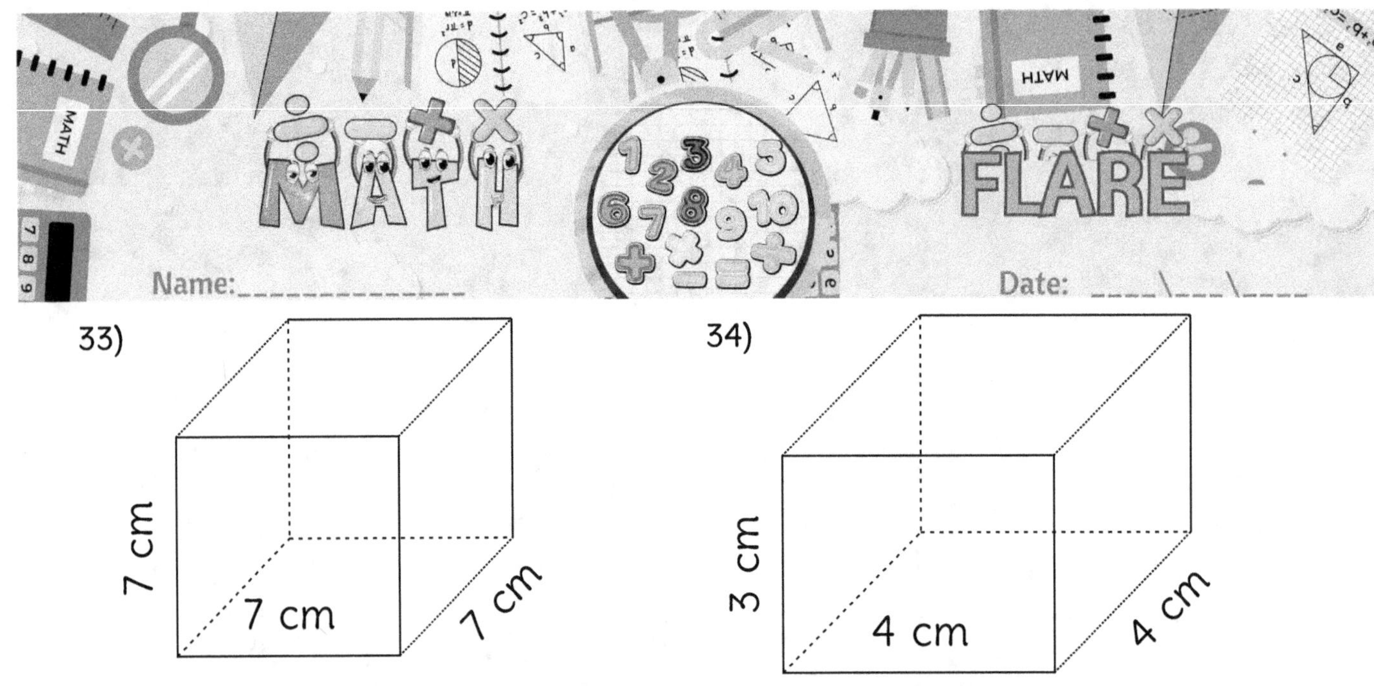

33)

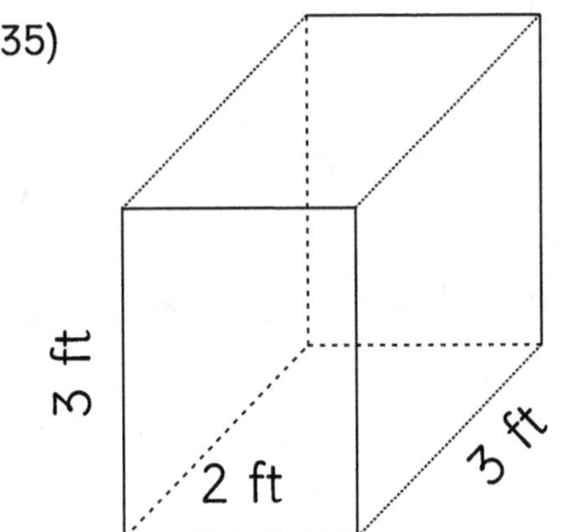

34)

35)

36)

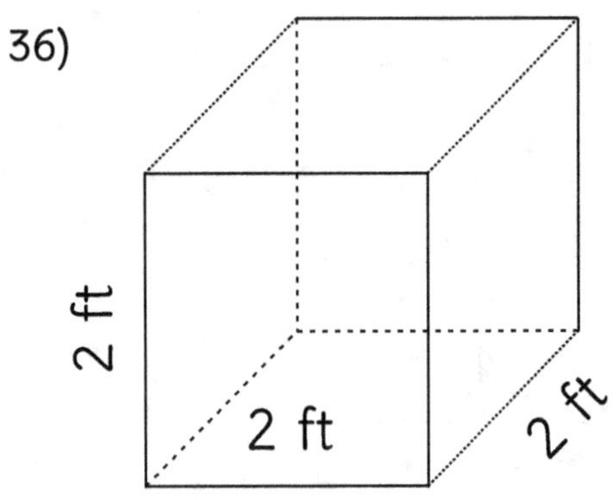

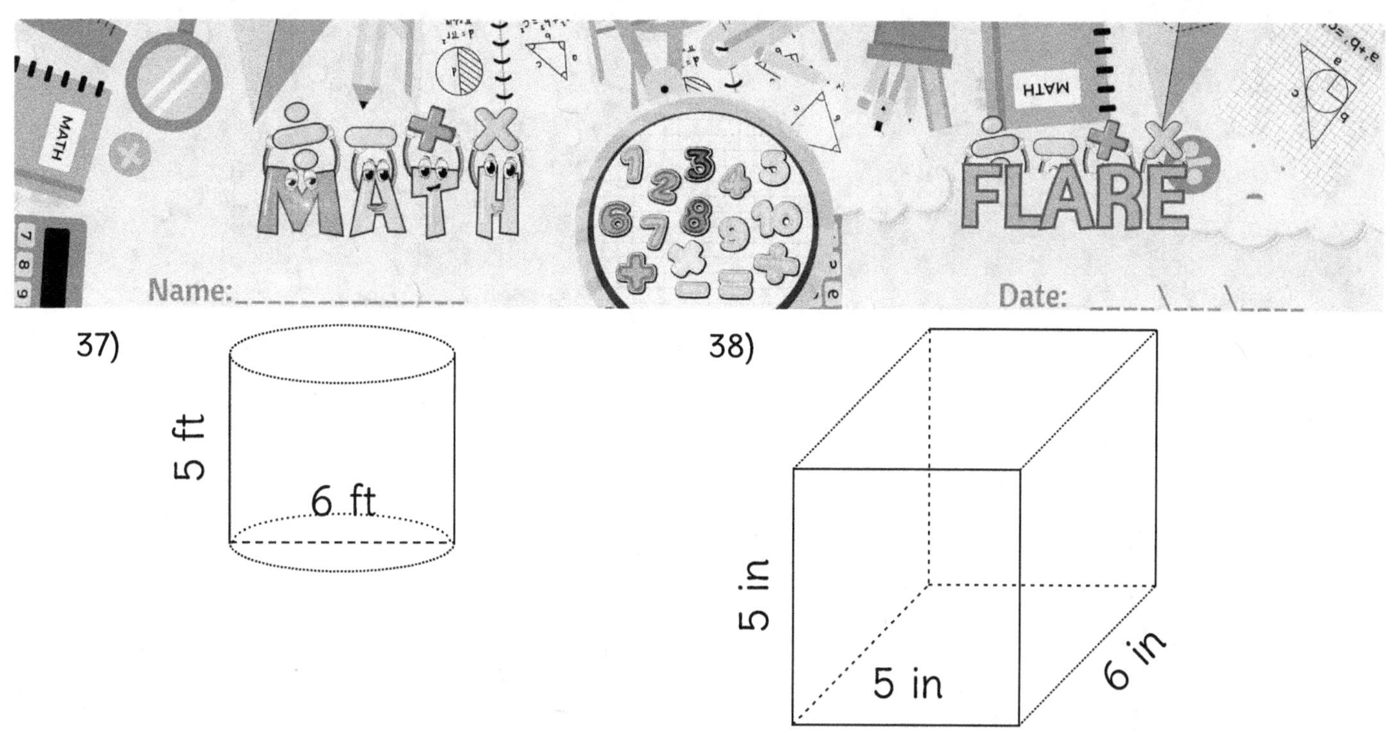

37)

38)

39)
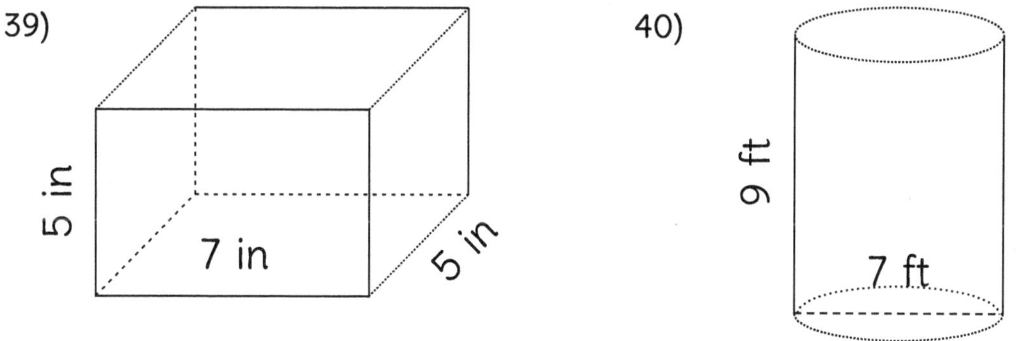

40)

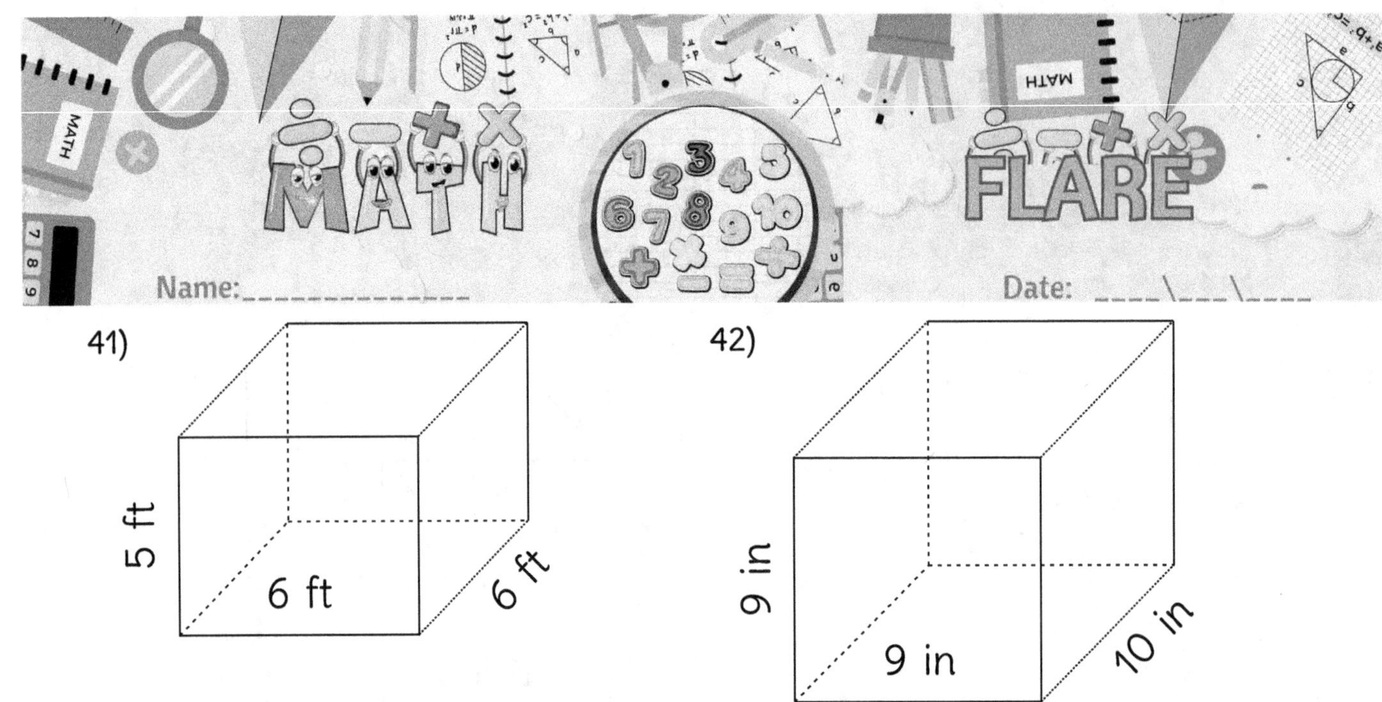

41)

5 ft

6 ft

6 ft

42)

9 in

9 in

10 in

43) 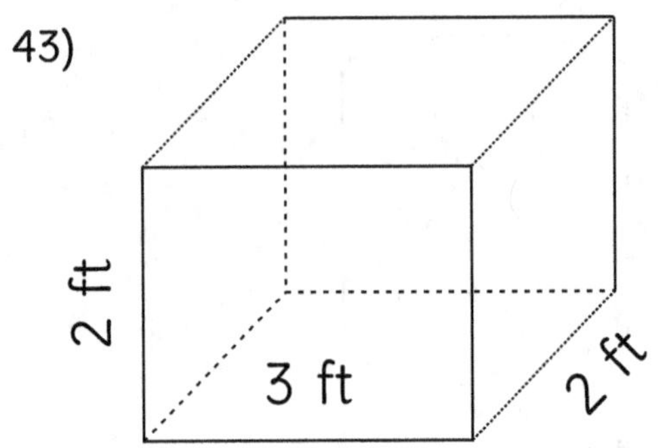

2 ft

3 ft

2 ft

44) 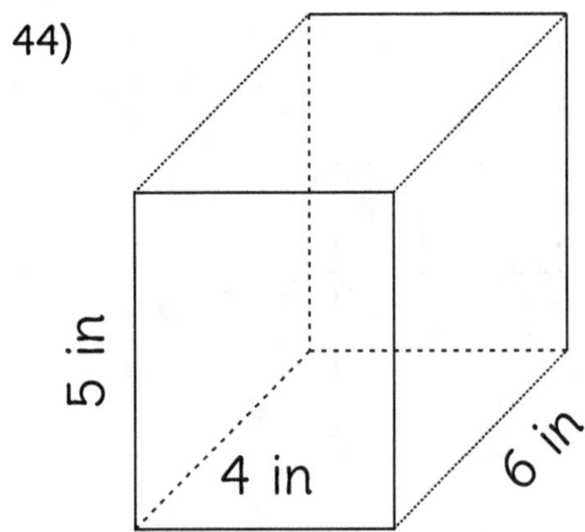

5 in

4 in

6 in

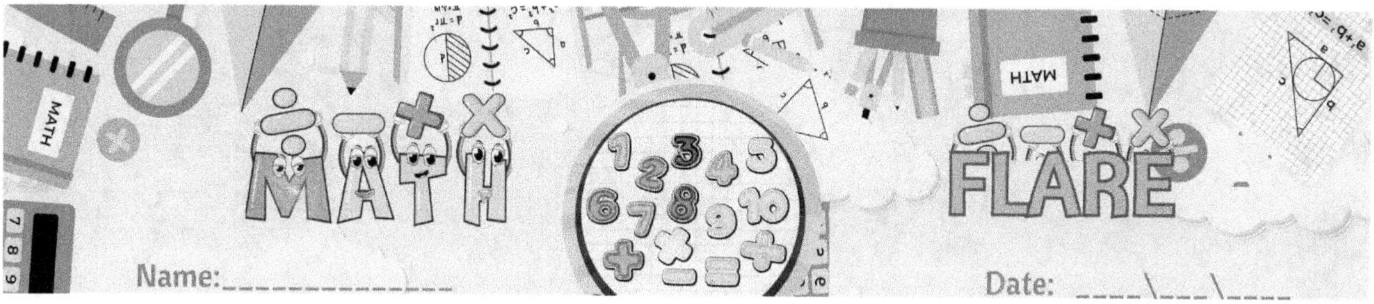
MATH
FLARE
Name:_______________
Date: ____________

45)

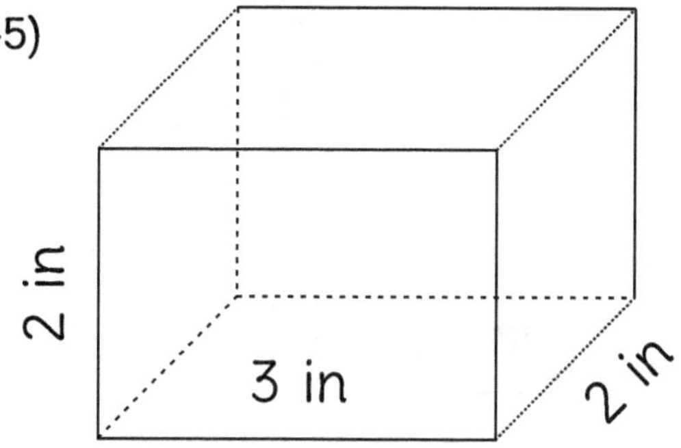
2 in
3 in
2 in

46)

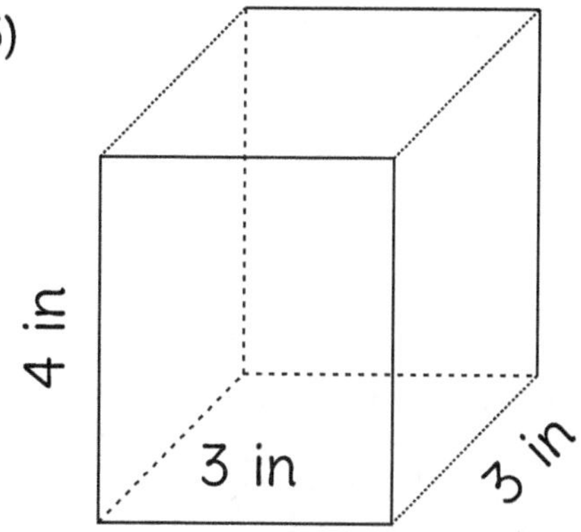
4 in
3 in
3 in

47)

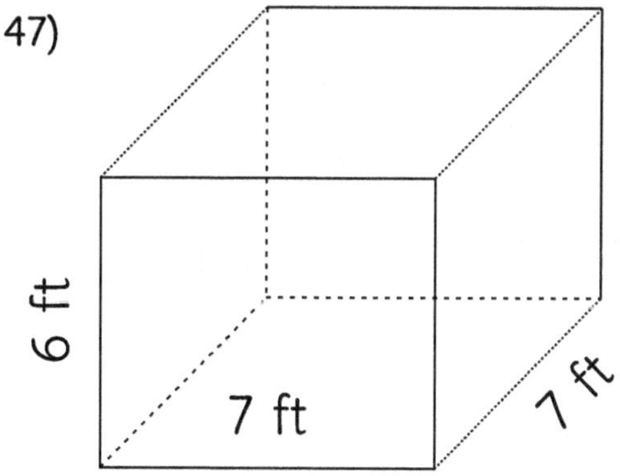
6 ft
7 ft
7 ft

48)

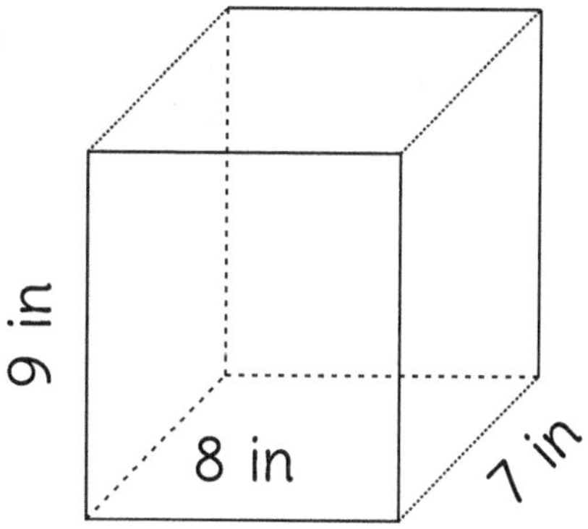
9 in
8 in
7 in

49)

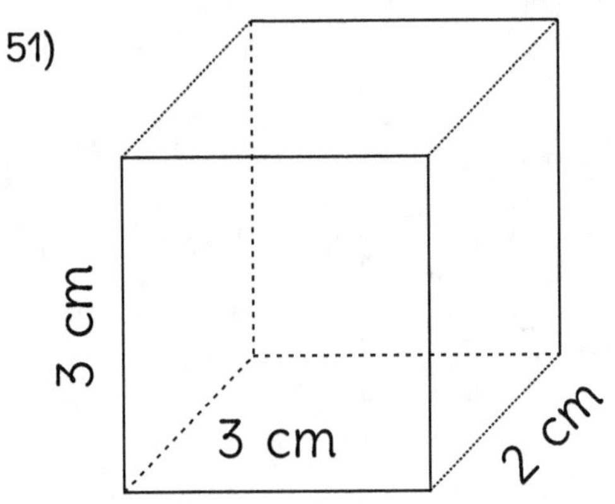

50)

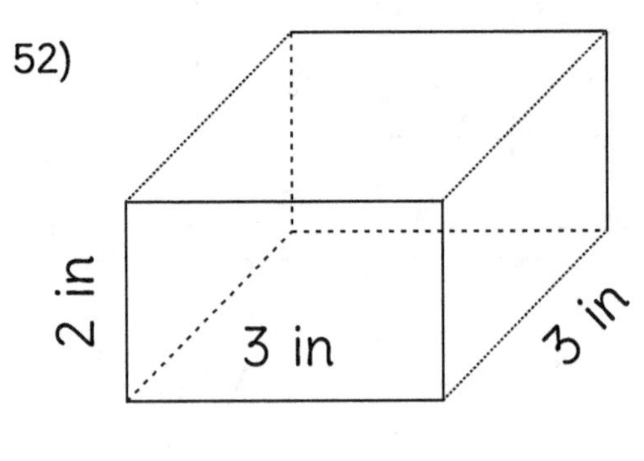

51)

52)

MATH
FLARE
Name:
Date:

53)

6 cm
9 cm

54)

5 ft
6 ft
4 ft

55)

3 ft
3 ft
3 ft

56)

7 cm
10 cm
9 cm

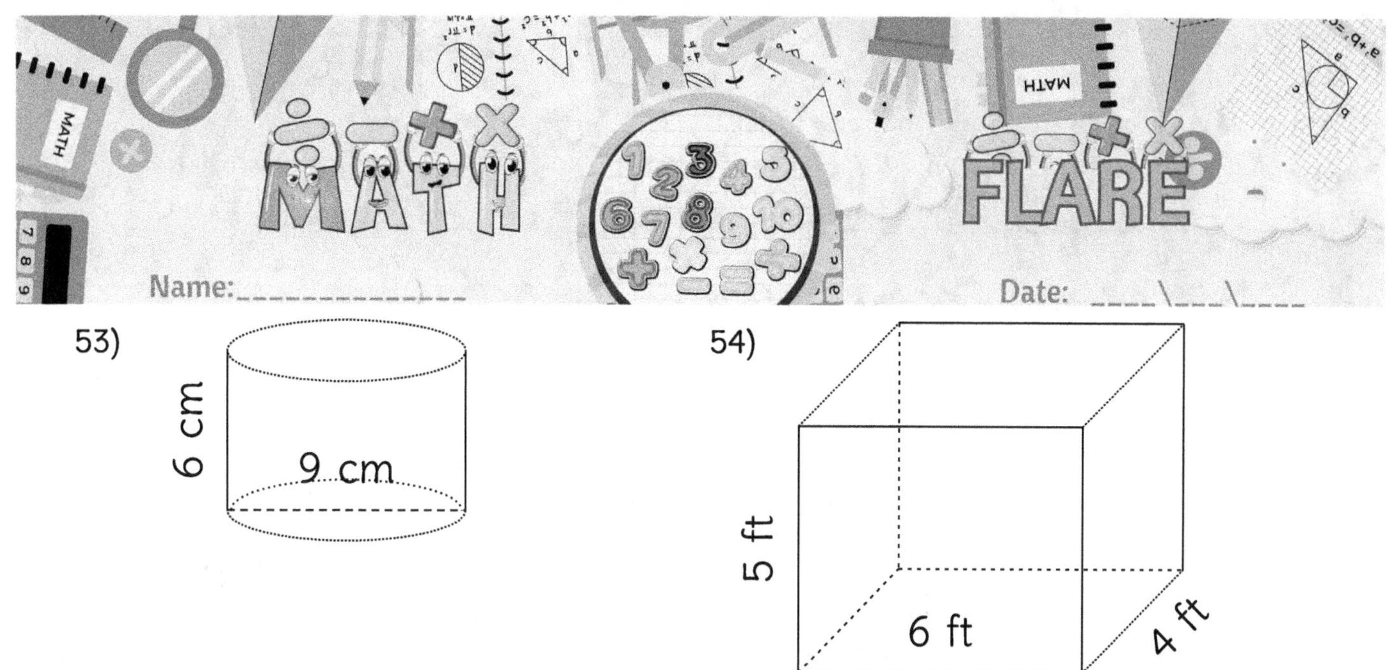

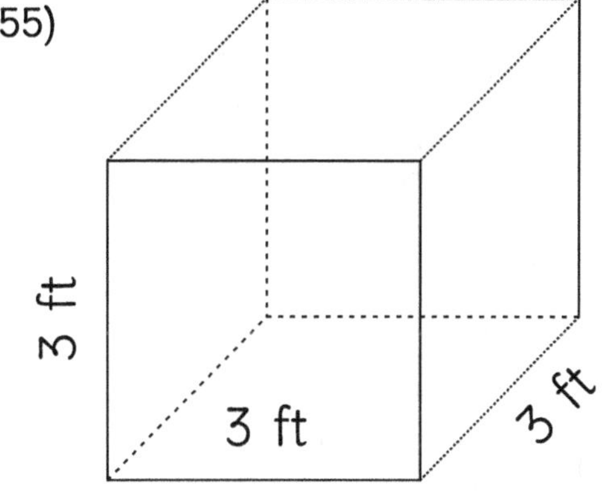

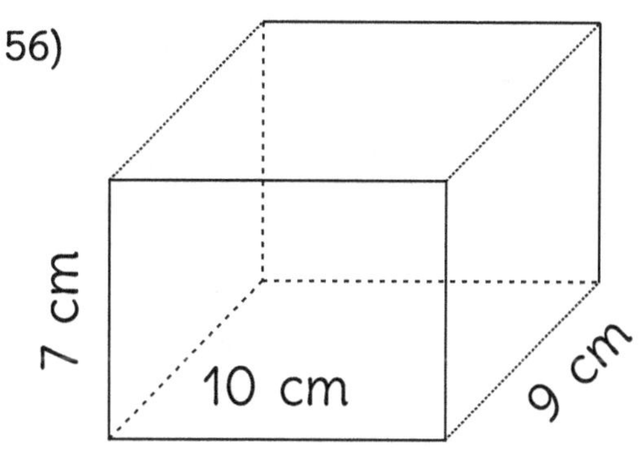

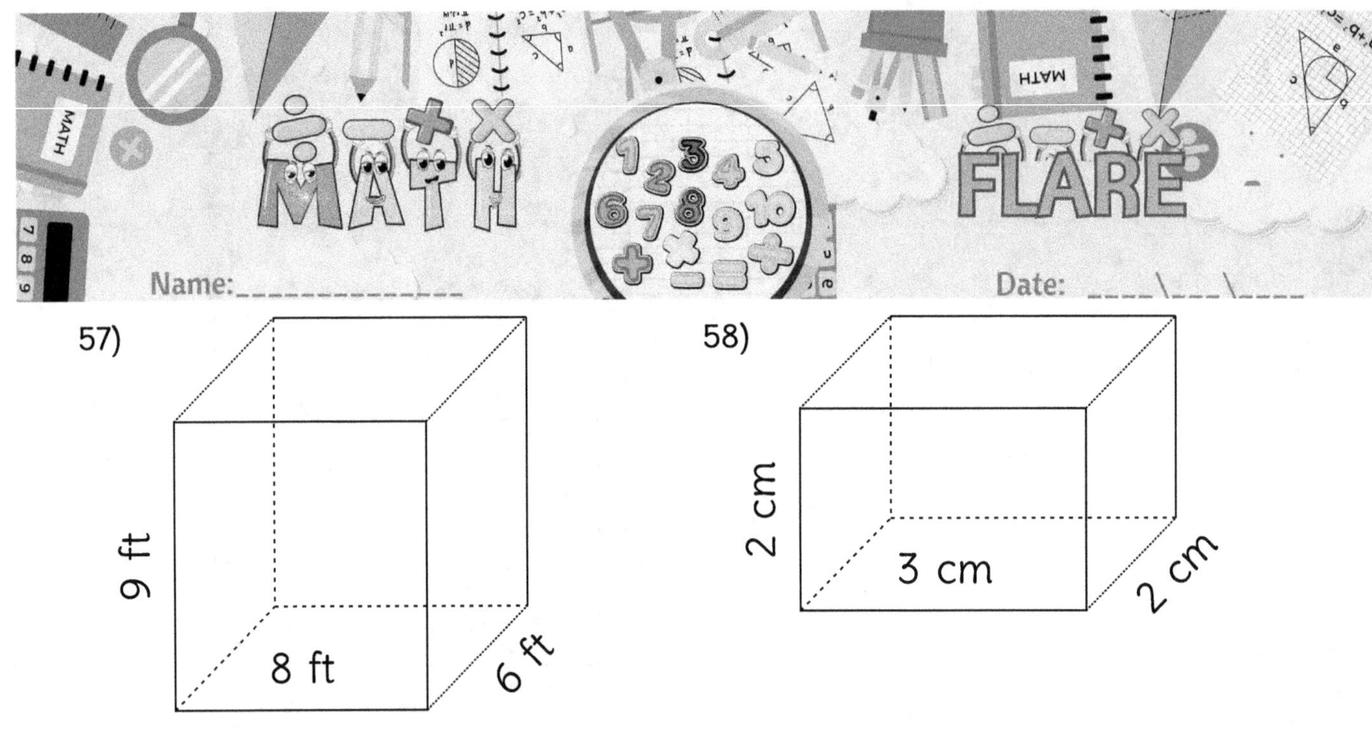

57)

58)

59) 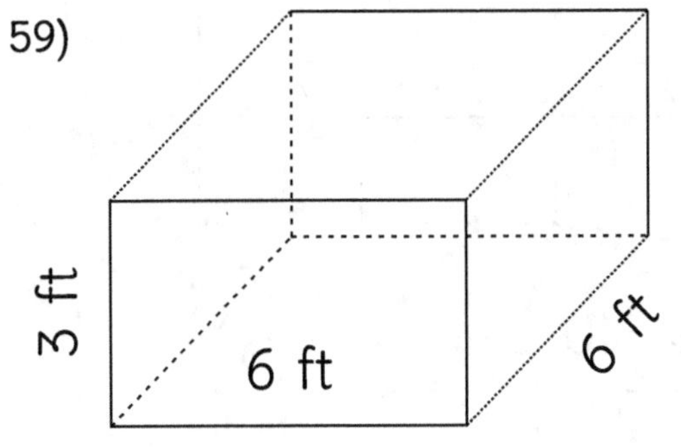

60) 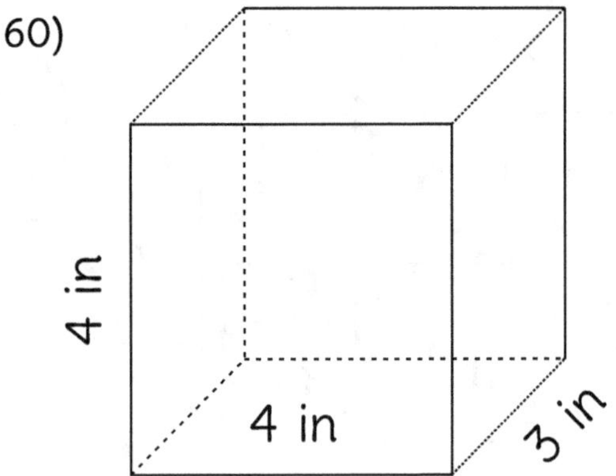

Chapter. 06
Statistics

Mean

The mean, also known as the average, is a measure of central tendency.

To find the mean of a set of numbers:

- Add up all the numbers in the set.
- Divide the sum by the total count of numbers in the set.

For example: consider the set of numbers: 70, 72, 49, 69, 27, 76.

$$\text{Mean} = \frac{70 + 72 + 49 + 69 + 27 + 76}{6}$$

$$= \frac{363}{6} = 60.5$$

Median

The median is a measure of central tendency that represents the middle value of a dataset when the values are arranged in ascending or descending order.

To find the median of a set of numbers:

- Arrange the numbers in ascending or descending order.
- If the total count of numbers is odd, the median is the middle value.
- If the total count of numbers is even, the median is the average of the two middle values.

For example: consider the set of numbers: 70, 72, 49, 69, 27, 76.

$$27, 49, 69, 70, 72, 76$$

$$\text{Median} = \frac{69 + 70}{2} = \frac{139}{2} = 69.5$$

Mode:

The mode in statistics refers to the value that appears most frequently in a given set of data.

Let's consider the following set of numbers:

$$\{2, 4, 4, 5, 6, 6, 6, 7, 8, 8\}$$

In this set, the number 6 appears three times, more than any other number. Therefore, the mode of this dataset is 6.

It's possible for a dataset to have more than one mode if two or more numbers appear with the same highest frequency. In such cases, the dataset is considered multimodal. If no number repeats, the dataset is considered to have no mode.

For example:

$$\{2, 4, 4, 4, 5, 6, 6, 6, 7, 8, 8\}$$

In this date set, 4 and 6 appear three times. Therefore, this dataset is multimodal.

Range:

In statistics, the range refers to the difference between the largest and smallest values in a dataset. It represents the spread or variability of the data.

For example, consider the dataset $\{68, 13, 30, 18, 45, 76, 11\}$:

To calculate the range:

1. Arrange the data points in ascending order.

$$11, 13, 18, 30, 45, 68, 76$$

2. Subtract the smallest value from the largest value.

- The smallest value is 11.

- The largest value is 76.

$$\text{Range} = \text{Largest value} - \text{smallest value} = 76 - 11 = 65.$$

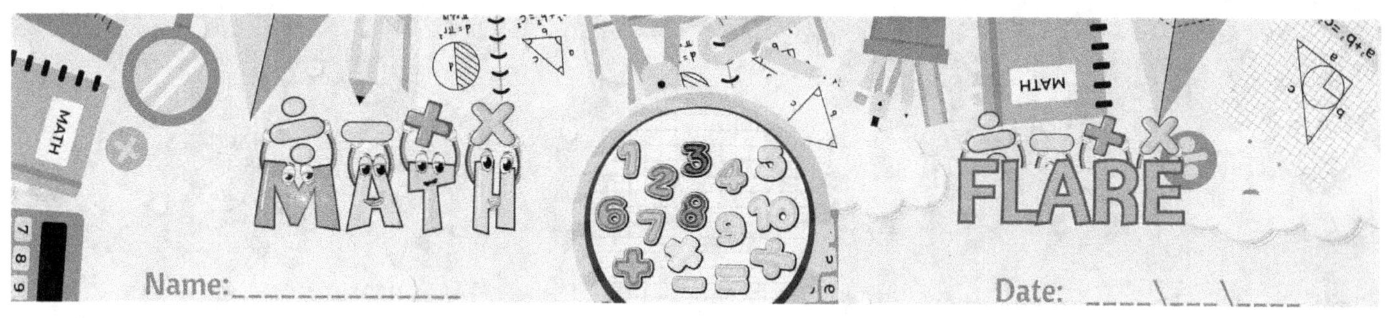

Mean, Median, Mode, and Range

Find the Mean, Median, Mode and Range of the following sets of data.

1) **68, 13, 30, 18, 45, 76, 11**

   Mean = 37.286   **Median =** 30

   Mode = none   **Range =** 65

$$\text{Mean} \quad \frac{68,\ 13,\ 30,\ 18,\ 45,\ 76,\ 11}{7}$$

$$= \frac{261}{7} = 37.3$$

11, 13, 18, 30, 45, 68, 76

$$\text{Range} = 76 - 11 = 65$$

2) 55, 28, 23, 49, 66, 9, 40

   Mean = _____   Median = _____

   Mode = _____   Range = _____

3) 29, 88, 50, 63, 40, 19, 65

   Mean = _____   Median = _____

   Mode = _____   Range = _____

4) 69, 57, 27, 5, 21, 84

   Mean = _____   Median = _____

   Mode = _____   Range = _____

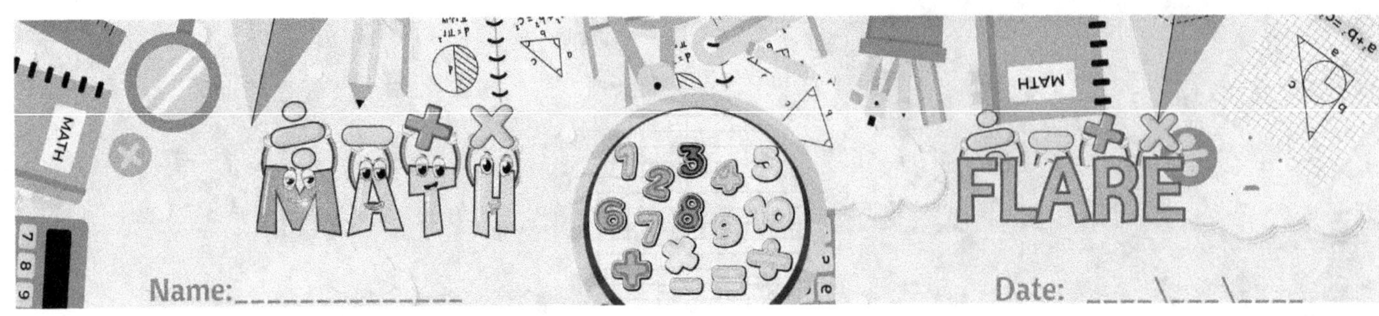

5) 17, 33, 23, 83, 30, 42, 33

Mean = _______   Median = _____

Mode = _______   Range = _____

6) 81, 78, 51, 65, 11, 69, 15

Mean = _______   Median = _____

Mode = _______   Range = _____

7) 45, 16, 46, 56, 61, 7

Mean = _____   Median = _____

Mode = _____   Range = _____

8) 98, 29, 92, 35, 37, 26

Mean = _______   Median = _____

Mode = _______   Range = _____

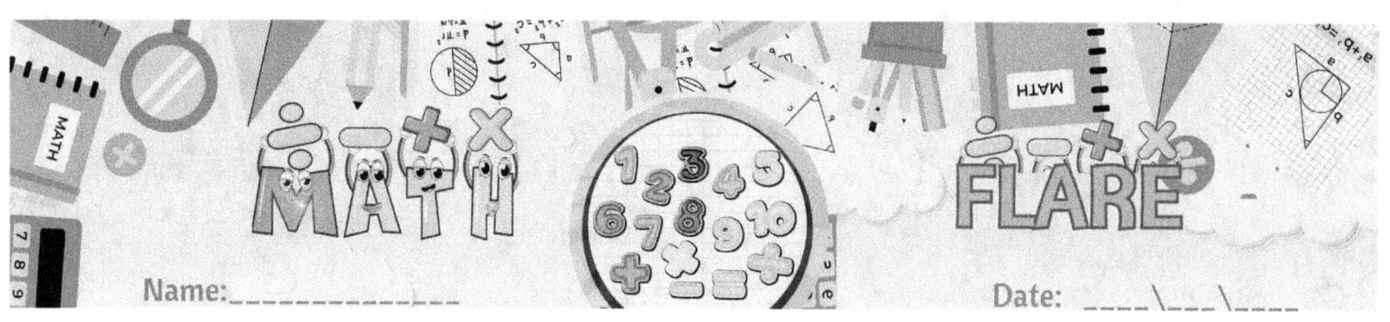

9) 53, 83, 98, 56, 4, 14, 24

Mean = _______   Median = ____

Mode = _______   Range = ____

10) 91, 94, 22, 5, 40, 20

Mean = _______   Median = ____

Mode = _______   Range = ____

11) 24, 76, 59, 51, 38, 85

Mean = _____   Median = _____

Mode = _____   Range = _____

12) 52, 71, 4, 21, 54, 11

Mean = _____   Median = _____

Mode = _____   Range = _____

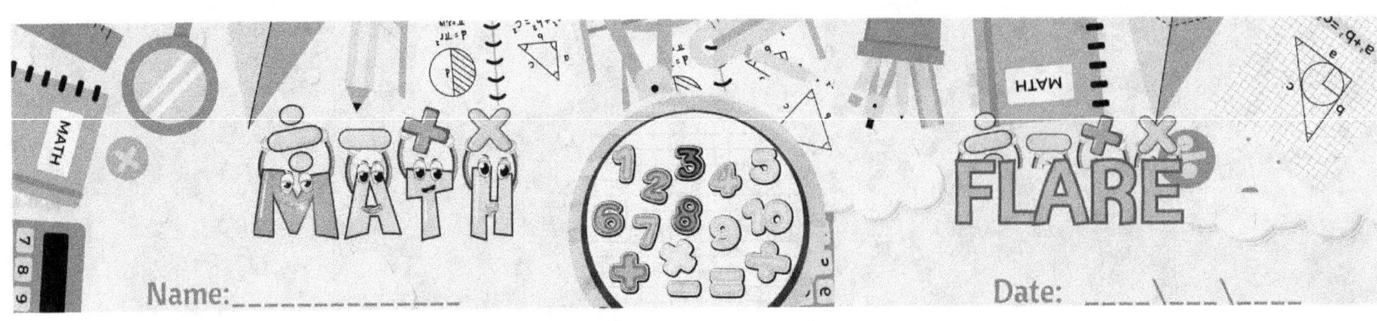

13) 70, 44, 15, 86, 87, 41

Mean = _______   Median = _____
Mode = _______   Range = _____

14) 87, 47, 4, 89, 49, 82

Mean = _______   Median = _____
Mode = _______   Range = _____

15) 23, 48, 51, 86, 77, 20

Mean = _______   Median = _____
Mode = _______   Range = _____

16) 23, 11, 7, 36, 37, 30, 39

Mean = _______   Median = _____
Mode = _______   Range = _____

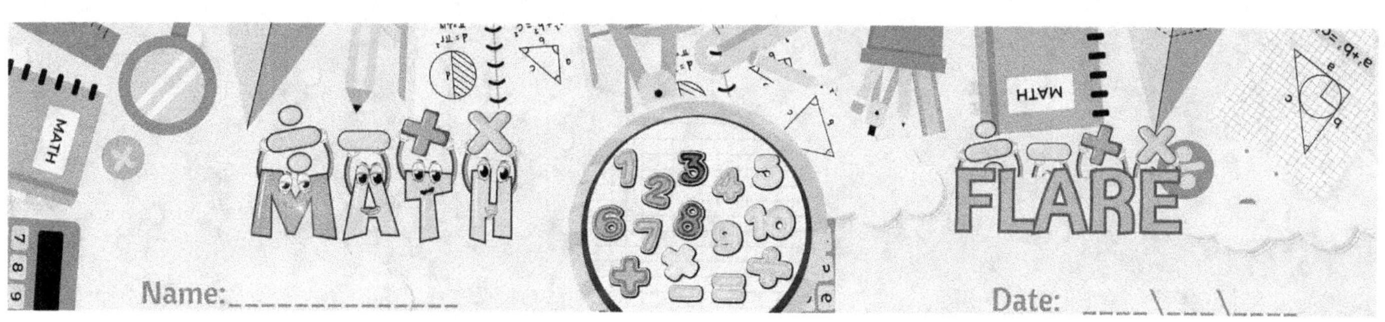

17) 78, 55, 50, 84, 55, 49

Mean = _______   Median = _____

Mode = _______   Range = _____

18) 63, 45, 45, 33, 70, 10, 6

Mean = _______   Median = _____

Mode = _______   Range = _____

19) 7, 81, 18, 93, 16, 35, 28

Mean = _______   Median = _____

Mode = _______   Range = _____

20) 76, 28, 89, 34, 66, 93, 83

Mean = _____   Median = _____

Mode = _____   Range = _____

21) 97, 43, 5, 34, 7, 84

Mean = _____   Median = _____

Mode = _____   Range = _____

22) 47, 10, 85, 38, 62, 49

Mean = _____   Median = _____

Mode = _____   Range = _____

23) 40, 85, 38, 78, 15, 80

Mean = _____   Median = _____

Mode = _____   Range = _____

24) 76, 72, 14, 41, 93, 13, 21

Mean = _____   Median = _____

Mode = _____   Range = _____

ANSWERS

Page 1: Positive and Negative Integers

1. 9	2. 6	3. -4	4. -4	5. 7	6. -8	7. -2	8. -8
9. 9	10. -19	11. 10	12. -6	13. 4	14. 7	15. -3	16. -11
17. 4	18. -4	19. 13	20. 8	21. 1	22. -10	23. 16	24. -4
25. 7	26. -9	27. -16	28. 6	29. 14	30. -3	31. 2	32. 8
33. 17	34. -3	35. 16	36. -17	37. -2	38. 6	39. -2	40. 5
41. -13	42. -2	43. 1	44. -12	45. 6	46. 4	47. -3	48. 14
49. -1							

Page 11: Exponents

1. 81	2. 1/289	3. 1/64	4. 100	5. 729
6. 1/16	7. 1/196	8. 1/125	9. 28,561	10. 3,375
11. 1	12. 1/9	13. 10,000	14. 49	15. 1/27
16. 4,096	17. 1/8	18. 16	19. 50,625	20. 64
21. 4	22. 6,859	23. 1,728	24. 36	25. 4,913
26. 27	27. 1/8000	28. 400	29. 1/512	30. 83,521
31. 1,296	32. 196	33. 1	34. 1/2744	35. 1/1000
36. 1/225	37. 1/256	38. 225	39. 1/324	40. 1/36
41. 1	42. 6,561	43. 1/1728	44. 1/4913	45. 130,321
46. 1/4096	47. 256	48. 104,976	49. 38,416	50. 1/4
51. 1/400	52. 65,536	53. 125	54. 1,331	55. 1/5832

56. 16   57. 5,832   58. 8,000   59. 1/3375   60. 144

61. 512   62. 1/49   63. 1   64. 1/169   65. 2,401

66. 1/729   67. 343   68. 9   69. 2,744   70. 625

71. 1/343   72. 361   73. 289   74. 121   75. 1/216

76. 1/25   77. 1/64   78. 8   79. 14,641   80. 1/6859

Page 19: Square and Cube Roots

1. 1   2. 3   3. 34   4. 10   5. 9   6. 86   7. 20   8. 3

9. 25   10. 22   11. 13   12. 2   13. 19   14. 8   15. 22   16. 4

17. 27   18. 9   19. 5   20. 7   21. 38   22. 67   23. 48   24. 49

25. 10   26. 1   27. 21   28. 2   29. 6   30. 11   31. 80   32. 6

33. 7   34. 4   35. 12   36. 64   37. 23   38. 16   39. 14   40. 5

41. 87   42. 8   43. 17   44. 32   45. 55   46. 15   47. 29   48. 69

49. 72   50. 18   51. 13   52. 97   53. 85   54. 20   55. 14   56. 12

57. 77   58. 68   59. 46   60. 42   61. 26   62. 59   63. 91   64. 31

65. 76   66. 39   67. 18   68. 84   69. 28   70. 11   71. 21   72. 44

73. 33   74. 58   75. 17   76. 19   77. 24   78. 90   79. 35   80. 92

81. 66   82. 82

Page 25: Factors

1. None   2. 2, 4, 8, 16, 32

3. None   4. 2, 3, 6, 9, 18, 27

5. 2, 5   6. 2

7. 3, 19

8. 2, 41

9. 3

10. 3, 11

11. None

12. 2, 3, 4, 5, 6, 10, 12, 15, 20, 30

13. 2, 37

14. 2, 4, 7, 8, 14, 28

15. 2, 4, 5, 10, 20, 25, 50

16. 2, 3, 4, 6, 9, 12, 18

17. 2, 31

18. None

19. 3, 9

20. 3, 5

21. 7

22. None

23. 5, 19

24. None

25. None

26. None

27. None

28. None

29. 2, 3

30. 3, 9, 11, 33

31. 2, 4, 23, 46

32. 2, 7

33. 2, 4

34. 2, 17

35. None

Page 30: Multiples

1. 50, 100, 150, 200, 250

2. 18, 36, 54, 72, 90

3. 68, 136, 204, 272, 340

4. 72, 144, 216, 288, 360

5. 64, 128, 192, 256, 320

6. 1, 2, 3, 4, 5

7. 31, 62, 93, 124, 155

8. 41, 82, 123, 164, 205

9. 98, 196, 294, 392, 490

10. 95, 190, 285, 380, 475

11. 78, 156, 234, 312, 390

12. 12, 24, 36, 48, 60

13. 14, 28, 42, 56, 70

14. 83, 166, 249, 332, 415

15. 79, 158, 237, 316, 395

16. 5, 10, 15, 20, 25

17. 39, 78, 117, 156, 195

18. 38, 76, 114, 152, 190

19. 42, 84, 126, 168, 210

20. 2, 4, 6, 8, 10

21. 86, 172, 258, 344, 430

22. 8, 16, 24, 32, 40

23. 57, 114, 171, 228, 285

24. 49, 98, 147, 196, 245

25. 19, 38, 57, 76, 95

26. 26, 52, 78, 104, 130

27. 6, 12, 18, 24, 30

28. 4, 8, 12, 16, 20

29. 3, 6, 9, 12, 15

30. 44, 88, 132, 176, 220

31. 52, 104, 156, 208, 260

32. 25, 50, 75, 100, 125

33. 99, 198, 297, 396, 495

34. 84, 168, 252, 336, 420

35. 88, 176, 264, 352, 440

Page 35: Order of Operations (PEMDAS)

1. 43
2. 1.2
3. 19
4. 280
5. 18
6. -9

7. 12
8. 23
9. 34
10. 119
11. 256
12. -4

13. 9
14. 17
15. 112
16. -8
17. 1,602
18. 24

19. 71
20. 60
21. 100
22. 63
23. 300
24. 260

25. 7
26. 582
27. -18
28. 112
29. 12
30. -7

31. 91
32. 205
33. 26
34. 27
35. 99
36. 6

37. 324
38. 24
39. 0.3
40. 18
41. 56
42. 369

43. 39   44. 169   45. 30   46. 17   47. 13   48. -4

49. 240   50. 40   51. 330   52. 8,105   53. 136   54. 27

55. 232   56. 16

Page 41: Solving Equations: (One Step)

1. $x = 209$ 2. $x = 17$ 3. $x = 4$ 4. $x = 216$ 5. $x = 6$

6. $x = 1$ 7. $x = 2$ 8. $x = 13$ 9. $x = 15$ 10. $x = 15$

11. $x = 12$ 12. $x = 15$ 13. $x = 17$ 14. $x = 10$ 15. $x = 120$

16. $x = 20$ 17. $x = 20$ 18. $x = 1$ 19. $x = 8$ 20. $x = 16$

21. $x = 19$ 22. $x = 72$ 23. $x = 16$ 24. $x = 4$ 25. $x = 9$

26. $x = 16$ 27. $x = 72$ 28. $x = 4$ 29. $x = 4$ 30. $x = 1$

31. $x = 10$ 32. $x = 20$ 33. $x = 96$ 34. $x = 18$ 35. $x = 17$

36. $x = 3$ 37. $x = 10$ 38. $x = 17$ 39. $x = 2$ 40. $x = 18$

41. $x = 8$ 42. $x = 70$ 43. $x = 51$ 44. $x = 19$ 45. $x = 14$

46. $x = 17$ 47. $x = 1$ 48. $x = 19$ 49. $x = 18$ 50. $x = 32$

51. $x = 6$ 52. $x = 18$ 53. $x = 8$ 54. $x = 10$ 55. $x = 13$

56. $x = 15$ 57. $x = 65$ 58. $x = 19$ 59. $x = 12$ 60. $x = 2$

61. $x = 8$ 62. $x = 19$ 63. $x = 12$ 64. $x = 11$ 65. $x = 6$

66. $x = 19$ 67. $x = 15$ 68. $x = 19$ 69. $x = 2$ 70. $x = 75$

71. $x = 19$ 72. $x = 11$ 73. $x = 8$ 74. $x = 2$ 75. $x = 7$

76. $x = 56$ 77. $x = 6$ 78. $x = 16$ 79. $x = 1$ 80. $x = 6$

81. $x = 3$ 82. $x = 3$ 83. $x = 20$ 84. $x = 1$ 85. $x = 144$

86. x = 7   87. x = 6   88. x = 1   89. x = 5   90. x = 2

91. x = 16   92. x = 7   93. x = 8   94. x = 8   95. x = 20

96. x = 1

Page 51: Evaluate Expressions
1. 2   2. 6   3. 13   4. -6   5. 34   6. 120   7. 52   8. 156

Page 52: Evaluate Expressions
1. 6   2. 16   3. 59   4. 33   5. -18   6. 90   7. 120   8. 62

Page 53: Evaluate Expressions
1. 39   2. 55   3. 60   4. 5   5. 10   6. 11   7. 13   8. 0

Page 54: Evaluate Expressions
1. 0   2. 71   3. 16   4. 54   5. -20   6. 56   7. 0   8. 12

Page 55: Evaluate Expressions
1. 1.8   2. 39   3. 752   4. 32   5. 41   6. 2.5   7. 39   8. 12

Page 56: Evaluate Expressions
1. 1.3   2. 8   3. 8   4. 0.8   5. 3   6. 20   7. 18   8. 17

Page 57: Evaluate Expressions
1. 32   2. 52   3. 11   4. 0   5. 16   6. 18   7. 0.9   8. 18

Page 58: Evaluate Expressions
1. 108   2. 8   3. -3   4. 157,464   5. 50

6. 2,304   7. 51   8. 10

Page 59: Evaluate Expressions
1. 144   2. 11   3. -16   4. 10   5. 66   6. 40   7. 729   8. 60

Page 60:   Evaluate Expressions

1. 5.3   2. 28   3. 0.6   4. 1   5. -2   6. 8   7. 1   8. 36

Page 61:   Solving Inequalities

1. y ≤ 2   2. y ≥ -1   3. z < 1   4. z < 1   5. k ≥ -3

6. x > -5   7. k > -9   8. k > -1   9. x ≤ 11   10. z > 1

11. m ≤ -2   12. x < 1   13. z < 6   14. y ≤ -11   15. y < -10

16. y ≤ 12   17. z ≥ 3   18. k ≥ -1   19. z > -12   20. m ≤ -1

Page 66:   Proportional Relationship

1. 1   2. 12   3. 50   4. 5   5. 8   6. 48   7. 9

8. 4   9. 3   10. 25   11. 24   12. 10   13. 49   14. 9

15. 3   16. 4   17. 8   18. 32   19. 4   20. 11   21. 11

22. 10   23. 20   24. 1   25. 7   26. 18   27. 3   28. 60

29. 72   30. 20   31. 8   32. 11   33. 3   34. 1   35. 42

36. 7   37. 10   38. 20   39. 16   40. 8   41. 12   42. 2

43. 10   44. 12   45. 20   46. 72   47. 18   48. 8   49. 4

50. 2   51. 9   52. 2   53. 100   54. 30   55. 8   56. 18

57. 18   58. 3   59. 5   60. 36   61. 18   62. 4   63. 120

64. 24   65. 100   66. 3   67. 4   68. 5   69. 8   70. 54

71. 88   72. 2   73. 45   74. 6   75. 3   76. 72   77. 2

78. 5   79. 15   80. 6

Page 74:   Ratio and Proportion Word Problems

1. 26.69   2. 2.83   3. 3.2   4. 22.68   5. 6

6. 37   7. 10.62   8. 11.69   9. 830.25   10. 28.67

11. 7.86   12. 2.35   13. 7   14. 8   15. 31.5

16. 13.75   17. 36   18. 9.91   19. 12.5   20. 18.67

21. 48   22. 218.67   23. 745.5   24. 20.5   25. 1.71

26. 10.77   27. 12.86   28. 240.75   29. 318.86   30. 22.86

Page 84: Percentage

1. 8   2. 16   3. 20%   4. 200   5. 48   6. 300

7. 100%   8. 60%   9. 700   10. 10   11. 75%   12. 300

13. 50   14. 1%   15. 70   16. 245   17. 480   18. 200

19. 20   20. 900   21. 30   22. 25%   23. 75%   24. 5%

25. 100   26. 800   27. 30   28. 900   29. 100   30. 6%

31. 100%   32. 800   33. 20   34. 900   35. 9%   36. 8%

37. 2%   38. 6   39. 25   40. 9   41. 900   42. 18

43. 15   44. 450   45. 400   46. 300   47. 200   48. 56

Page 88: Convert Percent and Decimals

1. 0.34   2. 86%   3. 0.03   4. 24%   5. 0.96   6. 81%   7. 0.78

8. 0.99   9. 0.48   10. 64%   11. 0.59   12. 70%   13. 0.8   14. 0.46

15. 0.11   16. 0.17   17. 0.95   18. 44%   19. 33%   20. 0.18   21. 0.35

22. 0.62   23. 0.29   24. 20%   25. 75%   26. 68%   27. 26%   28. 0.69

29. 0.36   30. 5%   31. 9%   32. 19%   33. 14%   34. 0.27   35. 10%

36. 71%   37. 97%   38. 4%   39. 7%   40. 0.87   41. 2%   42. 65%

43. 88%   44. 85%   45. 0.53   46. 84%   47. 0.58   48. 74%   49. 0.42

50. 77%   51. 0.31   52. 0.06   53. 8%   54. 0.28   55. 0.66   56. 0.22

57. 45%   58. 57%   59. 0.61   60. 0.41

Page 93:   Convert: Ratio, Fraction, Percent, and Decimals

1.

	Ratio	Fraction	Percent	Decimal
a.	18:18	18/18	100%	1
b.	10:14	10/14	71.4%	0.714
c.	5:6	5/6	83.3%	0.833
d.	10:11	10/11	90.9%	0.909
e.	1:6	1/6	16.7%	0.167
f.	12:19	12/19	63.2%	0.632
g.	9:19	9/19	47.4%	0.474
h.	1:19	1/19	5.3%	0.053
i.	1:2	1/2	50%	0.5
j.	5:19	5/19	26.3%	0.263
k.	9:16	9/16	56.2%	0.562
l.	1:11	1/11	9.1%	0.091
m.	3:9	3/9	33.3%	0.333
n.	1:4	1/4	25%	0.25
o.	7:8	7/8	87.5%	0.875

2.

	Ratio	Fraction	Percent	Decimal
a.	12:19	12/19	63.2%	0.632
b.	8:20	8/20	40%	0.4
c.	4:19	4/19	21.1%	0.211
d.	3:4	3/4	75%	0.75
e.	1:2	1/2	50%	0.5
f.	9:17	9/17	52.9%	0.529
g.	5:19	5/19	26.3%	0.263
h.	1:8	1/8	12.5%	0.125
i.	13:19	13/19	68.4%	0.684
j.	12:15	12/15	80%	0.8
k.	1:1	1/1	100%	1
l.	4:6	4/6	66.7%	0.667
m.	16:19	16/19	84.2%	0.842
n.	1:6	1/6	16.7%	0.167
o.	5:11	5/11	45.5%	0.455

3.

	Ratio	Fraction	Percent	Decimal
a.	1:1	1/1	100%	1
b.	6:14	6/14	42.9%	0.429
c.	1:2	1/2	50%	0.5
d.	3:4	3/4	75%	0.75
e.	1:14	1/14	7.1%	0.071
f.	1:3	1/3	33.3%	0.333
g.	4:5	4/5	80%	0.8
h.	6:16	6/16	37.5%	0.375
i.	5:19	5/19	26.3%	0.263
j.	5:18	5/18	27.8%	0.278
k.	2:8	2/8	25%	0.25
l.	13:19	13/19	68.4%	0.684
m.	4:14	4/14	28.6%	0.286
n.	14:19	14/19	73.7%	0.737
o.	11:20	11/20	55%	0.55

4.

	Ratio	Fraction	Percent	Decimal
a.	2:5	2/5	40%	0.4
b.	3:5	3/5	60%	0.6
c.	5:8	5/8	62.5%	0.625
d.	5:12	5/12	41.7%	0.417
e.	6:12	6/12	50%	0.5
f.	1:2	1/2	50%	0.5
g.	2:8	2/8	25%	0.25
h.	3:16	3/16	18.8%	0.188
i.	1:1	1/1	100%	1
j.	9:11	9/11	81.8%	0.818
k.	1:3	1/3	33.3%	0.333
l.	12:13	12/13	92.3%	0.923
m.	1:14	1/14	7.1%	0.071
n.	3:11	3/11	27.3%	0.273
o.	7:20	7/20	35%	0.35

5.

	Ratio	Fraction	Percent	Decimal
a.	6:13	6/13	46.2%	0.462
b.	12:13	12/13	92.3%	0.923
c.	2:3	2/3	66.7%	0.667
d.	1:6	1/6	16.7%	0.167
e.	3:4	3/4	75%	0.75
f.	5:5	5/5	100%	1
g.	7:10	7/10	70%	0.7
h.	6:14	6/14	42.9%	0.429
i.	5:9	5/9	55.6%	0.556
j.	12:16	12/16	75%	0.75
k.	1:16	1/16	6.2%	0.062
l.	11:13	11/13	84.6%	0.846
m.	18:20	18/20	90%	0.9
n.	2:14	2/14	14.3%	0.143
o.	2:4	2/4	50%	0.5

Page 98:   Area and Perimeter

1. P=51 A=112.5   2. P=31 A=40   3. P=34 A=48

4. P=42 A=78   5. P=40 A=58   6. P=64 A=186

7. P=24 A=24.5   8. P=34 A=72   9. P=76 A=256

10. P=46 A=91   11. P=28 A=29.52   12. P=36 A=61

13. P=60 A=124   14. P=30 A=36   15. P=36 A=55

16. P=27 A=25.74   17. P=26 A=34   18. P=66 A=180

19. P=30 A=43.3   20. P=46 A=111   21. P=27 A=32

22. P=23 A=25.16   23. P=48 A=143   24. P=82 A=240

25. P=34 A=42   26. P=68 A=182   27. P=34 A=70

28. P=58 A=144   29. P=41 A=71.5   30. P=20 A=16.32

31. P=35 A=48   32. P=80 A=225   33. P=38 A=69.18

34. P=20 A=12.38   35. P=36 A=62.35   36. P=39 A=73.18

37. P=28 A=44   38. P=48 A=101.82   39. P=26 A=28

40. P=21 A=17.82   41. P=25 A=29.02   42. P=50 A=136

43. P=39 A=66   44. P=27 A=32   45. P=26 A=28

46. P=82 A=252   47. P=33 A=45   48. P=44 A=74.52

49. P=29 A=36   50. P=33 A=28.7   51. P=36 A=62.34

52. P=25 A=20.9   53. P=33 A=52.39   54. P=39 A=66

55. P=24 A=36   56. P=19 A=12.24   57. P=24 A=24

58. P=19 A=15   59. P=27 A=32.80   60. P=32 A=53

61. P=32 A=43   62. P=38 A=49   63. P=44 A=72

64. P=30 A=43.3   65. P=32 A=49   66. P=28 A=27.6

67. P=50 A=102   68. P=41 A=70   69. P=58 A=130

70. P=22 A=14   71. P=56 A=120   72. P=29 A=36

73. P=32 A=42.56   74. P=72 A=259   75. P=46 A=88

76. P=22 A=22.26   77. P=22 A=21   78. P=60 A=154

79. P=46 A=112   80. P=50 A=100

Page 118:   Circumference and Area of circles

1. C=62.80 cm A=314.00 cm²   2. C=37.68 cm A=113.04 cm²

3. C=69.08 in A=379.94 in²   4. C=12.56 cm A=12.56 cm²

5. C=113.04 in A=1,017.36 in²   6. C=25.12 cm A=50.24 cm²

7. C=125.60 cm A=1,256.00 cm²   8. C=119.32 cm A=1,133.54 cm²

9. C=94.20 in A=706.50 in²   10. C=56.52 in A=254.34 in²

11. C=87.92 cm A=615.44 cm²   12. C=43.96 in A=153.86 in²

13. C=31.40 cm A=78.50 cm²   14. C=50.24 in A=200.96 in²

15. C=81.64 cm A=530.66 cm²   16. C=6.28 cm A=3.14 cm²

17. C=18.84 in A=28.26 in²   18. C=75.36 in A=452.16 in²

19. C=100.48 in A=803.84 in²   20. C=106.76 in A=907.46 in²

21. C=18.84 cm A=28.26 cm²   22. C=12.56 cm A=12.56 cm²

23. C=12.56 cm A=12.56 cm²   24. C=56.52 in A=254.34 in²

25. C=100.48 cm A=803.84 cm²   26. C=37.68 in A=113.04 in²

27. C=37.68 in A=113.04 in²   28. C=87.92 cm A=615.44 cm²

29. C=12.56 cm A=12.56 cm²   30. C=37.68 cm A=113.04 cm²

31. C=113.04 cm A=1,017.36 cm²   32. C=81.64 cm A=530.66 cm²

Page 126:   Classify and Measure Angles

1. 75° Acute   2. 135° Obtuse   3. 120° Obtuse   4. 95° Obtuse

5. 165° Obtuse   6. 125° Obtuse   7. 145° Obtuse   8. 40° Acute

9. 100° Obtuse 10. 235° Reflex 11. 75° Acute 12. 190° Reflex

13. 150° Obtuse 14. 225° Reflex 15. 55° Acute 16. 30° Acute

17. 15° Acute 18. 220° Reflex 19. 200° Reflex 20. 75° Acute

21. 275° Reflex 22. 155° Obtuse 23. 330° Reflex 24. 260° Reflex

25. 110° Obtuse 26. 95° Obtuse 27. 160° Obtuse 28. 305° Reflex

29. 265° Reflex 30. 120° Obtuse 31. 115° Obtuse 32. 200° Reflex

33. 285° Reflex 34. 355° Reflex 35. 70° Acute 36. 140° Obtuse

37. 105° Obtuse 38. 70° Acute 39. 205° Reflex 40. 90° Right

41. 120° Obtuse 42. 45° Acute 43. 290° Reflex 44. 115° Obtuse

45. 95° Obtuse 46. 45° Acute 47. 175° Obtuse 48. 225° Reflex

Page 138: Volume and Surface Area

1. V=252 cm³ cm³ SA=240 cm² cm²

2. V=36 ft³ ft³ SA=66 ft² ft²

3. V=18 cm³ cm³ SA=42 cm² cm²

4. V=307.88 in³ in³ SA=253 in² in²

5. V=113.10 cm³ cm³ SA=132 cm² cm²

6. V=75.40 ft³ ft³ SA=101 ft² ft²

7. V=80 in³ in³ SA=112 in² in²

8. V=12 in³ in³ SA=32 in² in²

9. V=150 cm³ cm³ SA=170 cm² cm²

10. V=144 ft³ ft³ SA=168 ft² ft²

11. V=226.19 ft³ ft³ SA=207 ft² ft²

12. V=452.39 in³ in³ SA=327 in² in²

13. V=392 cm³ cm³ SA=322 cm² cm²

14. V=100 cm³ cm³ SA=130 cm² cm²

15. V=197.92 ft³ ft³ SA=188 ft² ft²

16. V=27 in³ in³ SA=54 in² in²

17. V=336 cm³ cm³ SA=292 cm² cm²

18. V=785.40 cm³ cm³ SA=471 cm² cm²

19. V=157.08 in³ in³ SA=165 in² in²

20. V=445.32 cm³ cm³ SA=325 cm² cm²

21. V=230.91 in³ in³ SA=209 in² in²

22. V=720 ft³ ft³ SA=484 ft² ft²

23. V=630 cm³ cm³ SA=446 cm² cm²

24. V=36 cm³ cm³ SA=66 cm² cm²

25. V=192 in³ in³ SA=208 in² in²

26. V=12 in³ in³ SA=32 in² in²

27. V=60 cm³ cm³ SA=94 cm² cm²

28. V=343 in³ in³ SA=294 in² in²

29. V=402.12 cm³ cm³ SA=302 cm² cm²

30. V=150 cm³ cm³ SA=170 cm² cm²

31. V=50.27 ft³ ft³ SA=75 ft² ft²

32. V=18 ft³ ft³ SA=42 ft² ft²

33. V=343 cm³ cm³ SA=294 cm² cm²

34. V=48 cm³ cm³ SA=80 cm² cm²

35. V=18 ft³ ft³ SA=42 ft² ft²

36. V=8 ft³ ft³ SA=24 ft² ft²

37. V=141.37 ft³ ft³ SA=151 ft² ft²

38. V=150 in³ in³ SA=170 in² in²

39. V=175 in³ in³ SA=190 in² in²

40. V=346.36 ft³ ft³ SA=275 ft² ft²

41. V=180 ft³ ft³ SA=192 ft² ft²

42. V=810 in³ in³ SA=522 in² in²

43. V=12 ft³ ft³ SA=32 ft² ft²

44. V=120 in³ in³ SA=148 in² in²

45. V=12 in³ in³ SA=32 in² in²

46. V=36 in³ in³ SA=66 in² in²

47. V=294 ft³ ft³ SA=266 ft² ft²

48. V=504 in³ in³ SA=382 in² in²

49. V=48 in³ in³ SA=80 in² in²

50. V=64 in³ in³ SA=96 in² in²

51. V=18 cm³ cm³ SA=42 cm² cm²

52. V=18 in³ in³ SA=42 in² in²

53. V=381.70 cm³ cm³ SA=297 cm² cm²

54. V=120 ft³ ft³ SA=148 ft² ft²

55. V=27 ft³ ft³ SA=54 ft² ft²

56. V=630 cm³ cm³ SA=446 cm² cm²

57. V=432 ft³ ft³ SA=348 ft² ft²

58. V=12 cm³ cm³ SA=32 cm² cm²

59. V=108 ft³ ft³ SA=144 ft² ft²

60. V=48 in³ in³ SA=80 in² in²

Page 153: Mean, Median, Mode, and Range

1. Mean = 37.286, Median = 30, Mode = none, Range = 65

2. Mean = 38.571, Median = 40, Mode = none, Range = 57

3. Mean = 50.571, Median = 50, Mode = none, Range = 69

4. Mean = 43.833, Median = 42, Mode = none, Range = 79

5. Mean = 37.286, Median = 33, Mode = 33, Range = 66

6. Mean = 52.857, Median = 65, Mode = none, Range = 70

7. Mean = 38.5, Median = 45.5, Mode = none, Range = 54

8. Mean = 52.833, Median = 36, Mode = none, Range = 72

9. Mean = 47.429, Median = 53, Mode = none, Range = 94

10. Mean = 45.333, Median = 31, Mode = none, Range = 89

11. Mean = 55.5, Median = 55, Mode = none, Range = 61

12. Mean = 35.5, Median = 36.5, Mode = none, Range = 67

13. Mean = 57.167, Median = 57, Mode = none, Range = 72

14. Mean = 59.667, Median = 65.5, Mode = none, Range = 85

15. Mean = 50.833, Median = 49.5, Mode = none, Range = 66

16. Mean = 26.143, Median = 30, Mode = none, Range = 32

17. Mean = 61.833, Median = 55, Mode = 55, Range = 35

18. Mean = 38.857, Median = 45, Mode = 45, Range = 64

19. Mean = 39.714, Median = 28, Mode = none, Range = 86

20. Mean = 67, Median = 76, Mode = none, Range = 65

21. Mean = 45, Median = 38.5, Mode = none, Range = 92

22. Mean = 48.5, Median = 48, Mode = none, Range = 75

23. Mean = 56, Median = 59, Mode = none, Range = 70

24. Mean = 47.143, Median = 41, Mode = none, Range = 80